Latino Mennonites

YOUNG CENTER BOOKS IN ANABAPTIST & PIETIST STUDIES

Donald B. Kraybill, *Series Editor*

LATINO MENNONITES

Civil Rights, Faith, and Evangelical Culture

Felipe Hinojosa

JOHNS HOPKINS UNIVERSITY PRESS
Baltimore

Johns Hopkins University Press
2715 North Charles Street
Baltimore, Maryland 21218-4363
www.press.jhu.edu

Library of Congress Cataloging-in-Publication Data

Hinojosa, Felipe, 1977–
Latino Mennonites : civil rights, faith, and evangelical culture / Felipe Hinojosa.
pages   cm. — (Young Center books in Anabaptist & Pietist studies)
Includes bibliographical references and index.
ISBN-13: 978-1-4214-1283-2 (hardcover : alk. paper)
ISBN-13: 978-1-4214-1284-9 (electronic)
ISBN-10: 1-4214-1283-7 (hardcover : alk. paper)
ISBN-10: 1-4214-1284-5 (electronic)
1. Hispanic American Mennonites—History—20th century. 2. Hispanic Americans—Social conditions. 3. Race relations—Religious aspects—Mennonites. 4. Mennonites—United States—History—20th century. I. Title.
BX8128.H56H56 2014
289.7089'68073—dc23   2013027716

A catalog record for this book is available from the British Library.

Special discounts are available for bulk purchases of this book. For more information, please contact Special Sales at 410-516-6936 or specialsales@press.jhu.edu.

Johns Hopkins University Press uses environmentally friendly book materials, including recycled text paper that is composed of at least 30 percent post-consumer waste, whenever possible.

Dedicado a la vida y ejemplo de mis padres,
Conrado y Esther Hinojosa,

y el amor y apoyo de mi esposa y mis hijos,
María Maribel, Samuel Alejandro, Ariana Saraí

Contents

Part III BECOMING EVANGÉLICOS

Preface

I was raised in a family of storytellers. I grew up hearing my father's stories about his childhood in San Fernando, Tamaulipas, Mexico, and in South Texas. In the 1940s my father's family immigrated to the United States, where they found work in the vegetable and shrimping industries of South Texas. The family settled in Brownsville and lived off Coolidge Street in the area around what is known as el barrio de la Southmost. My mother, Esther Tijerina, was born and raised in Brownsville in a small home off Ringgold Street, not far from where my father grew up. Shortly after my parents married, they joined many other South Texas migrant families that every year journeyed north to work in the tomato fields of northwestern Ohio and the cherry fields around Traverse City, Michigan. In many ways the story of my parents' faith was shaped during those long trips north and in the hot days they spent working in the fields and raising a family.

My parents first met ethnic Mennonites in Archbold, Ohio, where they worked picking tomatoes on Mennonite-owned farms in the 1960s. My grandmother, Manuela Tijerina, liked that Mennonite farmers honored the Lord's day by not working on Sundays and that Mennonite missionaries offered church services in Spanish for migrant farmworkers. Since those days, both the Tijerina and Hinojosa sides of my family have been integrally tied to the Mennonite experience. That link strengthened when in the early 1970s my parents started a Mennonite Church in Brownsville. With the help of my grandfathers, Joaquin Hinojosa and Felix Tijerina, they organized a small church in the heart of the Southmost barrio. The small group of Mexican Americans that gathered those first few Sundays saw the Mennonite Church as more than an ethno-religious group with strong ties to the rural Midwest. Instead, they saw the Mennonite Church as many Latinos do today, as an *iglesia evangélica* (evangelical church) with a faith tradition firmly rooted in community, peace, and justice.

From about the time that I was in junior high school, I was aware that my family's faith traditions were different than those of my friends. Most of my friends were Catholic and often confused my dad, a "pastor," with a "priest." It was hard enough being Protestant, but to be associated with the Mennonite Church brought its own set of problems. My friends made good use of wordplay by accusing me of belonging to the "men of the night" church or, my personal favorite, the "Miller Lite" church. In reality, there was a part of me that wanted to be Catholic, for no other reason than to fit in. I remember asking my parents to teach me how to make the sign of the cross so that I could join my high school football teammates who did so before every game.

Questions of religious identity followed me into college. As an undergraduate at Fresno Pacific University, I read important books in Latino theology by scholars such as Justo González, Ada María Isasi-Díaz, and Virgilio Elizondo. But while these scholars examined theology and religious ethics, the everyday stories and complex historical experiences of Latino religious communities were not usually part of these theological works. Historical works, unfortunately, have not faired much better. For the most part, historians have overlooked the cultural identities, faith traditions, and faith-informed activism of Latino evangelicals in twentieth-century America. The few historical studies that exist tend to characterize *los aleluyas* (as Latino evangelicals are sometimes called) as either victims of Anglo Protestantism or irrelevant because of their relatively small numbers compared to the larger Latino Catholic population.

Such assumptions seemed to contradict what I saw growing up attending church every Sunday morning and night and every Wednesday night and countless youth group conferences every summer. Here I saw people who blended their faith and culture by incorporating the cultural elements of music, rhythm, dress, and language into their faith experiences. More important, the church that I grew up in expressed its faith through social action by opening a gym that gave barrio youth a place to play basketball and, in the 1980s and 1990s, provided shelter for a few hundred Central American refugees for weeks at a time. These experiences shaped my thinking but also led me to ask deeper questions about how Mexican Americans and other Latino evangelicals negotiate and blend their religious and ethnic identities. This book is an effort to better understand my own upbringing as a Mexican American *evangélico* in South Texas, but it also strives to extend our collective understandings of the relationships among Latino religion, identity, and civil rights politics.

Because of the broad and expansive nature of religious missionary projects, my research took me to church and organizational archives in South Texas, Indiana, Puerto Rico, Pennsylvania, and Kansas. Many of my primary sources are Spanish and English church newspapers, audio recordings, oral history interviews, meeting minutes, and correspondence. While I was certainly interested in institutional Mennonite Church records, I found that informal letters, speeches, and audio recordings often yielded the best source material for this project. Often this meant visiting people's personal collections, which were sometimes hidden away in basements or old filing cabinets. In the end, I was able to gain significant insights directly from Latinos and Latinas who participated in the Mennonite Church themselves and to uncover new source material that sheds new light on Latino Mennonites in particular and Latino evangelicals in general in twentieth century America.

~

Latino Mennonites is divided into three parts, covering three different historical periods. The first part, "Missions and Race," looks at the years between the 1930s and 1960s. Chapter 1 traces the origins and development of Mennonite missions in Latino communities in Chicago, South Texas, Puerto Rico, and New York City. Chapter 2 reveals how the missionary motives that prompted white evangelicals to oppose segregationist policies at home also moved white Mennonites to engage issues of racism within the church in the 1950s. This chapter documents the ways in which Latinos entered the debate, initially focused on blacks and whites, and fundamentally redefined how the church talked about race and civil rights.

Part II, "Black, Brown, and Mennonite," traces the development of the Minority Ministries Council (MMC) and the interethnic politics of black and brown Mennonites in the 1960s and early 1970s. Chapter 3 examines how debates over money, influenced by the politics of James Forman's "Black Manifesto," led to the coalition between black and brown Mennonites in 1968. Chapter 4 explores the contested politics that emerged during the Cross-Cultural Youth Convention in northern Indiana in 1972. Chapter 5 shifts from youth politics to the tense and conflicted relationship that emerged between the Mennonite Church and the farmworker movement in central California. Conflicts with Mennonite growers in central California as well as a long-standing aversion to union participation kept Mennonite Church leaders from fully supporting the movement for farmworker rights.

Part III, "Becoming Evangélicos," looks at the rise of Latino evangelical politics in the 1970s. Chapter 6 considers the role of Latinas in the Mennonite Church as concerns mounted over how committed white Mennonites were to Latino causes. In 1973, the increased participation of Latinas in the Mennonite Church led the shift toward Latino religious identity politics in the 1970s. Through culturally distinct forms of music, conferences in Spanish, debates around feminism, and promoting cultural values, Latinas rose to prominence at a moment when both Latino and African American men were beginning to question the viability of a black-brown coalition. More important, the roles that Latinas took in the church were undergirded by a belief that feminist thought could coexist with religious doctrine. These borderlands of faith and feminism defined the contradictory positions that Latinas took with regard to traditional gender norms in the home and questions of women in leadership in the church.

Chapter 7 examines how Latino Mennonites took the lessons from the civil rights movement to mobilize their own movement for inclusion in the church in the 1970s. The politics of becoming "evangélicos" challenge the ubiquitous notion that American religion took a decidedly right turn in the late 1970s. For Latino evangelicals, the 1970s was a critical decade that gave rise to the development of bilingual educational programs, culturally relevant church curriculum and music, and programs to help serve Spanish-speaking communities. The book ends with Latino Mennonites' celebration of their fiftieth anniversary in 1982 with a conference commemorating their important milestones.

The conclusion synthesizes the major ideas of the book and closes with an examination of how the politics of belonging have defined the struggles of Latino evangelicals. Whether in terms of religious faith and identity, race, immigrant rights, or sexuality, the politics of belonging continue to present both challenges and possibilities for Latino evangelicals in their quest to belong in the religious landscapes of twenty-first-century America.

Acknowledgments

This book began as a graduate seminar paper for a class on comparative race and ethnicity taught by Luis Alvarez at the University of Houston. It has been a long road from there, but every step of the way I had the support and encouragement of friends, colleagues, and family. At the University of Houston, I was fortunate to work under the guidance of Guadalupe San Miguel Jr. I am thankful to Lupe for all our great conversations, his pushing me to clarify my writing, and the multiple lessons he provided on the varying styles and rhythms of Tejano music. For these, and for his belief in this project, I am eternally grateful. Raúl Ramos and Luis Alvarez were great mentors and friends who consistently challenged me to think about how my ideas fit into the larger scope of Chicano and Latino history. Other former and current faculty at the University of Houston—Todd Romero, Andrew Chesnut, Gerald Horne, Landon Storrs, Monica Perales, Eric Walther, and Tom O'Brien—were critical to my development during my graduate school years. Of course, my years at UH would not have been complete without the friendships I forged through our graduate student group, La Colectiva.

At Texas A&M University my colleagues Carlos K. Blanton, Glenn Chambers, Lisa Ramos, Armando Alonzo, Adam Seipp, Ernest Obadele-Starks, Hoi-eun Kim, Kate Engel, Angela Hudson, Rebecca Schloss, Jason Parker, Harold Livesay, Albert Broussard, Walter Buenger, and David Vaught have supported this project and helped make my transition from graduate student to assistant professor an enjoyable one. At every step of the way, this project has benefited from the help of historians such as Arlene M. Sánchez Walsh, Timothy Matovina, Juan F. Martínez, Paul Barton, Anne M. Martínez, Daniel Ramírez, Donald Kraybill, Miriam Pawell, Deborah Kanter, Tom Dunlap, Phil Sinitiere, Carlos K. Blanton, Trinidad Gonzales, Jesse Esparza, Victor Gomez, Sonia Hernandez, Jimmy Patiño, Albert Rodriguez, Catalina Bartlett, Rod Janzen, Kevin Enns-Rempel, Steve Nolt, and, of course, the editorial expertise of Ulrike Guthrie. I am also very grateful for the feedback I received from all the great scholars who participated in the Teaching the Latino Midwest Seminar at the University of Iowa. In particular I would like to thank the organizers, Omar Valerio-Jiménez, Claire Fox, and Santiago Vaquera-Vásquez, for helping uncover the hidden histories of Latinos in the Midwest.

Special thanks also go out to my good friends and fellow historians Roberto Treviño and Tobin Miller Shearer. I first introduced myself to Roberto over the phone after reading his excellent book *The Church in the Barrio*, and over the years I have benefited from his wisdom, compassion, and sharp intellect. Roberto read multiple drafts of each chapter and always challenged me to connect my work to larger themes in Chicano history and US religious history. Tobin also read multiple drafts of each chapter and always pushed me to think deeper about Mennonite history, race, and identity and how my story fit in the larger historiography of race in America. This book is better because of the careful oversight Roberto and Tobin provided. Of course, any shortcomings in this book are my responsibility.

I would also like to thank several resource persons at the various archives I visited. I enjoyed working with Dennis Stoesz and Colleen Mc-Farland at the Mennonite Church USA Archives; James Lynch and John Thiesen at the Mennonite Library and Archives in North Newton, Kansas; Grace Charles at Texas A&M, Corpus Christi; and all the great people I met at the Lancaster Mennonite Historical Society (Lancaster, Pennsylvania), Eastern Mennonite Missions (Salunga, Pennsylvania), and the Universidad de Puerto Rico (Mayagüez, Puerto Rico).

This book benefited from the financial assistance of several organizations. A fellowship from the Hispanic Theological Initiative in 2008 helped support this project during its earliest phase and allowed me to conduct much of the research. In 2010 a First Book Grant for Minority Scholars from the Louisville Institute allowed me to make the final push to complete the manuscript. I was especially grateful for the Louisville Institute's Winter Seminar, where my work received feedback from fellow scholars and where I had the opportunity to network and meet people in the fields of religious studies and history. I would also like to thank the Texas A&M history department and the Melbern G. Glasscock Center for Humanities Research at Texas A&M for their guidance and financial support.

This book would not have been possible without the grace and courage of the people who actually lived this history. In South Texas, Lupe Garcia, María De León, Rosario Vallejo, Perfecta De León, Lupe De León, Ted Chapa, Jesus "Chuy" Navarro, and Dan and Mary Miller welcomed me into their homes, shared their stories with me, and showed me their stacks of photo albums. In Ohio, Indiana, and Michigan, Yvonne Diaz, Gilberto Perez, Seferina De León, José M. Ortíz, Samuel Hernandez, Carlos Romero, Rafael Barahona, Gilberto Flores, Ruperto "Tito" Guedea, Paul and Anne Conrad, Raul and Vanita Tadeo, Dan Shenk, and John and Shirley Powell all opened their homes to me, shared their stories and pictures, and fed me some wonderful meals. In Puerto Rico, I spent memorable days with Gracie and Neftali Torres in 2007. As we sipped *café con leche*, we talked about Puerto Rican identity, church politics, and the redemptive power of history.

My parents, Conrado and Esther, and my sisters and brothers—Esther and Larry, Conrado R. and Teresa, Diana, Elizabeth, Anna and Albert, Dina and Jerry—always provided fantastic meals, lots of laughs, great coffee, and unwavering support for my project. I am who I am today because of them. My wife, Maribel, and my children, Samuel Alejandro and Ariana Saraí, have lived with this project from the beginning. I first met Maribel on a cool summer evening in a small church in Orange Cove, California, in 1996. We became friends that summer and married four years later. As this book's first editor, Maribel read every chapter, provided critical feedback, and encouraged me through my many frustrations and discouragements. I simply could not have done this without her. Gracias, mi amor. And for my children who continually asked me, "Papi, are you still working on that book?" I love you more than you know.

Abbreviations

CCYC   Cross-Cultural Youth Convention

CESR   Committee on Economic and Social Relations

CPS   Civilian Public Service

MBM   Mennonite Board of Missions

MBMC   Mennonite Board of Missions and Charities

MCA   Mennonite Church USA Archives, Goshen, IN

MCC   Mennonite Central Committee

MLA   Mennonite Library and Archives, Bethel College, North Newton, KS

MMC   Minority Ministries Council

NFWM   National Farm Worker Ministry

UFW   United Farm Workers

URC   Urban Racial Council

VS   Voluntary Service

VSer   Voluntary Service worker

WMSA   Women's Missionary and Service Auxiliary

WMSC   Women's Missionary and Service Commission

Latino Mennonites

Introduction

Interethnic Alliances, Sacred Spaces, and the Politics of Latino Evangelicalism

The Mexicans are waiting for you, dear friends, if your purpose is strong and true. . . . If you know the truth that makes men free, and with skill can bring it to view, the Mexicans are waiting for you, dear friends, the Mexicans are waiting for you.
—HARRY NEUFELD, Mennonite Brethren missionary, 1947

As a young boy in South Texas in the 1950s, Samuel Hernandez liked going to the theater every Saturday to watch cowboy and Indian movies. The serials that ended with dramatic cliffhangers kept him coming back week after week. So when a good friend told him that the local Mennonite Church was going to show a movie—for free—he could not pass it up. The church was a short walk from his house, so he followed his friends with the hope that people at the church might also serve Kool-Aid and cookies.

Going to church was nothing new for Samuel. "Every Sunday my grandmother made me go," he remembered. "She pulled me by the ears and made me confess all my sins to the priest. . . . There weren't that many, so I had to invent some to make it worthwhile." So when Samuel first walked into the small Mennonite Church with his friends, he was surprised to find walls with no religious art or portraits of a crucified Jesus.

All he found were two Mennonite missionaries, Elvin Snyder and Weldon Martin, preaching to a group of children with a reel-to-reel recorder capturing their booming voices. At first, Samuel believed the reel-to-reel device was the film projector and that eventually the preaching would stop and the film would begin. But no film was shown that night. Later that evening on his way out of the church, one of the Mennonite missionaries approached him and asked, "You're coming back, aren't you?" As a shy 11-year-old, Samuel felt he had to say yes even though he was disappointed that no movie was shown. "I was 11, but I had to keep my word," Samuel admitted, "so I went back to Sunday school at the Mennonite Church." Disregarding his grandmother's repeated warnings not to attend the Mennonite Church, Samuel continued and was eventually baptized two years later.[1]

Samuel was only one of a handful of children who joined the Mennonite Church at a young age in the small South Texas town of Mathis. In the years following World War II, communities in South Texas joined places such as Chicago; La Plata, Puerto Rico; and New York as a popular destination for Mennonite missionaries who were interested in working with Spanish-speaking communities. In these communities, white Mennonites hosted a mix of evangelical and social programs that included vacation Bible schools, kindergarten education, health care, and a slew of other programs that caught the attention of Mexican Americans and Puerto Ricans who "did not understand why they [Mennonites] were so nice."[2]

Understanding the multiple layers and complex undertones of being Latino and Mennonite is the principal motive of this book.[3] It focuses on the experiences of Mexican Americans and Puerto Ricans who in the mid-twentieth century joined the Mennonite Church after participating in its programs and being intrigued by its belief system. Central for those who joined the Mennonite Church was the question of how best to reconcile their new religious faith with their ethnic identity. In other words, what did it mean to be Latino and Mennonite? This question is complicated by how the faith traditions of Mennonites are tied to both their ethnicity and their religious beliefs as members of a historic peace church. Historically, white Mennonites have described their movement as an alternative to either Protestant or Catholic Christianity.

In their theology of nonresistance, pacifism, and aversion to politics, Mennonites have held a middle ground as Anabaptists, or as one scholar phrased it, "neither Catholic nor Protestant."[4] However, where Mennonites have fit historically has varied and changed across space and time. As a tradition rooted in the reform movements in Europe during the sixteenth century, Anabaptism emerged as an alternative to Catholicism and as a radical extension of the Protestant Reformation. But the distinctions of Anabaptism as a "third way" have not always been clear, especially when we consider the history of Latino Mennonites. As Latinos and Latinas adopted Mennonite beliefs, they did so with an evangelical influence that better reflected their own cultural context. In other words, being Latino and Mennonite also meant being part of a larger family of *evangélicos* (Latino evangelicals) that included their Pentecostal and mainline Protestant neighbors. Driven by a desire to refashion the contours and expressions of Latino religious and ethnic identity, Latino Mennonites have historically straddled the border of evangelicalism and Anabaptism.

Latino Evangelicals: From the Cold War Politics of Race to Identity Politics in the 1970s

Tracing the intersections of civil rights, faith, and evangelical culture among Latino Mennonites is the focus of this book. I argue that the civil rights movement, from the black freedom struggle to the Chicano and Puerto Rican movements, played a central role in helping shape and define ethnic and religious identity for Latinos in the Mennonite Church. During the 1960s and 1970s, the politics of the Chicano, Puerto Rican, and black freedom struggles captured the imagination of Mennonite religious leaders, who belonged to a church known more for rural and peaceful agrarian life than social protest. Exploring the civil rights politics that emerged in the Mennonite Church provides a new perspective on religion and civil rights by showing how the Chicano and Puerto Rican movements fostered an eclectic mix of religious activists in unexpected places.[5] This book shows how the discursive power and political hopes of the Chicano and Puerto Rican movements inspired faith-informed activism in churches across the Midwest, beyond their geographic strongholds in the Southwest and Northeast. The civil rights movement placed Latino Mennonites at the center of discussions of racial justice in the church. These discussions led Latinos in the Mennonite Church to establish their own organizations in the 1970s, when the identity politics of race, gender, and

faith became central in their quest to belong. In other words, the entan-
gled politics of civil rights and religious faith helped shape how Latinos
thought about and practiced their faith as evangelical Mennonites.

In recent years Latino religious communities have played a key role in
national politics. In the 2012 presidential election, for example, Latino
Catholics and evangelicals made up 94 percent of the Latino electorate.
Latino evangelicals, whose numbers have reached 10 million, garnered
national attention from politicians of both parties who were eager to gain
the trust of an electorate with a history of varying political allegiances.[6]
The high profile of Latino religious communities in American politics,
however, has a longer history that dates back to the mid-twentieth century, when they were thrust into the political fray by the energy and moral
rhetoric of the civil rights movement. By the late 1960s both Latino Catholics and evangelicals had organized faith-informed movements in an effort to make their churches more diverse and inclusive spaces. What began
as movements for church reform in the 1960s have since blossomed into
national movements in which Latino religious communities have proven
to be important voices for immigrant rights.

From organized church reform movements to cultural forms of resistance like the images of the Virgin of Guadalupe along the United States–
Mexico border, Latino religious communities have a long history of political and religious participation in their quest to build a better and more
equitable society. Building on this legacy, historians have stressed how
Latino religious activism has ranged from small church movements to national religious movements like the National Farm Worker Ministry and
the National Council of Churches' Council on Hispanic American Ministries. These larger national movements brought together a broad array
of Latino faith communities from Catholics to United Methodists as they
worked for social change in the vegetable and fruit fields of California and
within their own religious structures.[7]

While these works have provided new lenses with which to view and
understand the civil rights movement, they often ignore how the broader
engagement of Latino evangelicals with the Chicano and Puerto Rican
movements was often filled with missteps, multiple political orientations,
organizational struggles, and sometimes tense interethnic alliances. In an
effort to recount the positive impact of religion on civic activism, scholars have in turn created a linear narrative that fails to incorporate the pit-

falls and complexities of Latino civic and religious engagement.[8] While Latinos worked to end racism in their own church traditions, the internal questions around the role of women, church missions, and the place of religious activism often made the road toward self-determination bumpy. The case of Latinos in the Mennonite Church uncovers how the struggles over race, gender, culture, and faith coalesced to give rise to a movement for racial justice in the church in the years after World War II.

This study reassesses the motivations, politics, and contradictions of Latino religious activism by approaching the topic across a wider demographic lens and a longer time frame. These themes are addressed through the two central goals of the book. First, the book centers the role of the black, Chicano, and Puerto Rican freedom struggles and the influence these movements had on the coalitions forged between Latino and African American Mennonites. By examining the interethnic coalition Latinos forged with African Americans through the Minority Ministries Council (MMC), this study moves beyond a single-ethnic-group approach and shows how closely linked black and brown concerns were within the Mennonite Church. As one of the few interethnic religious groups of its kind in the United States, the MMC was influential in challenging white Mennonites to incorporate nonwhites into their institutions and in rethinking the role of white missionaries in Latino and African American contexts.[9]

Historians have noted the influence of Latin American liberation theology on Latino civil rights efforts in Catholic and Protestant churches. Important works by Latino and Latina religious scholars have called attention to the role religion played "in the formation of a movement value system focused on social justice."[10] In theological studies, scholars have examined "the ties that bind" Latino and African American theologies based on historical oppression and an exclusion in theological discussions on the nature of God and biblical interpretation.[11] As important as these contributions have been, they leave us with an incomplete picture of the civil rights struggles that emerged in Latino religious communities, especially for Latino evangelical leaders who resonated with the preaching and theology of Martin Luther King Jr. I contend that it is impossible to understand the rise of Latino Mennonites in particular and Latino evangelicalism in general without taking into account the interethnic coalitions that developed during the civil rights movement.[12]

A comparative approach to religious and historical studies is especially important today given rapidly changing demographics and the political necessity of civil rights activists to engage the energy and creativity that can come from interethnic politics. As historian Luis Alvarez argues, a comparative approach moves Chicano and Latino studies beyond "a kind of silo or vertical model of organization . . . [that] produce[s] knowledge on a particular race or ethnic group without much consideration to how different groups engage one another."[13] Considering the interaction among different groups helps to widen the lens, as historian Mark Brilliant argues, of civil rights history in terms of both geography and demographics.[14] Both are true in this case as black and brown Mennonites engaged one another in a mostly white and Midwestern religious context. Certainly, interethnic movements present unique challenges and conflicts, especially within a religious context riddled with theological and cultural concerns. In this regard, the case of the MMC is no different. But interethnic movements, and the case of the MMC in particular, also reveals the possibilities and hope that black-brown coalitions offered during the civil rights movement in general and in religious contexts in particular.

The second central goal of this study is to extend and disrupt the traditional civil rights narrative by discussing the changing nature of Latino religious activism before and after the turbulent 1960s. These are elements that have remained largely unconnected to the traditional civil rights narrative and have recently begun to be reevaluated or reformulated by scholars as part of the historiography of the "long civil rights movement."[15] In the late 1940s and 1950s white Mennonites began to engage the race question as fears surfaced that segregation at home might hinder missionary projects overseas. What historians call the Cold War politics of race forced white evangelicals to rethink their relation to African Americans, but it also raised the important question about the place of Latinos in American racial politics at midcentury.[16]

Fast-forward to the mid-1970s when Latinos in the Mennonite Church joined a broad chorus of Latino evangelicals who pressured religious leaders to be more responsive to the cultural, educational, and political needs of Spanish-speaking communities. The Reverend Leo Nieto, who self-identified as a Chicano Protestant pastor, stressed the influence of the Chicano movement when he noted that "the Movement of Chicanos, in turn, helps those of us who call ourselves Christians, those of us who know about and talk about resurrection, to see an example of what it means to fight for justice."[17] Much of this activism rested on the rising sense of a shared Latino identity that was beginning to play out in both Latino Catholic and evangelical churches.

Contrary to the belief that the identity politics of race and feminism were "corrosive" and disrupted the possibility of a unified evangelical left in the 1970s, this book shows how the politics of identity served as a tool for political and religious mobilization.[18] In the case of Latino Mennonites, it led to a coalition movement with African Americans and other people of color that positioned Latinos and Latinas in church leadership. It also counters the ubiquitous notion that in the 1970s American religion took a decidedly conservative turn. In fact, the 1970s were a time when the creative energies of Latino Mennonites and other evangelicals emerged as a greater political and religious force in the United States. By examining this trend, this study provides yet another dimension to current scholarship that is recasting our understanding of US civil rights history.

Creating an Evangelical Culture

A focus on religion and the civil rights movement provides an important contribution to the fields of Chicano and Latino history. Much of the written history has largely disregarded the role religion has played in the movements that led to ethnic studies programs, labor rights for farmworkers, urban reforms, and Chicana feminism in the 1960s and 1970s. As Mario García argued in his essay "Religion and the Chicano Movement," religion remains one of the most overlooked aspects of Chicano history.[19] But more than telling a story that has not been told, a focus on religion is important because it helps reveal the ideological complexity and national scope of the Chicano and Puerto Rican movements. Historian David Montejano has examined how Catholic Church schools in San Antonio have provided "an educational alternative to the segregated and underfunded public school system" that in the end helped disrupt the city's caste structure.[20] Examples like this showcase the unlikely alliances that emerged between religious organizations and Chicano and Puerto Rican activists across the country. This book highlights only one piece of this important relationship, but it represents part of a larger project to insert Chicano and Puerto Rican history into the broader history of American religion and social movements of the 1960s and 1970s.[21]

For this reason, this book is more than a history of Latinos in the Mennonite Church. It is a social history that provides what Peter Goodwin Heltzel calls "a new genealogy of evangelicalism" that reveals the complex interplay between religion and identity politics.[22] As Heltzel argues in *Jesus and Justice*, the problem with popular definitions of "evangelicalism" is that they often do not go far enough in engaging social and cultural politics. In other words, socially contextualized definitions of evangelicalism that explore the complexities of this religious movement from the perspective of Latinos, African Americans, Native Americans, and Asian Americans are rare.[23]

Part of the problem, as Arlene M. Sánchez Walsh has argued, is that Latinos are left out of a "holistic approach to discussing American evangelicalism" that either categorizes them as victims of Anglo Protestantism or as an extension of conservative and white evangelicalism in the United States.[24] The reality is much more complicated. Like African American evangelicals, Latino evangelicals have their own history, which speaks to the importance of race, citizenship, and culture along with religious devotion, spirituality, and church missions.[25] While this book focuses on Latino Mennonites, it also attempts to broaden the narrow interpretation of "evangelicalism" as yet another code for white Protestant American identity.

Without question, the term "evangelical" remains contested among religious studies scholars. I have no intention of settling the debate here, but I will clarify my use of the term "evangelical" rather than terms such as "Pentecostal" or "mainline Protestant." I use "evangelical" in a broad sense to include Latinos and Latinas who identify as "born-again" Christians.[26] I label Latino Mennonites "evangelicals" or "evangélicos" because, in ways that will become clear in this book, they had more in common with their mainline Protestant and Pentecostal neighbors than they did with white Mennonites from the rural Midwest.[27] Obviously, there are many varieties among the faith traditions of Latino evangelicals, from Pentecostals (who comprise multiple varieties themselves) to mainline Protestant groups. I do not mean to diminish the complexities within each tradition, but I do believe that there exists what I call a *cultura evangélica* that unites these multiple groups and broadens the boundaries of belief and culture. Often these have to do with the central tenets of evangelicalism: conversion, biblical inerrancy, church missions, and belief in Christ's sacrifice on the cross and resurrection.[28]

But perhaps even more important than religious belief are cultural elements such as holding church services in Spanish, lively and animated worship, belief in faith healing, and a focus on social needs of the community. To varying degrees, these are characteristics of an evangelical culture that can be found in both Latino Pentecostal and mainline Protestant churches. They reveal a unique closeness that bridges differences along the lines of doctrine and denominational loyalty. In other words, religious affiliations are not fixed identities. Evangelical culture reveals how people's choices regarding where they choose to congregate has more to do with community, familiarity, and culture.[29] Lupe De León, who joined the Mennonite Church as a young boy in South Texas, highlighted this point when he asserted that "when Latinos leave the Catholic Church to become Protestant, we break up our extended family because we are no longer going to *quinceañeras* and *bailes* [dances]. . . . Our *tios* [uncles] and *tias* [aunts] no longer invite us because we are the do-gooders, *los aleluyas* [the halleluiahs]. . . . Our family becomes the church."[30]

The physical space of the church, in other words, is not only the place where people worship God, ask for the forgiveness of sins, or meet each other on Sunday mornings. The church is also a place where community concerns are shared, where people come to pray for changed realities, and where people understand their theology as a message of hope, peace, and dignity. It is a space where community initiatives are born and where people ask deep philosophical questions about suffering and the nature of God. Moreover, the geography of Spanish-speaking churches, many of which are located "in the heart of the Chicano barrio," also places churches in the middle of communities where social justice struggles open opportunities for the church and its congregants to form "a vital part of people's lives."[31] For example, in the late 1960s young Mexican Americans in South Texas pushed for "Latin pastors for Latin churches" in a move to dismiss the mostly white Mennonite leadership that had dominated churches in South Texas. It was an effort that reflected the broader trends of Chicano activism that emerged in churches in the 1960s and 1970s. Throughout much of the history of Latinos in the United States, the space and geographic placement of the church has provided room for cultural expression, social interaction, and political engagement. This is the hidden history of Latino religion that, as Otto Maduro has argued, often flourishes outside of the traditional boundaries of institutional religion.[32]

Rethinking the history of evangelicalism can also open new possibilities for understanding the history of race, gender, and social movements in religious and multiethnic contexts. This book begins that work by unraveling a new genealogy of evangelicalism that explores how questions of faith, identity, and social activism flourished in a religious context that some jokingly referred to as the "black bumper" Mennonites—because some could only purchase cars with black bumpers, no chrome. Doing so forced Latinos to address cultural markers such as patterns of dress, views on military service, and a rural lifestyle that shunned extravagance. Esther Ventura, a Mexican American woman from Chicago, expressed this best when she noted that Mennonite "culture is so much a part of the religion. . . . We get confused which is the culture and which is the doctrine?"[33] Becoming Mennonite meant coming face to face with the theological currents and strong ethnic ties of Mennonites, but it also moved Latinos and Latinas to negotiate their religious identities as evangélicos and aspiring Mennonites, especially as the rumblings of the freedom movements loomed large in the 1960s.

Mennonites: Reluctant Evangelicals

Mennonites were relative latecomers to evangelical missions in the mid-twentieth century. Aside from the foreign missionary work in India and Argentina in the early twentieth century, Mennonite missions were often reserved for people within their own ethno-religious group who they believed had gone astray.[34] But by the 1920s Mennonites had caught wind of the fundamentalist movement and began to criticize themselves for not being evangelical enough. The debate over the lack of evangelical thrust within the Mennonite Church highlights a very real tension between those who desired to remain "the quiet in the land" and those who believed a stronger emphasis should be placed on evangelical missions.[35] These tensions characterized the uncertainties Mennonites faced in the 1940s and 1950s as they felt the pull of evangelicalism even as they struggled to hold an Anabaptist identity rooted in sixteenth-century Europe.

Historians place the beginning of the Protestant Reformation in 1517 when Martin Luther posted his Ninety-Five Theses at Wittenberg University in Germany.[36] Luther advocated the reformation of church politics, economics, and other social factors that he believed were leading the Christian church toward ecclesiastical ruin. Luther's theses were not without context. Throughout the medieval period, church leaders supported an ecclesiastical reform that resembled the pre-Constantinian Jesus movement. But it was not until Luther posted his theses that real institutional change occurred in the church on a broad scale. Luther's theses challenged church hierarchy and became associated with *protest*, which led to the reformers being called *Protestants*.

Although the Protestants challenged many aspects of church corruption during this period, there were some who felt that Luther and other reformers did not go far enough. This sparked the radical reformation around 1525. These new radical reformers advocated rebaptizing adult believers, or ana-baptizing them. Rebaptizers, or Anabaptists, believed in what they termed the "priesthood of all believers," which challenged church hierarchy by allowing all to be ministers instead of a select few.[37] Anabaptists argued for a more literal reading of the Bible, especially chapters 5, 6, and 7 of the Gospel of Matthew, which outline the ethic of nonviolence, the sharing of possessions, and the importance of conversion from a life without God to a life led by God. Anabaptists also advocated nonparticipation in secular government and military service.

In 1530 a new movement was born when a young Catholic priest named Menno Simons was influenced by a segment of the Waldensians, a movement within Anabaptism, to leave the Catholic Church. Simons agreed with the Waldensians that military service, the taking of oaths, and infant baptism were contrary to the teachings of the Bible. Those who followed Menno's teachings and writings eventually came to be known as Mennonites. The story of the Mennonites in Europe is long and complex and full of religious schisms. The largest and most meaningful schisms took place in North America and south Russia (Ukraine) during the latter part of the nineteenth century. These schisms gave birth to the three largest groups of Mennonites in the United States: the Mennonite Brethren, General Conference Mennonites, and the "Old" Mennonite Church.[38]

While this book focuses on the missions and politics of the "Old" Mennonite Church, Mennonite groups in general experienced a crisis mid-twentieth century as some within their ranks questioned the church's commitment to preaching the Gospel. During this time, Mennonites entered a period of missionary zeal that made it difficult to distinguish Mennonites from other evangelical missionary groups of the period. This reality has forced scholars to rethink the place of Anabaptism in the American religious landscape, especially in its relationship to evangelicalism. As it turns out, the relationship between evangelicalism and Anabaptism has been closer and more collaborative than previously thought.[39]

This close relationship also raises an important point about the centrality of race and racism in Mennonite history. In general, historians have argued that questions about nonresistance, peace, and political engagement were at the heart of Mennonite theology and identity throughout much of the twentieth century. However, a closer look at the evidence suggests that the intersections of evangelicalism and race, not peace and nonresistance, have been at the center of evolving notions of Mennonite theology and identity. Throughout most of the twentieth century, race and church missions forced an ethno-religious group with strong ties to its German Swiss and Russian roots, to acknowledge both its affinity for American evangelicalism and its whiteness.[40] White Mennonites who entered Latino communities in the 1930s and 1940s were part of a wave of Mennonites who were willing to stretch the boundaries of their identity as ethnic Anabaptists to embrace the promises of white evangelicalism. It is no coincidence that as missions to Latino communities expanded in the years after World War II, Mennonites began to rethink their relationship to society through higher rates of urbanization, church growth, and political engagement. This shift is one of the reasons white Mennonites became so enamored with the rising evangelical movement in the years after World War II. Like Mennonites, the neo-evangelicals were expanding their church base by distinguishing themselves from the fundamentalist movement, increasing the focus on church missions and engaging society on important cultural issues.[41]

The case of Latino Mennonites sheds light on important debates around religion and interethnic politics, faith-informed activism, and church reform movements. But this book carries broader implications for the study of religion, race, and civil rights beyond the case of Latinos in the Mennonite Church. Specifically, it explores the idea that the "long civil rights movement" played an important role in shaping how Latino religious communities thought about and practiced their faith, culture, and politics. The close relationship between civil rights politics and religious faith opened a space for Latinos, African Americans, and progressive whites to form interethnic coalitions as they worked to make the church a more inclusive space. A focus on religion and interethnic politics can expand the boundaries of evangelicalism and Latino civil rights history and reveal new areas of study. In order to tell one story of Latino civil rights, this book provides a study of the dynamic relationships among civil rights, faith, and evangelical culture in twentieth-century America.

Part I

⤳

MISSIONS AND RACE

CHAPTER 1

Building Up the Temple

Mennonite Missions in
Mexican and Puerto Rican Barrios

*Satan has worked among the Mexicans a long time, and as we go about
giving out the gospel we find the results of his work, and how difficult it
is at times for these people to meet scriptural demands.*
—Amsa Kauffman, Mennonite missionary, Tuleta, Texas, 1941

Esta gente come mucho pan. (These people eat a lot of bread.)
—Ofelia Aguilar Garcia, Mathis, Texas, 1950s

Becoming Mennonite

On the morning of March 10, 1936, Mennonite missionaries T. K.
Hershey and William G. Detweiler loaded up their Ford V-8 pickup,
bid farewell to their families in Pennsylvania, and began their trip to the
borderlands of the United States and Mexico. From Texas to California,
Hershey and Detweiler surveyed the Southwest in hopes of beginning a
mission among the growing ethnic Mexican population. After traveling
more than 7,000 miles, the missionary duo decided that the South Texas
region (just south of San Antonio) was an ideal spot to begin their work, as
there resided a "good class of Mexicans, mostly pure Mexicans not Spanish Americans, which are harder to reach."[1]

Their trip, although somewhat late in the missionary timeline, continued a long tradition of missionary activity in the Southwest borderlands dating back to the late nineteenth century.[2] For Hershey and Detweiler the desire to evangelize the borderlands represented not only their own missionary zeal but also a belief that the Mennonite Church as a whole was not doing enough to spread the Gospel. Shortly before their trip, Detweiler expressed his frustration to Hershey: "I do believe that the greatest sin that we as a Mennonite Church are guilty of is the failure to render greater obedience to the Great Commission."[3]

With an eye toward better understanding Latino religious identity, this chapter explores Mennonite missionary projects in Chicago, South Texas, Puerto Rico, and New York City from the 1930s to the 1960s. Mennonite missionaries entered Mexican and Puerto Rican communities cautiously. Mennonites were conflicted over their relationship to American society in general and to American evangelicalism in particular. These debates over religious and ethnic identity prominent in the mid-twentieth century were evident in mission stations throughout the country, where Mennonites practiced a two-tier approach to church missions that combined evangelicalism with an ethic of social service.

For Latinos, becoming Mennonite not only led to new definitions of religious identity but also propelled them to engage questions about military service, patterns of dress, and the role of the church in society. Nevertheless, religious conversion was not an all-encompassing experience. Latinos filtered and adjusted aspects of the Mennonite faith they deemed culturally irrelevant or simply shifted religious allegiances to something that better reflected their cultural experience. These religious transitions were the breeding ground for the blending of evangelicalism and Anabaptism that formed the basis for Latino Mennonite identity in the mid-twentieth century.

"The Stranger within Our Gates"

Among the first three Mennonite volunteers who arrived in South Texas in 1952 was a young Mexican American from Chicago, Ray Vallarta. From the time he was a young boy in the 1930s, Vallarta attended the Mennonite Mexican Mission on Roosevelt Avenue in Chicago's Near West Side. That Vallarta ended up in South Texas as a volunteer says a lot about how connected he felt to the Mennonite Church even as a young man. His experience, however, was not unique. Along with Vallarta, the small Mennonite mission to the ethnic Mexican population in Chicago attracted a good number of Mexican families, most of whom had immigrated to Chicago in the early twentieth century as a result of revolutionary turmoil in Mexico.[4]

With the growth of Mexican immigrant communities in Chicago, Mennonites focused their mission program in the 1920s on Mexican immigrants who settled in the city's Near West Side. With a small following of Mexican families, the Mennonite mission in Chicago formed a congregation called La Iglesia Menonita Mexicana (the Mexican Mennonite Church) in 1942. Although the mission was initially small in scope, Chicago became a launching pad for Mennonite missionaries who were intent on founding missions among the growing population of Mexican immigrants, or what they referred to as "the stranger within our gates."[5]

Between 1910 and 1930 Mexican immigrants settled in three locations in Chicago: the South Side, the Near West Side, and the Back of the Yards / Packingtown area. In these neighborhoods Mexican immigrants often lived side by side with African American, Polish, Italian, and Irish communities. For Mexican immigrants, the interaction with their white ethnic neighbors served as one way to position and assert their notions of belonging within the American nation. Historian Gabriela Arredondo states that in these interactions, Mexicans "were presented with a moment that held at least the possibility of a process of adjustment with the potential for Mexicans to become white and thereby become American alongside their newly arrived Polish and Italian neighbors."[6] This moment, Arredondo argues, faded during the interwar period, as race relations between Mexican immigrants and white ethnics defined Mexicans as nonwhite. The issues that caused the most friction revolved around housing, employment, and national belonging.

Even in the small confines of the Mennonite mission in Chicago, questions of belonging and group identity surfaced as the church became yet another contested space. For example, racial tensions developed when white ethnic parishioners refused to attend church with Mexican immigrants. In a letter to the mission board, Mennonite missionary Edwin Weaver suggested moving Spanish services "some where over in their section [because] so many of them hate the Mexican people."[7] Weaver described how white ethnics had begun to circulate a petition forbidding Mennonites to do mission work among the Mexican population.

This worried missionaries who, on one hand, wanted to expand their missionary efforts in the Mexican community but, on the other, did not want to jeopardize their ongoing mission efforts with white ethnics. As a result, the Illinois Mennonite Conference agreed that it was appropriate to hold services for Mexican immigrants separate from whites. Conference leader F. D. King asserted that "in connection with Mexican work [I] never was strong for mixing Mexicans into our church building with our whites. . . . Our attendance generally slumped from about then on; the separate place for worship for the Mexicans was to my mind wise, in fact imperative."[8]

Mennonite missionary P. A. Friesen agreed. Friesen believed that allowing Mexicans into the congregation would only serve to fracture the church, which he believed harbored "so much race prejudice." On the other hand, Friesen knew that his congregation would have no problem supporting the mission to the Mexican population as long as it gathered in another place. In the end, the church followed the mandates of white ethnics in Chicago, but Friesen admitted that while the racial tensions necessitated a split, ethnic Mexicans were often "better behaved than some who have white faces."[9]

For Mennonite missionaries, ethnic Mexicans posed a race problem infused with conflicts over language and culture. Initially, none of the Mennonite missionaries spoke Spanish, and none had any experience working with non-European immigrants. To address this shortcoming, the Mission Board enlisted the help of former and current missionaries to Argentina who spoke Spanish and had some experience working in Latin American contexts. J. W. Shank was one of the first to organize Sunday school programs and charity programs that provided clothing, food, and other supplies for Mexican families in Chicago struggling with the economic hardships brought on by the Great Depression.[10] Before long, Mexican families began trickling into Mennonite church services and other activities. By 1932 missionary reports revealed that close to 50 people were attending the Spanish Sunday school classes, but hostile relations between ethnic Mexicans and their Polish, Italian, and Irish neighbors often tempered glowing reports of church growth. In 1933 Nelson Litwiller, another Argentine missionary on furlough, arrived in Chicago and continued holding church services for the Mexican population on Sunday afternoons and a couple of evenings during the week.[11]

The work remained under the purview of white Mennonites until Litwiller became acquainted and began working with a young Pentecostal preacher named David Castillo. Castillo became interested in the Mennonite Church, and before long Litwiller arranged for Castillo to study at the Mennonite seminary in nearby Goshen, Indiana. In 1934, two years after Mennonite missionaries received threats from whites in the neighborhood, the mission moved to the heart of Latino Chicago, the neighborhood in Chicago's Near West Side along Roosevelt Road, where it flourished under Castillo's leadership.[12] Drawn by the neighborhood's "ethnic familiarity" and "availability of Spanish-speaking services," the Near West Side was an important destination point for Mexican and Puerto Rican immigrants in the mid-twentieth century.[13] It was also the neighborhood home of Saint Francis of Assisi Catholic Church, also known as "the Mexican cathedral," which served as an important cultural and religious home for immigrants in the Near West Side.[14]

As the church grew and attracted large numbers of Mexican children, mostly looking for activities to pass the time, it became clear to neighborhood residents like Esther Ventura that being part of the Mennonite Church had deep implications for one's identity. In 1973 Ventura talked about this in an interview she gave as part of a Mennonite oral history project:

> I had thought that, well not that I was blonde and blue-eyed, but I had always felt that I was a Mennonite in culture and religion, and at the same time I knew I was different by the way I looked. . . . You grow up in an environment that is very religiously structured and then all of a sudden you realize that you aren't of German extraction, that you are Mexican. I have a lot of conflict with the Mennonite Church because like I said I had grown up in it and felt a part of it, but when I was with Mennonites in another setting away from the city I saw how I was not like them.[15]

While in the mission field Mennonites behaved very much like their Protestant counterparts, in their ethnic enclaves of Pennsylvania, Indiana, and Kansas, they were an ethno-religious group with a certain disdain for outsiders. In Chicago, for example, Mennonites often discouraged church members from listening to or playing Mexican music.[16]

Like some other Protestant missionaries, Mennonites did not allow instruments in their churches. They required that new converts—especially women—adopt conservative dress, and they insisted that new converts relinquish such vices as dancing, tobacco, alcohol, and playing billiards. The requirements of personal change, as historian Paul Barton has shown, reflected a moral code that was based on an Anglo cultural worldview perceived to be inherently necessary for the religious conversion of ethnic Mexicans to Protestantism.[17]

Love, Race, and Mennonite Missions

But there was more to the moral code than this. Notably, Mennonites prohibited interracial love and marriage. This came into focus when in 1936 David Castillo became a licensed minister in the Mennonite Church. His rapid rise to leadership in the church was tempered only by his growing admiration for Elsa Shank, the young daughter of missionary J. W. Shank. While Mennonites promoted a strong sense of responsibility in mission work among ethnic Mexicans, interracial love often brought out the fears and racist undertones of Mennonite missions in nonwhite communities.

The romance between Castillo and Shank quickly grabbed the attention of Mission Board secretary S. C. Yoder. In a letter to J. W. Shank, Yoder concluded that if Castillo and Elsa Shank were to marry, they should consider moving out of the country. "It seems to me," wrote Yoder, "that for their own good, it would be better for them to move to Argentina and work there where there is not the discrimination against mixed marriages that there is here in the U.S."[18] Castillo eventually married Elsa, and in 1940 they moved to La Junta, Colorado, where to a limited extent they continued ministry work among Spanish-speaking communities in the Denver area.

The issues that the union between Castillo and Shank raised among Mennonite leaders highlighted the uneasy relationship Mennonites had with the Mexican population in Chicago. It also raised broader concerns about the possibility that interracial unions might disrupt the sanctity of the tightly knit Mennonite community. Until then, much of the concern about marriage had to do with marrying outside of the Mennonite faith.

Many of the statements on marriage put forth by Mennonites since the early twentieth century focused solely on the importance of Mennonites marrying other Mennonites. As historian Tobin Miller Shearer found, this internal focus resulted in few statements on the church's stance on interracial marriage. That changed in the 1950s when articles on the subject began appearing in church periodicals sparked in part by the marriage of an African American man named Gerald Hughes and a white woman named Annabelle Conrad.[19]

Their marriage initiated a broad debate between black and white Mennonites about the role of race in the church. But more than a decade before the marriage between a black and white Mennonite, the church's response to a marriage between a Mexican American and a white Mennonite was to suggest the couple relocate to a faraway place like Argentina where they would be out of the purview of most Mennonite communities. After becoming the first Mexican American ordained in the Mennonite Church, David Castillo was mostly disregarded, as his marriage to Elsa Shank posed a threat to the emerging views of Mennonites on race and marriage. After that, Castillo's involvement in the Mennonite Church never quite lived up to the expectations others had of him when he first started as a fiery Pentecostal preacher in 1930s Chicago.

Conflicts over interracial romance, however, did little to stop ethnic Mexicans from attending Mennonite Sunday school classes every week. Many of the families from Chicago, such as the Ventura and Tadeo families, left the Pentecostal Church to attend the Mennonite Church and take advantage of the resources they offered. For example, the Ventura and Tadeo children enjoyed the trips to the countryside with Mennonites as part of the "Fresh-Air" program in the 1940s. Fresh-air programs started in the latter part of the nineteenth century when evangelists attempted to expose urban dwellers to the benefits of country living. Mennonites in the Chicago and Pennsylvania areas began hosting their own fresh-air programs for black and Latino children in the late 1940s and 1950s.

One of those participants was Raul Tadeo, a Mexican American child from Chicago. "The fresh-air program in Chicago left a tremendous impact on my life. I remember thinking to myself this is the kind of home that I want to have. That's what I remember most when I first met that family." Tadeo would often spend two weeks at a time in the home of a Mennonite family in rural Illinois.[20] Experiences like this, along with many other social resources Mennonites offered, convinced families like the Tadeos to leave the Pentecostal churches they attended to join the Mennonite Church.

These religious conversions reflected a broader trend among ethnic Mexican families, who often switched between and across religious affiliations in order to position their families for the most benefit. Historian Vicki Ruiz illustrated this well in her examination of the Houchen Settlement House in El Paso. Ruiz found that Mexican women often accepted the resources offered by Protestant groups while all along rejecting the theology of their benefactors. In other words, decisions about religious conversion were sometimes based more on physical needs than on genuine conviction of faith.[21]

But while that certainly was the case for some, religious conversion did often produce an authentic belief system and a lifelong commitment to the church. Regardless of how ill-prepared Mennonite missionaries were for an urban environment, the resources and help they offered to Mexican immigrants helped sustain the mission and spur on its growth. Like the members of La Iglesia Menonita Mexicana in Chicago, Mexican Americans in South Texas were also confronted with becoming Mennonite. But the experiences were by no means similar. In South Texas, where the realities of Jim Crow segregation and discrimination against Mexican Americans were common practice, becoming Mennonite would raise important questions about negotiating religious identities as evangélicos and Anabaptists.

"They Come Running to Gather Up Every Prayer": South Texas, 1936–1945

On the evening of October 16, 1936, about 25 Mexican Americans gathered in the small town of Pettus, Texas, where they listened to Mennonite missionary T. K. Hershey read from the Gospel of John and preach a sermon on "new life" in Christ. Located about 75 miles south of San Antonio along Highway 181, Pettus was the first of three towns where Mennonite missionaries focused their efforts. The next two, Tuleta and Normanna, were already home to some Mennonite churches attended by people who had moved to the area in the early twentieth century. Some Mennonites came to South Texas as dairy farmers, while others had moved to the region to escape the cold and retire in a warmer climate.[22]

On a typical Sunday, Hershey organized two evangelical services at which he preached to small groups of Mexican Americans. Whereas church services in Normanna were held in the local "Mexican school," in Pettus services were held in the home of a Catholic woman named Eulalia Valdez. Valdez, whom Mennonite missionary David Alwine called only by her Christian name, "Beulah," supported the work of Protestant missionaries in part because she had family members who were Protestant. Alwine described Valdez's as a "typical Mexican home," with one small room for a "wood stove, a small table, and a few boxes on the wall for cupboards" and another room to sleep. The humble living conditions of Mexican Americans in these small towns shocked both Alwine and Hershey. In one report, Alwine noted his disbelief at "how they [Mexicans] live in their small huts of one or two rooms."[23]

Around the same time that Mennonite Church missionaries worked in small towns south of San Antonio, another missionary—Harry Neufeld, from the Mennonite Brethren Church—arrived in the small border town of Los Ebanos, Texas. The Mennonite Brethren Church and Mennonite Church were two separate denominational groups that for the most part did not interact, but both succeeded in attracting new members. Neufeld reported that 17 people attended the first Sunday school program in 1937 and that the second week 49 people attended despite being what he called "a people over whom the enemy rules with all his strength."[24] Hershey reported that on the first Sunday in January 1938, 11 Mexican Americans were baptized in Tuleta and well over 100 more were recorded attending Sunday school programs in Pettus, Tuleta, and Normanna.[25]

The religious environment that white Mennonites encountered in South Texas already had a long history of Protestant missions among Mexican Americans that stretched back to the nineteenth century.[26] While the numbers of Mexican American Protestants remained low even into the 1930s, in places across South Texas the legacy of Protestantism had taken root. In Beeville, Texas, close to where Hershey initiated his work, the local Baptist and Pentecostal churches each had about 30 Mexican American attendees every week, while the well-established Presbyterian Church attracted more than 100 Mexican Americans.[27]

Even with a strong Protestant presence, white Mennonites were puzzled by the religious mixing and shifting they observed among the Mexican American population. "This community seems to have an unusual mixture of Protestantism and Catholicism," wrote David Alwine. "Both are good, they think, for we all worship the same God."[28] Another Mennonite missionary, Amsa Kauffman, focused on the religious practices he witnessed among some Mexican American Protestants in South Texas, from *altarcitos* (altars) in homes to consistent and fervent prayers to the Virgin of Guadalupe. Unable to understand people's religious choices, Kauffman attributed the Protestant and Catholic mix to confusion and added, "Many of these people do not know where they stand when it comes to religion."[29]

In the South Texas border town of Los Ebanos, Harry Neufeld focused his attention on the "peculiar and superstitious beliefs" of the community and his early interaction with *curanderos* (folk healers). He described local *curanderos* as "people [who] pose as being from another world . . . endowed with gifts from heaven and hav[ing] the power of healing . . . who work their hocus pocus remedies, give some kind of medicine which possibly has no healing potencies or ingredients in it and send people home."[30] In his book *Eight Years among Latin-Americans*, Neufeld added:

> Missionaries to Africa write about this and how the natives there are bound by it. Naturally living in a civilized country it is not expected here, but believe me it is here among this people. Some of them live without hope of ever being saved because they have sold themselves to the devil and they worship him in all sincerity, and that in the worst form namely, sex.[31]

If race had dominated the missionary efforts in Chicago, it became an even more pronounced reality in South Texas. In the 1930s, Mennonite missionaries entered a complex society with a rigid racial code that structured the relations between Anglos and Mexican Americans. One major reason, as historian David Montejano has argued, was the rise of commercial farms in South Texas that simultaneously boosted the economy and heightened racial antagonisms between Mexicans and Anglos in the region. The new "social arrangements of the farm order," were clearly reflected in the substandard working and living conditions of many Mexican Americans, a reality that Mennonite missionaries saw as a consequence of living a Godless life.[32] "In nearly every town we visited," Amsa Kaufman wrote, "we saw evidence of the low moral life of these people. . . . You could better understand what I mean if you could see one of these communities across the road from one of our prosperous Mennonite communities."[33] The general dislike for the cultural and religious blending of Mexican Americans hindered the early attempts to plant churches in South Texas.

These issues were compounded during World War II when Mexican American families who had attended Mennonite churches reverted to familiar religious traditions. Kauffman complained that many of the people he baptized had now returned to the "mysterious ceremonies, [and] prayers to the Virgin and to the Saints" as a way to cope with the stress of wartime.[34] In addition to complaints about religious backsliding, Kauffman expressed his frustration with how the wartime labor shortage spurred Mexican American families to leave Mathis and surrounding communities for longer periods of time. Kauffman wrote: "No time since we are on the field have we experienced such migration of entire families and in some cases almost entire communities, as during the past summer. This has come about because of the shortage of labor in the various farming communities of the country."[35] Shortly after he made these comments, in 1943, Kauffman moved to Indiana and left the Mennonite mission work in South Texas lacking direction. The Mennonite Brethren mission also lost its first missionaries in the 1950s when Harry and Sarah Neufeld left the South Texas border mission under suspicious circumstances. "He [Neufeld] told us one thing," remembered Mexican American pastor Alfredo Tagle, "but we all knew that the reason he left was because his son Gordon had fallen in love with a Mexican girl, and Neufeld did not believe in the mixing of the races."[36] Despite these departures, and even as the missionary efforts in South Texas dwindled, the booming commercial farming industry in the nearby town of Mathis helped resurrect the missionary hopes of white Mennonites in South Texas.

Saving Souls and Doing Justice in South Texas, 1947–1955

In 1946 Ernesto and Luciana Gonzalez moved to Mathis from nearby San Patricio. A year later Mennonite missionary Florence Lauver and his family arrived in Mathis and set up a mission program immediately across the street from the Gonzalez home. The families soon became acquainted, and the Gonzalez family became the first family in Mathis to attend church services at the small Mennonite mission. Although the families had come to Mathis for different reasons, they joined a larger movement of people coming to Mathis eager to find agricultural work in South Texas.

In the mid-twentieth century, Mathis was in the midst of an agricultural transformation. A big part of the economic boom came in 1950 when F. H. Vahlsing purchased 7,000 acres in and around Mathis and built irrigation systems, wells, and packing gins, which made Mathis a major hub for the distribution of staple crops such as spinach, onions, carrots, cabbage, and cotton. Vahlsing's growing corporation attracted a large number of Mexican migrant families and boosted Mathis's population from 1,950 in 1940 to 6,075 by 1960.[37] Many of the workers who arrived in Mathis came from northern Mexico and the Rio Grande valley. For them, Mathis became yet another stop along the annual migration paths that followed cotton to West Texas and fruit and vegetable crops across the Midwest.[38]

The local paper, the *Mathis News*, attributed most of the population gains to Vahlsing's corporation, noting that, "although Vahlsing was not the first to market vegetables from Mathis, he can largely be given credit for pushing it into the big place the industry now occupies."[39] The economic opportunities and population growth caught the attention of Mennonite missionaries and traveling evangelists who came to Mathis to bring salvation to farm laborers. The local newspaper frequently promoted tent revivals in the area sponsored by various Protestant denominations, including Mennonites. Every week new evangelists from the Baptist, Pentecostal, or Mennonite traditions came to Mathis to bring salvation to the growing number of Vahlsing workers.[40]

The days when missionaries like T. K. Hershey and William Detweiler worried about the evangelical pulse of the Mennonite Church seemed now like a distant memory. By the 1950s Mennonites were fully engaged in missionary projects that extended beyond their traditional ethnic enclaves. The annual meetings of the Mennonite Board of Missions and Charities (MBMC) heard a stream of reports from missionaries working in predominantly African American and Latino communities across the Midwest and Southwest. In these regions, the tactics and approaches of missions resembled those of other evangelical groups. Nelson Kaufman, the head of the MBMC during this time, believed that Mennonites had found "a great deal in common with the objectives and ... work of other evangelical groups."[41]

Mennonite missionaries lead a Bible study in the home of a Mexican American family in Mathis, Texas, 1955. (Courtesy of Rosario G. Vallejo)

In South Texas, Florence Lauver spent his days "sowing the precious seed among the Mexicans" just as he had done as a Mennonite missionary in Argentina. The responses from Mexican Americans in Mathis, however, were often mixed. In one case, he arrived at a home to escort the children to church, and "the mother had them combed and ready." In another case, "a painted lady who does not lead a good life" rejected Lauver's offer to purchase a new Bible. When that same woman learned that her neighbor had purchased a Bible from Lauver, she laughed it off, saying, "She is so bad that she should buy a pile of Bibles with a minister sitting on top of them." In addition to going door to door to invite people to church, Lauver spent time preaching to workers during their breaks, selling Bibles, and traveling to nearby Corpus Christi, where he envisioned another Mennonite mission.[42]

Lauver's work exemplifies the rising evangelicalism in the Mennonite

Church, but at every step of the way there was a parallel desire to establish social service projects. For some white Mennonites, it was clear that strict focus on church missions might alienate a large number of conscientious objectors who were eager to serve in the church after World War II. It was also clear, as missionary Elvin Snyder pointed out, that a social service program might help Mennonites move beyond simply "competing with Baptists, Pentecostals, and Catholics in trying to get folks to come to Sunday school and church services."[43] In 1952 MBMC leaders did just that and instituted a Voluntary Service (VS) program in Mathis as a way to capitalize on one of the strengths of the Mennonite Church: volunteerism.[44]

The mix of evangelicalism and social services that emerged in South Texas joined "orthodoxy to social compassion," as Paul Toews has argued, and provided a much-needed boost to the Mennonite mission. In January 1955 leaders broke ground for a new church building in Mathis. At the height of its popularity, Iglesia Menonita del Calvario (Calvary Mennonite Church) attracted over 200 Mexican Americans every Sunday morning. The growth of programs such as VS provided opportunities for young Mennonites to be "volunteers," or "VSers," as they were called, instead of "missionaries."[45]

VSers, Race, and Religious Identities

From the beginning it was clear that the VSers had entered a racially hostile community in Mathis, where Mexican Americans were relegated to poor working conditions, segregated schools, and a poor health care system. These realities led the VS program to institute three important programs: a maternity clinic, vacation Bible school, and kindergarten education. Each of these programs followed what a League of United Latin American Citizens (LULAC) investigation had revealed in 1948: the segregation of Mexican American school children, decrepit labor camps, and a public health crisis that was fueled by the poor working conditions.[46]

LULAC leaders noted that segregation in local schools was based "solely on the basis of [students'] Mexican descent, without the slightest effort being made to give them a language test." The Mexican Ward School System had approximately 800 Mexican students who were taught by 16 teachers with an average of 50 students per teacher. To make matters worse, the school buildings were "improperly lighted, over-

Church members outside Iglesia Menonita del Calvario in Mathis, Texas, 1950s.
(Courtesy of Mennonite Church USA Archives, Goshen, Indiana)

crowded, poorly equipped, with practically no sanitary facilities whatso-ever." By contrast, the school that Anglo children attended consisted of 12 classrooms, music rooms, a two-story redbrick elementary school building, a football field, tennis courts, and playgrounds, all for an estimated 250 Anglo students.[47]

South Texas also suffered from one of the highest infant mortality rates in the nation. In Texas, which in the 1940s had the sixth-highest infant mortality rate in the country, Mexican Americans had "an above-average child mortality rate" even though they made up only 11 percent of the state's population.[48] The problem immediately caught the attention of Lela Sutter, who in 1953 joined the VS program as a registered nurse from Hopedale, Illinois. In 1954 Sutter convinced VS program leadership to open a maternity clinic in Mathis to address the pre- and postnatal needs of Mexican American women. That year the clinic opened in the section

of town where most Mexican Americans lived and immediately attracted
women from Mathis and surrounding communities. In an average month,
nurses treated around 20 women, and by 1959 nurses had helped deliver
nearly 1,000 babies. When families could not afford to pay the clinic, they
often showered the nurses with onions, watermelons, cantaloupes, and
cucumbers. In return, nurses read Bible passages to the families and invited them to the Mennonite Church.[49]

But by far the most popular program was vacation Bible school. A typical five-day Bible school program attracted nearly 160 Mexican American children every day.[50] It was during vacation Bible school that children
came face to face with Protestant religious teachings and Mennonite culture. For many of the children who attended the vacation Bible school,
the pleasant behavior of the VSers came as a shock. "I really did not understand why they were so nice," remembered Perfecta De León, "because
white people in Mathis were so mean—they would spit at us and treat us
badly and didn't let us play with them."[51]

By contrast, VSers often invited families for lunch on Sunday afternoons and shared the food they were accustomed to eating in their midwestern homes. "We had never eaten bread rolls," recalled Perfecta De
León, "and the first time we went, my sisters ate the entire loaf with but-
ter and they thought it was funny, but my mother was fuming."[52] For the
young VSers who came to South Texas it was an experience unlike any
other. Some described South Texas as being "as much like foreign work as
one can get without going outside of the United States."[53]

If South Texas seemed "foreign" to white Mennonites, the reverse also
proved true. The young Mexican American children who first met the
VSers were both impressed and confused. Rosario Vallejo remembered
how the VSers "came with their long and plain-colored dresses and long
sleeves . . . and I started dressing like them as well because I saw it and
thought, are we supposed to wear that?"[54] The newly arrived VSers were
the only white people living in Mathis's west side—the Mexican American side of town—and their friendliness seemed quite strange to Rosario.
Growing up in Mathis, even as a little girl, Rosario clearly understood her
place as a Mexican American. "In Mathis they [Anglos] didn't greet us
and we didn't greet them; they did their thing and we, well, we were shy,
but when the volunteers arrived they showed us no prejudice."[55]

What distinguished the Mennonite experience for young women like

Mexican American parents look on as their children present what they are learning in
the Mennonite kindergarten program, 1950s. (Courtesy of Rosario G. Vallejo)

Rosario and Perfecta found expression through the body. Becoming Mennonite meant no shorts, no short sleeves—a conservative dress that mir-
rored how Mennonites themselves dressed—no dancing, no Mexican
music, and of course, no facial makeup.[56] This represented a fundamental
shift for most families, like Rosario's, who often attended the festive *bailes*
(dances) in ranching communities around Mathis. Rosario's father quit
being a musician because it meant going to dances that sometimes lasted
several nights. "When we came to town and met the missionaries, my dad
stopped playing, and my mom stopped using makeup," noted Rosario,
"because we saw how the Mennonites lived and the example they gave
us. . . . I never used makeup because of the VSers."[57]

For many Mexican American youth the VSers became models for how
to live a Christian life. They were white, seemed not to be troubled with
financial needs, dressed simply, and were always available to help. But
even as relationships were good-natured, VSers complied with the established racial codes in South Texas. Ted Chapa, who attended the vaca-

tion Bible school as a young boy, remembered that "the Mennonites would preach to us and live in our community . . . but if one of their sons or daughters wanted to marry a Mexicano or Mexicana, that was a no-no and they would open the Bible and explain why that should not happen."[58] The VS program prohibited white Mennonite women from coming too close to Mexican American boys and instituted a policy that advised young women to "be friendly to everyone, but single boys."[59]

These policies, however, did not stop some VSers from forging relationships with Mexican Americans. VSers did have some flexibility, given their status as religious practitioners and outsiders that allowed them to befriend and work with Mexican Americans in ways that did not pose a threat to the local racial structure. But these relationships were rare and often caused more grief than anything. For the sake of the mission, it was important for VSers and Mennonite missionaries to maintain strong relationships with the local Anglo community. Without the support of local Anglos, Mennonite missions might not have enjoyed the success they did in the 1950s and early 1960s.[60]

Budding Pentecostals, Hesitant Peacemakers

For Mexican Americans who joined the Mennonite Church, becoming Mennonite presented new challenges and opportunities. Samuel Hernandez and Lupe De León, both of whom joined the church as teenagers, generally liked the Mennonite position on peacemaking, but they struggled with the quiet and reserved worship services they attended four times a week. For Samuel and Lupe, Mennonite worship services were bland, and both seemed to be more attracted to the fast-paced rhythms and animated styles of their Pentecostal neighbors. Their appreciation for Pentecostal styles led them to a Mennonite turned Pentecostal named Gerald Derstine, who they heard organized camp revival meetings in Minnesota. Derstine was a controversial figure in the Mennonite Church. In 1956 he was removed from his pastoral duties at Strawberry Lake Mennonite Church in Ogema, Minnesota, because he refused to admit that speaking in tongues and charismatic worship were "activities of the devil."[61]

Against the advice of VSers and Mennonite missionaries, Lupe, Samuel, and his brother Raul Hernandez hit the migrant trail in the late 1950s to work the sugar beet fields of Minnesota and catch a glimpse of Derstine at his nightly revival meetings. One night a chance meeting with a group of Pentecostal Mennonites from Mexico spurred their interest in attending a Bible school in La Paz, Baja California. Not long after, Lupe claimed to have had a prophetic vision about that same Bible school: "In the vision, I saw Jesus beckoning me to go to school in La Paz, Baja California. And along with Raul we both left Mathis in the fall and went to Baja California. We studied in Spanish and lived in poor conditions, and later Raul's brother Samuel Hernandez joined us as well. After we returned I married Seferina Garcia."[62]

While in Bible school, Lupe, Raul, and Samuel were summoned to appear at the local draft board in San Patricio County. They obliged, but they did so with the intent to register as conscientious objectors because of their commitment to Mennonite peace theology and their desire to serve in the church instead of fighting in Vietnam. A small number of Mexican Americans registered as conscientious objectors, but in each case the young men volunteered as medical assistants, church leaders, or youth leaders.[63] The decisions these young people made demonstrate the seriousness with which they integrated their newfound faith. They aligned themselves with Mennonite peace theology while at the same time rejecting the slow pace and quiet nature of Mennonite worship services.

Integrating the Pentecostal experience was one way Mexican Americans hoped to transform the Mennonite Church and push it to further expand its strict religious boundaries. The following years would see a new cadre of Mexican American leaders emerge from South Texas. In the 1960s people like Ted Chapa, Criselda Garza, Manuela García, and Chuy Navarro, all of whom had grown up attending Mennonite churches in South Texas, emerged as leaders who continued to push the church to further immerse itself within the cultural geography of South Texas.

Mennonite Missions in Puerto Rico and New York

While missions in Chicago and South Texas were grounded in an emerging evangelical consciousness, Mennonite missions in Puerto Rico started through a government program for conscientious objectors during World War II. Born out of the Selective Service and Training Act of 1940, the Civilian Public Service (CPS) program made it possible for conscientious objectors to serve their country during wartime "under civilian, as opposed to military, administration."[64] The first CPS group to enter Puerto Rico was the Brethren Service Committee in 1942, followed by the Mennonite Central Committee and the Friends Service Committee, who in 1943 joined the work in Castañer, Puerto Rico. With nurses and doctors among the ranks of volunteers, CPS established a fully functioning hospital in the town of La Plata in 1944. Known as the Mennonite General Hospital, it treated more than 1,000 patients a year and provided both minor and major surgeries.[65]

The work of the CPS program was in part a continuation of the New Deal policies that extended into Puerto Rico in the 1930s. In 1935 President Roosevelt instituted the Puerto Rican Reconstruction Administration (PRRA) as a means to address the social and economic problems of Puerto Rico.[66] By 1938 the PRRA, also known as the Caribbean "mini–New Deal," had invested nearly 120 million dollars to improve the island's infrastructure, and by the 1950s the PRRA had built 178 rural and urban schools and instituted recreational programs in the arts, clubs, and sports in Puerto Rico.[67] These changes were hard to miss. After a return trip to Puerto Rico in the 1950s, former CPS volunteer Dr. H. Claire Amstutz reported to Mennonites in the United States "that there have been changes in the economic picture in Puerto Rico. . . . In the cities and along the highways many of the houses were painted and had television aerials. There were many more cars and less oxcarts."[68]

When the CPS program ended in 1947, Mennonite missionaries joined former CPS volunteers to forge missionary programs, build churches, and continue the social services work that had made the CPS program so popular.[69] Unlike missions in Chicago and South Texas, Mennonites were familiar in Puerto Rico as a result of their work through the CPS program. Their popularity reached the halls of government when in 1954 Governor Luis Muñoz Marín called on Puerto Ricans to "help the Mennonites continue their valuable medical and hospital services to our people in these communities."[70]

Part of that appeal had to do with the fact that many CPS volunteers were young and energetic and lived in the communities where they served. As a child growing up in the small town of Coamo Arriba, José Ortíz remembered how "the Catholic priest came around in a black Chrysler Imperial with a red interior and stayed briefly, and then here come the Mennonites in an old Jeep, saying jump on there's room for one more, while the

Puerto Rican parents and children pose with Mennonite missionaries in Guavate,
Puerto Rico, 1950s. (Courtesy of Mennonite Church USA Archives,
Goshen, Indiana)

priest never bothered."[71] The differences between the role of institutional
Catholicism and Mennonite CPS workers seemed to be as stark as night
and day for the local population. "They were gringos and affluent," remembered Ortíz. "They had cameras, eye glasses, shoes, equipment, and
in Puerto Rican society if you have money and gadgets you have status.
They were wearing good shoes, blue jeans and white T-shirts."[72] This ap-
pearance of "status" and the sense that the institutional Catholic Church
was irrelevant led Ortíz to "give his life to Christ" and join the Mennonite
Church in 1952 at the age of thirteen.

With a new religious identity came certain economic sacrifices for
Ortíz's family. None was bigger than when his father quit planting tobacco because it went against the family's new religious beliefs. "People
thought my father was crazy," remembered Ortíz, "because he was leaving
the cash crop." The logic behind this move made little sense to neighbors,

but it certainly resonated with Ortíz's father, who did not want to be associated with what many evangelical Mennonites in the United States considered a vice. The irony here, however, came years later when Ortíz moved to Lancaster County in Pennsylvania. There he discovered the large plantations where Mennonite and Amish farmers were making a comfortable living planting and harvesting tobacco.[73]

Missionaries, Gender Roles, and Conscientious Objectors in Puerto Rico

The goodwill and trust that CPS workers built up in the 1940s, however, gave way to the sometimes disparaging assessments of Puerto Rican families by Mennonite missionaries. In the late 1940s and 1950s, when Mennonite missionary work spread throughout the small and mostly rural communities, Mennonite missionaries organized workshops that focused on child care and hygiene for Puerto Rican women, whom they characterized as "dirty and unkept. . . . Some are addicted to smoking and chewing tobacco, and some of the young girls have temptations to go to places of worldly amusement."[74] In the communities of La Plata and Rabanal, Mennonite missionary Marjorie Shantz reported that "the women of Puerto Rico, even the Christians, lack a knowledge of their responsibility to their children in the spiritual and physical realm."[75] In her report on Mennonite-organized workshops, Shantz noted that some Puerto Rican women were suspicious at first but eventually did join, as they were "willing to listen to the Gospel in their homes or attend other church services."[76]

If working with Puerto Rican women meant preparing them to be "domestic" missionaries, working with men carried greater implications for leadership in the church. Mennonite missionaries often established "training-in-service" workshops that helped train Puerto Rican men in the intricate ways of church leadership and doctrine. The hope, as described by missionary John Driver, was to establish "a strong indigenous church . . . in Puerto Rico."[77] Men who showed interest in pastoral leadership often received opportunities to attend Mennonite colleges in the United States or local Bible colleges on the island. But as an unspoken prerequisite for Mennonite church leadership, Puerto Rican men also had to accept the pacifist beliefs so crucial to Mennonite religious identity. As Mennonite missions expanded, Puerto Rican men were compelled to think about their choices, as American citizens, with regard to military service and war in the 1950s.[78]

While the records show that several Puerto Rican men made the decision to become conscientious objectors, they reveal little else about those men's lives or how they came to their decisions. Julio Rivera of the Palo Hincado Mennonite Church became the first Puerto Rican conscientious objector to appear before the federal hearing officer in San Juan in 1950. Two more Puerto Ricans, Esteban Rivera and Fidel Santiago, soon followed. Santiago served as secretary and receptionist at La Plata Mennonite hospital, and Rivera served as cook for the hospital and service unit. Rivera, originally from La Plata, was the son of a farmer, and after his 1-W term (the replacement program for CPS) ended in 1955, he went on to become copastor of the Rabanal congregation.[79] Some of the young men completed their 1-W terms in places as far away as Colorado and continued from there to participate in church leadership once they returned to Puerto Rico. Like Mexican Americans in South Texas, the commitment made by young men who registered as conscientious objectors revealed how influential Mennonite peace theology was for some Puerto Ricans.

With an emerging cadre of dedicated leadership and the strong legacy of the CPS program, the scope of missions in Puerto Rico grew far larger than in Chicago and South Texas combined. By the early 1960s, the Puerto Rican Mennonite Church grew to nearly 500 members and 12 congregations across the island. In addition to organizing churches, Mennonites opened a 32-bed hospital in the town of Aibonito, a number of clinics in rural communities, a Mennonite school in Pulguillas, and a successful radio program called *Luz y Verdad* (Light and Truth) that reached Mexican Americans as far away as South Texas.[80]

Yet Mennonite success in Puerto Rico played out amid a larger backdrop of increased mechanization and industrialization on the island. These developments affected all Puerto Ricans, but those who lived in rural communities were hit the hardest by these economic changes. The booming postwar economy of the United States lured Puerto Ricans struggling to make ends meet to the ports and industrial sectors of places like New York City, Philadelphia, and Chicago, where a majority of the more than 1 million Puerto Rican migrants lived in 1960.[81]

From Puerto Rican to Nuyorican

Mennonite missionaries understood postwar Puerto Rican migration as largely a result of Christian conversion: "As they become saved they desire to rise to a higher standard of living," noted Lester Hershey.[82] But in reality, the factors that led to the midcentury migration of Puerto Ricans to the mainland were more complex. Historian Virginia Sánchez Korrol attributes the migration of mostly rural and working-class Puerto Ricans to the controversial plan known as Operation Bootstrap. The plan was an extension of the PRRA in its attempt to industrialize Puerto Rico by luring "U.S. corporate and manufacturing interests to the island in exchange for lucrative tax benefits, and a cheap Puerto Rican labor pool that was educated and Americanized."[83] It was during this time that a "modernizing elite" came to represent the future track of Puerto Rico's economic and political development.[84] For a vast number of Puerto Ricans, however, the future was in New York City.

In 1950, along with thousands of other Puerto Ricans, Neftali Torres moved with his family to New York City. Even though he was only seven at the time, Torres admitted that the move from the island to the mainland was something he "never fully recovered from."[85] Puerto Rican migrants like the Torres family settled into patterns established by Puerto Ricans who had been coming to New York City since the early twentieth century. The Torres family settled in East Harlem's burgeoning Puerto Rican community, known as El Barrio. Near the navy shipyard where many Puerto Ricans found work, El Barrio was a community in transition in the 1950s.[86]

The newly arrived Puerto Rican migrants replaced the European immigrants who first settled the area: Irish, Italians, Germans, and Poles. Aside from the fistfights Torres had with white ethnic youth in the neighborhood, the harshness of the move to East Harlem was eased somewhat by Torres's father, who, as a local grocer, often provided his family with familiar foods from Puerto Rico. For the vast majority of Puerto Ricans, adjusting to life in East Harlem meant organizing a strong sense of community through mutual aid societies, trade unions, and fraternal groups where migrants found support.[87]

But alongside the trade unions and mutual aid societies were churches throughout East Harlem and Brooklyn that served as a bridge between the island and the mainland. In her book *Oxcart Catholicism on Fifth Avenue*, Ana María Díaz-Stevens explores the role and ministry of the Archdiocese of New York in helping to settle Puerto Rican migrants.[88] But beyond the formal church institutions was a dynamic and vibrant religious economy that Puerto Rican migrants re-created as an extension of their Pentecostal and mainline Protestant traditions on the island.

In her book *The Transnational Villagers*, sociologist Peggy Levitt shows how churches often operate as transnational networks that link "migrants into a powerful, resource-rich network they can access regardless of their political citizenship."[89] These migrant networks proved useful to Mennonite missionaries from Puerto Rico who followed the migration patterns north.

In 1957 Gladys Widmer, one of the best-known Mennonite missionaries in Puerto Rico, contacted Aquilina and Angel Torres, who had recently arrived in Brooklyn. Although Aquilina had not attended the Mennonite Church in Puerto Rico, her mother was a longtime member, and it did not take long for Widmer, together with missionary John Driver, to baptize Aquilina and Angel Torres in their small Brooklyn apartment. Sometime later, several other Puerto Ricans made the decision to join the new Mennonite community forming in and around the emerging Puerto Rican neighborhood in Brooklyn.[90] Widmer's work with Puerto Rican families in the area eventually led to the establishment of the Primera Iglesia Evangélica Menonita (First Evangelical Mennonite Church) in Brooklyn in 1957. While Widmer's work was the first by missionaries sponsored by the MBMC, other Mennonite groups were already active in the area. In 1946, the Lancaster and Franconia Mennonite conferences held open-air meetings in Queens and the Bronx hoping to appeal to Puerto Rican migrants. In this way, the work of Mennonite missionaries joined a vibrant religious marketplace in the boroughs of New York City where Puerto Ricans were settling in large numbers.

In East Harlem especially, Puerto Rican Pentecostals made up the essence of what Gastón Espinosa has called "Nuyorican religion."[91] Referencing a popular radio ad, Puerto Rican poet Piri Thomas wrote that in East Harlem, "We got more storefront churches than Carter has liver pills."[92] Thomas was right. The large numbers of Puerto Rican Pentecostals and the ubiquitous storefront churches highlight the prominent and quite influential religious movement among Puerto Ricans during the 1950s and 1960s.

In general, Latino evangelical churches did not see much growth until the late 1940s when several Spanish-speaking churches surfaced in Manhattan. The bulk of the growth concentrated in East Harlem, where an estimated 48 percent of the Puerto Rican population of New York City lived and where nearly 60 percent attended one of the approximately 32 Pentecostal churches in the neighborhood.[93] In 1949 another study found that nearly 50 percent of Puerto Ricans were married in Protestant churches, while only 27 percent of weddings took place in Catholic churches. The church helped newcomers like Neftali Torres's family adjust to their new surroundings. For Puerto Ricans adjusting to life in East Harlem, Pentecostal churches represented an important center of life and social activity. "Church was good for us kids," Neftali recalled. "For us non-English-speaking kids this was the one place where communication was all in Spanish, and the church gave us continuity." Pentecostal churches often had services every night of the week, along with recreational activities for youth and children after school hours.[94]

Building a religious avenue of cultural continuity between New York and Puerto Rico helped smooth the transition for many migrants. This resource-rich network aided families in finding housing, employment, and even free loaves of bread every Wednesday. "The bread delivery would drive up halfway through the sermon," remembered Torres, "and just when the pastor was saying amen, he would drive up and deliver day-old bread, raisin bread, and doughnuts. . . . We loved it." The power of continuity, personal relationships, and migrant networks served as powerful motivators for the growth of Puerto Rican Pentecostalism in New York.[95]

But even as powerful a force as the church was, it was not enough to keep Torres off the streets of El Barrio. As a teenager, Torres strayed from his Pentecostal upbringing for a life on the streets and a lifestyle that included drug use. Torres remembered spending almost every night at the local Pentecostal church as a young boy. But by the time he was a teenager, he and his two brothers spent more time on the streets than in the church. That would change one night after he had been stabbed and almost bled to death on the corner of 110th Street and Lexington Avenue. As he lay on the sidewalk, he remembered the "prophetic vision" that a woman in the church had been trying to share with him:

> The pastor's wife at our church came to my mom and said, "You know, I need to talk with Neftali because God has said something to me." My mother said that to me, and I said I don't want to hear it. After a few weeks the woman told my mother, "If Neftali will not come to me, I'll talk with you and you can tell him." Turns out the pastor's wife had seen me in a vision where I was hurt and bleeding on a street corner. That didn't mean anything to me until one Saturday night I got into a fight and I was stabbed. There I am, kneeling on 110th Street and Lexington Avenue, and I'm gushing with blood. At that moment I remembered what the pastor's wife had told my mother.[96]

Finding God on an urban street corner after a knife fight helped change Torres's life, but it also became part of a larger narrative for Latino Pentecostals. Nowhere is this better represented than in the film *The Cross and the Switchblade*, which documents the life of Puerto Rican gangster turned Pentecostal evangelist Nicky Cruz. The film, which stars Pat Boone as evangelist David Wilkerson and Erik Estrada as Nicky Cruz, highlights how the crimes of black and Nuyorican (Puerto Ricans living in New York) gangs could be redeemed through "salvation in Jesus Christ."[97] In many ways Torres's life followed the script of *The Cross and the Switchblade*: Puerto Rican youth gone bad finds redemption in Jesus. But Torres's life would take a different path.

A year after his religious experience, Torres found his way back to church. Instead of trips to dance clubs or the beach, Torres, now married to Gracie, began to organize trips to Times Square with youth groups. There they stood with signs that read, "Christ is the Answer." But as Torres recommitted his life to the Pentecostal Church, the massive movements for social change in the 1960s also began to capture his attention. On one occasion Torres and his newfound faith came face to face with the Vietnam War protesters. His group of about 35 youth was lined up on the steps of the New York Public Library holding their signs as thousands of antiwar activists marched in front of them. "We were swarmed with all these people," Torres explained, "and to my surprise those people were inviting us to join them and protest the war . . . and I thought should we as Christians be protesting war?"[98]

That question took on new meaning after Torres met John Smucker and John Freed, two young Mennonites at a drug rehabilitation center called Hope Christian Fellowship. Torres became affiliated with the rehabilitation center as a volunteer through his friend Sammy Santos, whom he had met while taking classes at a Pentecostal seminary in New York City. Torres noted that on meeting Smucker and Freed, he found them "different . . . white, middle-class, educated, and they simply didn't belong there; they walked around in coveralls and carried hammers."[99] The Mennonites in coveralls with hammers he met at the Hope Christian Fellowship displayed a political and religious orientation that he admired.

In the late 1960s, without knowing much about the Mennonite faith, Torres abandoned his Pentecostal affiliation and joined the Mennonite Church. With his seminary training, it did not take long for Mennonite leaders to credential him as a minister in the Mennonite Church. In a twist of fate, his first ministerial assignment was in Chicago at the very same church that Mennonites had started for ethnic Mexicans back in 1932. The church in Chicago provided a place for Torres to step out of El Barrio in East Harlem and come in contact with a Mexican American congregation where he met people who, unlike him, had grown up in the Mennonite Church. "Every Sunday we had potluck dinners with *pan dulce* [sweet bread], tacos, or tamales, and they would tell us stories," remembered Torres. "Those people had tradition, and it made us look into our tradition quite a bit."[100] Through his pastoral role in Chicago, Torres and his wife, Gracie, became affiliated with another Latino couple, Lupe and Seferina De León from Mathis, Texas. During the next four years, the Torres and De León families would have a significant influence on redefining Latino culture and faith in a Mennonite context.

～～

The cities and regions covered in this chapter represent the most important centers of Mennonite missionary activity in Latino communities during the twentieth century. The regions were tied together by a cadre of Mennonite missionaries who for the most part spoke Spanish and had some experience as missionaries in Argentina during the early part of the twentieth century. Even with the racist missteps and paternalistic pat-

Young men outside the Hope Christian Center, 1960s. It was here that Neftali Torres and Sammy Santos first met and interacted with Mennonite VSers. (Courtesy of EMM photo archives)

terns of Mennonite missionaries, they managed to organize the largest cluster of Latino Mennonite churches in the country. These churches then produced a core of Mexican American and Puerto Rican leadership that emerged in the Mennonite Church during the 1960s and 1970s. This helped keep much of the Mennonite Church focus tied to these regions and also provided a platform for churches in these communities to advocate for church resources. As these churches grew and developed Latino leadership of their own, smaller missions sprung up in places such as Colorado, Florida, Ohio, California, and Iowa, where churches were planted among migrant farmworkers and immigrant communities.

More important than the size or scope of the churches during the mission period between the 1930s and 1960s, however, are the ways in which Latinos forged a religious identity as Mennonites. Even with a strong push to plant churches and replicate the mission work of other Protestant groups, Mennonites managed to impart an ethic of peace, service, and simplicity in the communities where they worked. These were not imparted explicitly as much as they were passed on through Mennonite forms of dress and behavior and Mennonites' stance on military service. Mexican American and Puerto Rican women began to dress like VSers, young men signed up as conscientious objectors, and some took the opportunity to attend a Mennonite college in Kansas during the late 1950s.

But these visible markers of religious conversion are only part of the story. For Mexican Americans and Puerto Ricans who were baptized in the Mennonite Church, religious conversion was a significant experience but not an all-encompassing one. Becoming Mennonite challenged Latinos to think differently about pacifism, the role of the church in society, and even how they dressed, but it also moved them to think about ways to make the Mennonite experience more culturally relevant. In other words, religious conversion signified a new way for Latinos to view and understand the world around them, but it did not eliminate a strong desire to remain tied to their ethnic identities.

The Latino Mennonite experience represents one part of a larger movement of Latino evangelicals and Catholics who in the 1950s and 1960s redefined their religious and ethnic identities. Shaped first by the reforms of Vatican II in Latin America and later by the civil rights movement across the United States, these struggles challenged Latino religious communities to rethink the relationship between culture and religion and inspired many to become agents of social and religious change. But even as Mexican American and Puerto Rican youth came of age in the 1960s, the Mennonite Church was also experiencing its own changes. Since at least the mid-1950s, Mennonite leaders engaged in discussions about the issue of race and racism in the church. In 1955 Mennonite leader and peace activist Guy F. Hershberger drafted a statement on race entitled "The Way of Christian Love in Race Relations." That document would serve as a catalyst for the ensuing discussions of the workings of race in the Mennonite Church and in the urban church context. The following chapter documents how these events led to the formation of the Urban Racial Council in 1968 and the role Latinos and Latinas played in expanding conversations on race beyond black and white.

$\mathscr{X}$ CHAPTER 2 $\mathscr{X}$

Missionary Motives

Race and the Making of the Urban Racial Council

If we, as a peace church, can find no way to become true peacemakers in this revolution against the evil of segregation, let us cease to call ourselves a "peace" church and hand the title over to our Negro brothers who have surely earned it.
—DELTON FRANZ, 1963

Church Missions and Race

Speaking at the Conference on Race Relations in Atlanta in 1964, Mennonite pastor and civil rights activist Vincent Harding shared the story of Presbyterian minister Eugene Carson Blake. In 1963 Blake had joined demonstrators in Baltimore who had long felt the stinging force of the fire hoses, racial segregation, and low wages. "As he joined the demonstration line with fellow ministers," Harding recounted, "he said to those who had already borne the heat of many battles, 'we come late, but we come.'"[1]

Blake's story resonated with Harding, who in the late 1950s challenged white Mennonites to begin moving away from the "hills of Virginia and Pennsylvania" in order to better comprehend the issues affecting African Americans in urban communities. While Mennonites were not totally ignoring the problem of race, Harding believed that "like Blake, we Mennonites come late, very late. . . . While others are acting, we are only now investigating."[2] A few months after giving this talk, Harding left the Mennonite Church altogether, citing his frustration with white Mennonites, who he felt were not ready to commit fully to the black freedom struggle.[3]

That Mennonites were late to the civil rights scene was not a shock to Harding as much as were the internal politics that dominated this distinct ethno-religious group. Steeped in rural traditions, a "quiet in the land" reputation, and overwhelmingly white, Mennonites struggled with how best to engage the civil rights movement without betraying their belief in cultural separatism. This dilemma emerged around the time that Mennonites were embroiled in an intense debate over their role in American society and their history as a "people apart." As historian Paul Toews has argued, the conflict over separation and engagement raised important questions and new possibilities for Mennonites in the years immediately following World War II.[4] Nowhere was this clearer than in the revivalist fervor that swept the nation—and the Mennonites—in the 1950s. As a result, mission programs to Latinos and African Americans in both urban and rural areas grew substantially. Between the 1940s and 1960s, Mennonites helped organize roughly 26 African American and 17 Latino churches across the United States and 12 churches in Puerto Rico.[5]

But churches in black and Latino neighborhoods did more than add new converts to the Mennonite Church. They also raised important questions about race relations in the church and what if any role white missionaries should have in these contexts. These questions formed part of a larger identity crisis for white Mennonites in the 1950s.[6] Central to this crisis was how Mennonites would reconcile their Anabaptist roots of service and discipleship with the waves of revivalism and mission programs shaping the church. More important, how would the church survive the steady rise of rural Mennonites moving to American cities? And how would they justify civic participation?

Mennonite historians have for the most part agreed that World War II was a watershed event in that it transformed how white and mostly rural Mennonites fashioned their belief systems. Cultural markers such as modes of dress gave way to an ideology of "servant activism" that redefined Mennonite identity in the postwar era.[7] But as this chapter demonstrates, a more significant transformation came from the debates Mennonites had in the 1950s over how to improve race relations in the church and society. The "race crisis" became the defining issue for Mennonites and other white evangelicals who were seen as central to sustaining the

"American way of life."[8] Through the flurry of service and evangelistic activities—from Africa to the American Deep South—Mennonites and other evangelical groups were unwillingly thrust into a conversation over segregation, race, and power. Behind this evangelical engagement with race was a potent mix of religion and Cold War politics that helped shape postwar Christianity in America.

In the years after World War II, the United States emerged as a global superpower set on suppressing communism and spreading democracy. These aspirations, however, also exposed the nation's own shortcomings of racial segregation and poverty on the home front.[9] Mennonites and other evangelicals, who during these years launched elaborate global missionary projects, worried that inequalities at home might threaten their ability to share the Gospel as a uniquely democratic narrative. These concerns were enough to convince Mennonites and other evangelicals to begin conversations about race and segregation and in some cases actively work to end racial segregation.

In what historian David Chappell has called the "missionary motive," white churches were forced to draft statements in support of desegregation efforts at home in order to clear the way for church mission programs around the globe. Groups like the Southern Baptist Convention, which in 1956 had $2 million invested in 248 missionaries in Africa, subsumed its concerns about racial supremacy in order to protect its missionary investments.[10] This did not suggest that white churches were any less racist than white politicians, but it does show just how critical it was for white churches to work against racial segregation. More important, the movement of white evangelicals on race further revealed that the "historically significant thing about white religion in the 1950s and 1960s is not its failure to join the civil rights movement . . . [but] that it failed in any meaningful way to join the anti–civil rights movement."[11]

The Mennonite Church followed suit in the 1950s by organizing a series of "race conferences" that addressed racism in the church and church missions and raised questions about the level of involvement of white Mennonites in the civil rights movement. Each step of the way, however, the question of how race relations hindered or bolstered church missions remained central to the discussion. It is no coincidence that most of the race conferences organized in the 1950s and 1960s were under the missionary arm of the church, the Mennonite Board of Missions and Charities (MBMC).

These discussions eventually led to the establishment of the Urban Racial Council (URC) in 1968, which brought together African American and Latino leaders to work for greater integration of nonwhite people into the Mennonite Church. But even before white Mennonites launched into serious discussions on race and church missions, a larger church debate emerged about the importance of Anabaptist identity and a fear that the future of the Mennonite Church pointed ever fervently toward American evangelicalism.

The Anabaptist Vision and Mennonite Identity

In 1942 Harold S. Bender delivered the presidential address to the American Society for Church History. The speech, entitled "The Anabaptist Vision," became a rallying cry for Mennonites who were concerned that core theological values were being subsumed under a more general notion of American evangelicalism. According to Bender, Anabaptism—the movement that gave birth to the Mennonites in sixteenth-century Europe—embraced "discipleship," "a new church, separated from the world," and an ethic of "love and nonresistance that applied to all human relationships."[12] While these core values were all significant in their own right, how exactly they fit together would profoundly challenge Mennonite identity. In general, Mennonites struggled to reconcile how to remain "separated from the world" while actively engaging it through domestic and global missionary projects in the mid-twentieth century.

Bender's speech, however, reflected the aspirations of many white Mennonites who believed in maintaining strong ethnic ties, a commitment to peacemaking, and an ethic of service rooted in Anabaptist theology. Nowhere was this more visible than during World War II when 12,000 young men and women registered as conscientious objectors and committed themselves to working in Civilian Public Service (CPS) between 1941 and 1947. The CPS program was so popular among white Mennonites that it later served as a model for church programs like Voluntary Service (VS) in places such as South Texas and New York City.[13]

Similarly, but on a much larger scale, the Mennonite Central Committee

(MCC) sent hundreds of volunteers around the world to work for peace and provide relief services for communities in need.[14] In the 1940s alone, Mennonites spent more than $12 million for relief and development work around the world. They also organized three biblical seminaries by 1955 for young Mennonite intellectuals who wanted to explore the contours of Mennonite and Anabaptist beliefs. Social service organizations such as the domestic VS program and the global reach of the MCC represented the "servant activism" philosophy prominent among white Mennonites during the 1940s and 1950s. But even as Mennonites maintained their core values of peace and service, a parallel movement emerged that drew support from a growing cadre of Mennonites who believed in a broader engagement with the world around them through church missions and, in some cases, saving souls in open tent revivals.[15]

Revivals, Race, and Mennonite Identity

In the open fields of Lancaster and Franconia, Pennsylvania, Mennonites gathered for religious revivals in the early 1950s. Only two years after Billy Graham launched his first crusade in Los Angeles, Mennonite evangelist George Brunk II began preaching to large crowds of Mennonites during the summer of 1951. Sunday evening crowds often swelled to between 10,000 and 12,000 Mennonites gathered at the open field outside the Lancaster airport.[16] They sang hymns a cappella and heard fiery sermons from Brunk, who often pleaded, "I wish every one of you would say Amen," during his famous sermons on topics such as "God's Supreme Position of Power." Each revival ended with a "neither prolonged nor tedious" invitation to accept Jesus Christ as personal savior. According to reports, "Everything was done decently and in order."[17] It was revival Mennonite style.

Those who criticized Mennonite revivals were often chastised for being "helpers of the devil and his gang" or "defenders of the old ways."[18] As Mennonites more forcefully engaged Cold War–era revival in America, the "old ways" referred to the quiet and isolated existence in which many Mennonites lived in rural towns across the Midwest. Mennonite beliefs in simplicity, humility, and silence stood in stark contrast to the new and public demonstrations of faith, the fiery sermons, and the large crowds that Brunk and other Mennonite evangelists attracted. But by the 1950s,

Mennonites had become much more comfortable with public expressions of faith and joined a broad chorus of "new evangelicals" that rose to prominence against the backdrop of Cold War politics and a "Godless" communist threat.[19]

With the charismatic Billy Graham as its most visible leader, this new brand of evangelicalism branded itself as a more open and inclusive movement. It emerged as a middle-ground movement between an emerging Protestant left and paranoid religious leaders who believed communists were plotting a global takeover. Religious scholar George Marsden includes Mennonites in this mix of theological perspectives that often ranged "from Pentecostals to Mennonites" and that "maintained the so-called 'pietist' position that churches and religious leaders should stay out of politics and confine themselves more strictly to spiritual matters."[20]

With a focus on spiritual matters, the Mennonite Church experienced an awakening of sorts in the years following World War II.[21] In addition to increased missionary work on the American home front, Mennonites initiated missionary work in Latin America, Europe, Asia, and Africa. By the end of the 1950s, Mennonite missionaries were active in more than 15 countries around the world. To solidify their reach and influence, they established evangelistic radio programs such as *The Mennonite Hour, Luz y Verdad,* and the *Navaho Bible Hour.* They did all this with steady financial support from an increasingly wealthy constituency. Between 1950 and 1954 contributions to the MBMC nearly doubled to well over $1 million for the first time in its history.[22]

Much of this new wealth came from Mennonite farmers who saw their profits skyrocket as demand and produce prices doubled during World War II.[23] As contributions to missionary efforts increased, Mennonite leaders placed a greater emphasis on professionalism. Gone were the days of well-intentioned missionaries with little or no formal education. When J. D. Graber assumed the role of executive secretary of the MBMC in 1944, he represented this shift as the first executive secretary with substantial missionary experience in India, a paid salary, and a Princeton education.[24]

If the tensions around Anabaptism and evangelicalism revealed changing theological currents in the mid-twentieth century, increased urbanization and engagement with American pop culture revealed the rapid pace of Mennonite assimilation into American society. The move to the city began in earnest in 1945, when 8 percent, or 4,569 Mennonites resided in cities. By 1960 this figure jumped to 11 percent, or 8,187 out of a total membership of 73,576.[25] But increased urbanization revealed only one part of a broader assimilation pattern that white Mennonites experienced at midcentury. Historian Perry Bush has shown how everything from radio and film to the rising popularity of the American car in the 1950s helped accelerate patterns of assimilation. Some Mennonites welcomed these changes, while others were deeply troubled. Add to that list the move from German to English, which began in earnest in the 1930s and became a reality by the 1950s, and a clearer picture emerges that shows how a generation of Mennonites closed the gap of separation between American society and their ethnic enclaves in Pennsylvania, Kansas, and Indiana.

The changing patterns of cultural assimilation, fueled by a growing fascination with American pop culture, became even more visible when young Mennonites moved away from their strict dress codes. Everything from the length of a woman's hair to the styling of the "plain coat" for men changed as young Mennonites left behind their conservative fashions, which for most of the twentieth century had been visible markers of identity. Lee Lowry, an African American pastor from Saginaw, Michigan, remembered how as a child he and his friends "used to laugh at the funny white 'hats' the Mennonite ladies wore and the fact that you couldn't tell who the preacher was, because all the men wore the clerical coat and looked alike."[26]

While the changes in fashion raised the ire of conservative Mennonite groups, those who were new to the church and witnessed the transformation expressed even more disappointment. For Mexican Americans in South Texas, the changes came as a shock. When Lupe and Seferina De León from Mathis, Texas, who had first encountered Mennonites as teenagers, arrived as students at Hesston College in Kansas, they were surprised at how quickly patterns of dress had changed. For most at this small college, head coverings, long dresses, and absence of facial makeup were things of the past. The shock was especially pronounced for Seferina: "The Mennonites stressed to us a lot . . . [that] you don't go to the movies, you don't wear makeup, you don't go to the dances, you don't drink or smoke, you don't cut your hair. . . . So when we got to Hesston, here we see these Mennonites with short dresses, short hair, makeup, and I felt like we were lied to. . . . And they're Mennonite? Look at the way they are dressed!"[27] Chuy Navarro had a similar reaction when he noticed the new fashions of VS workers in the 1960s: "All of a sudden they arrived with long hair, cutoffs, and sandals . . . they all wanted to be flower children." Lupe De León noted that in contrast to the white T-shirts and clean-cut jeans of the 1950s, the volunteers in the 1960s arrived with "their record albums, their miniskirts, and fellows with bell-bottom trousers and long hair. They have shown us—ten years after they taught us differently—that Mennonites have sinful tendencies just as the rest of us have."[28] These comments by Mexican Americans show how deep and visible the changes were, but they also reveal how white Mennonites had developed a much broader and sophisticated engagement with American culture by the 1950s.

In short, the push of evangelicalism and the pull of the "Anabaptist Vision" coupled with a deeper engagement with American pop culture signaled a new era for white Mennonites. While they sought their Anabaptist roots, they also benefited from church budgets that were at an all-time high, larger missionary programs, and an active engagement with American culture and politics as a result of World War II. These were all new developments that brought enormous change to this once tight-knit ethno-religious community. The changes through technological advances such as radio, television, cars, and fashion trends all point to the ways in which Mennonite identity transformed during these years. But perhaps what had the greatest impact on radically shifting the direction of Mennonite culture, theology, and practice had to do with the mission programs that put white Mennonites in close contact with mostly African American and Latino communities in urban areas. More than changing fashions or the "servant activism" alive during World War II, church missions in nonwhite communities thrust Mennonites into uncharted waters in the postwar era.

Mennonites and the Race Question

The religious resurgence that swept the nation—and the Mennonites— was aided by an economic upswing that helped pull the United States out of its Depression-era struggles. This new prosperity gave rise to global missionary initiatives like World Vision, which emerged in the 1950s. The rise of World Vision was only one example in an era that saw evangelicals increase their missionary budgets and global reach as they promoted "a new evangelical optimism eager to save the world."[29] The clearest evidence for this new evangelical optimism was reflected in the nearly 30,000 American missionaries that worked around the world planting churches and spreading the Gospel. Along with increasing their missionary budgets, evangelical groups across the country invested millions of dollars building new churches or remodeling their old buildings. The new spaces of worship helped accommodate the growing number of Americans who attended church in larger numbers in the 1950s and 1960s.[30]

Global missionary projects were developed alongside home missionary projects in mostly black and Latino neighborhoods. Much of this focus in the 1950s followed the migratory path of Latinos and African Americans who, attracted by the promise of employment in the booming war and agriculture industries, moved to northern and western cities. As African Americans moved out of the Deep South, more than half a million Mexicans, some as part of the US-Mexican Bracero Program, migrated to cities across the Southwest and Midwest. On the East Coast, the controversial program to industrialize Puerto Rico—Operation Bootstrap—brought as many as 32,000 migrants every year to cities like Chicago and New York City in search of employment.[31]

Many of these migratory movements did not go unnoticed. As early as 1936, Mennonite missionary T. K. Hershey wrote about the urgent need to begin mission work among Mexicans, who "are . . . right at our door [and] who are ignorant of the Gospel. . . . This million and a half Mexicans in the United States stands as a challenge to the Mennonite Church."[32] For Mennonites, it was the perfect time for a coming-out party. With revenues for missionary organizations at an all-time high, Mennonites launched new missionary projects in 52 regions across the globe between 1946 and 1966, most of them in the 1950s, which saw a variety of Mennonite groups launching 37 new mission projects from South America to Asia. This was the period of internationalization for Mennonites, as they broke away from their traditional and quiet communities in rural America.[33]

In both rural and urban areas across the Midwest and Southwest, the MBMC organized missionary work in African American and Latino neighborhoods. In some cases it was Latino and African American Mennonites themselves who were the missionaries. In 1944 James and Rowena Lark moved to Chicago's Near Southside neighborhood to start a vacation Bible school program among African American children. Around the same time, David and Elsa Castillo moved to Denver to plant a church among the Latino community there.[34] In Puerto Rico, white Mennonites led the charge as they took advantage of the success of the CPS program during World War II.

With the initial success of Mennonite home mission programs in Latino and African American communities came increased concern over how the politics of race might hinder their ability to carry out missionary projects. Home mission programs gave white Mennonites a front-row view of racial injustice and segregation, but they also raised concerns about the appropriate roles for white Mennonites in civil rights struggles. In fact, many remained conflicted about how best to respond or whether they should involve themselves in civil rights struggles at all. For some, like Mennonite historian Irvin Horst, the appropriate way to address the race question should be rooted in a larger concern "to bring the Gospel to all the world" and not in community or street politics.[35]

Following Horst's advice, and with an eye toward protecting their missionary investments, white Mennonites organized two important gatherings to talk about race in 1951 and 1955. The latter meeting helped produce the doctrinal statement "The Way of Christian Love in Race Relations," written by peace activist Guy F. Hershberger.[36] The statement was significant because it revealed the official stance of the church and identified segregation, discrimination, and prejudice as "sin."[37] The statement prompted other branches of the church to make similar declarations. In 1959 a sister denomination, the General Conference Mennonite Church, adopted its own statement denouncing racism and segregation. In the following years, the MCC and the MBMC adopted statements as well as a host of other Mennonite colleges and church conferences.[38]

These first two meetings were followed by a series of gatherings that took place throughout the late 1950s and 1960s. In each gathering black and white Mennonites debated, drafted denominational statements, and listened intently to charismatic leaders who outlined important reasons why the Mennonite Church should commit more fully to the struggle for black civil rights. These meetings were particularly remarkable because they showcased the theological orientations and physical spaces where black and white Mennonites talked about race. In "homes and sanctuaries" across the Midwest, the civil rights movement captured the theological sensibilities of white Mennonites even as black Mennonites challenged them to leave behind visible and cultural markers of identity. At the forefront of this movement was Vincent Harding, an African American Mennonite, who in 1959 called on white Mennonites to "break down the wall of German-Swiss-Dutch backgrounds . . . [and] lose the cultural stereotype of Mennonitism . . . for there are some baptized here who are my color, whose parents or grandparents never came near Germany or Switzerland or Holland or Russia."[39] Harding's call was less an indictment of Mennonite identity politics than it was about moving the Mennonite Church to a place where the growing number of African Americans members could feel welcome.

As early as 1955, Lee Roy Bechler counted a total African American Mennonite membership of nearly 400, with the number of those who attended regularly totaling to more than 1,500 nationwide.[40] The growing number of African American Mennonites did more than fill the pews of the churches. They led the charge in the 1950s and 1960s to make the Mennonite Church a more inclusive place, and they formulated theological points that expanded and moved Anabaptism from a theology of "the quiet in the land" to one that stressed a racialized critique of American society. No one was better at this than Harding. He captured the attention of white Mennonites by reminding them that working against racial discrimination was not only their responsibility but a foundational part of their history as nonconformists and Anabaptists.

For Harding and other African American leaders, the Anabaptist heritage of Mennonites placed them in a unique position to address racial injustice. Believing that the country's racial struggles signified being "in a time of war," Harding called on white Mennonite leaders to see themselves as "ministers of reconciliation" and acknowledge that the time for peace "is for now or never." Harding's push to recognize the important role of the Anabaptist tradition was an important move that helped frame "the race question as a moral and spiritual problem."[41] In the larger spiritual tradition of the civil rights movement, Harding elevated the question of racism in America to a central moral dilemma. Doing so helped make the civil rights movement in the church and society a powerful religious movement in the 1950s and 1960s.

By joining "traditional black cultural and religious themes with ideas and strategies of social movements around the world," Michael Omi and Howard Winant argued, black civil rights leaders raised the issue of racism and segregation in America to one that embodied a deep reflection on religious ethics and social change.[42] But Harding took it one step further in the Mennonite Church. By equating the "race crisis" with "war," Harding appealed to the moral underpinnings of Mennonite theology and presented a challenge to white Mennonites that they could not turn down.

The theological creativity and moral push of black Mennonites reveal two important points. First, white Mennonite intellectuals like Harold Bender and Guy F. Hershberger did not have a monopoly on Anabaptist theology. African American leaders like Harding often cited Anabaptist history and theology when they "appealed to love, long-suffering, and nonconformity."[43] Second, black Mennonites believed that because of their history of peacemaking and struggle, Mennonites were especially well placed to address questions of power and race in society. How white Mennonites felt about this, however, was another matter entirely.[44]

The irony, of course, was that the insular attitudes of white Mennonites promoted "non-conformity to the ways of the world, [while they] slavishly and silently conformed to the American attitudes on race and segregation."[45] White Mennonites did not so much disagree with black civil rights leaders as they feared what civil rights engagement might actually mean for them. White Mennonites questioned whether they were suited for political protest on the streets or promoting legislative action. In 1963 Mennonite historian Cornelius Dyck characterized this concern perfectly when at a Mennonite race conference in Indiana he highlighted the limitations of the Anabaptist tradition: "For the Anabaptist the way to his neighbor seldom goes over Washington. But when we do these things at the local level as we are able, our Negro brothers think we are doing too little, too late. They want legislation. . . . If legislation is the answer, perhaps Mennonites do not have that answer theologically."[46] Contrary to the political work that went into organizing a fair and just policy for conscientious objectors during World War II, engaging a legislative struggle or joining street protests was not something white Mennonites considered part of their call for racial justice.[47] In short, Mennonites struggled with how to approach the question of civil rights. As one person summarized, "Many Mennonites are good, but not brave."[48]

Missionary Motives

While the race conferences of the 1950s and 1960s involved mostly black and white Mennonite leaders, their frank conversations spilled over into the church press. Between 1957 and 1969, 114 articles about race were published in the church magazine, the *Gospel Herald*.[49] In 1963 alone "eighty-five reports, editorials, profiles, and opinion pieces" were published in church newspapers across the country.[50] Most addressed the plight of African Americans, while others highlighted the supposed positive achievements that Mennonite churches had made with regard to racial integration. In one article published in 1949, historian Melvin Gingerich noted that in places from Chicago to Ohio, churches had "Mexican, Negro, and white members . . . and in Ohio we have a summer camp for Negro children."[51] The leading Mennonite intellectual on matters of peace, Guy F. Hershberger, asserted in another article that "to take part in any form of race discrimination and oppression is . . . a contribution to war."[52] The excitement over their perceived racial progress was often against the backdrop of other Protestant groups whom Mennonites criticized for having made minimal progress in "breaking down the barriers of discrimination."[53]

For white Mennonite leaders, concerns over how to engage the civil rights movement were overcome by a deeper desire to protect their missionary investments and a belief that the success of church missions hinged on the ability of white Mennonites to work against racism. Black leaders and pastors, who in the 1950s continually pushed back and questioned the place of white missionaries, often confirmed this sentiment. In 1954, L. C. Hartzler reported on a gathering of mission leaders where an African American minister stood up and asked the group of white missionaries: "How can you expect people of other countries and races to take seriously the preaching of the Gospel by your missionaries when you have segregation of races in your own country?"[54] Questions like these forced white Mennonites to think more critically about their role in the civil rights movement. But they were not the only ones. In the 1950s other white churches were also caught in a moral dilemma over how to respond to the practices of segregation and racial injustice.

In the years following the 1954 landmark case of *Brown v. Board of Education*, groups like the Southern Baptist Convention, southern Presbyterians, Congregationalists, Methodists, Lutherans, and Episcopalians issued doctrinal statements in support of the court's decision to require desegregation of public schools. Before this, the more progressive National Council of Churches declared that "the pattern of segregation is diametrically opposed to what Christians believed about the worth of a person." Southern Presbyterians took a similar stand when they declared that "no artificial man-made class or caste can be justified before God." The central motivating factor was the inability of white Protestants to find a biblical justification for segregation.[55] It was a point that the theologian Robert J. McCracken argued vehemently in the pages of the *Gospel Herald* in 1962: "There is no Christian argument in defense of racial discrimination."[56]

Without a clear Christian and biblical argument for segregation, white churches had no choice but to follow the mandates of the *Brown* case in 1954. According to historian David Chappell, the support that came for the *Brown* decision revealed that the white church would not be the place where anti–civil rights crusaders would find a home.[57] But beyond a sense of concern for Supreme Court mandates, white churches, including the Mennonite Church, had a much larger concern that affected them directly: their domestic and foreign missions. During a time of increased missionary zeal, racial segregation at home was an embarrassment for missionaries who were organizing churches overseas, especially in places like Africa. Most white churches had no choice but to at least to present the semblance that they believed in "justice for all." Racial segregation at home limited America's ability to counter communism and spread democracy overseas as much as it hindered white missionaries from spreading Christianity. The two were inseparable.

How racial segregation hindered the work of white missionaries overseas was a central concern for Mennonites but one that has often been overlooked by historians who have given more attention to the theological and political side of the debate.[58] Historian Perry Bush, for example, has argued that the politicization of race talk within the Mennonite Church in the 1950s had much to do with what Mennonites had learned during their legislative battles for conscientious objection during World War II. Similarly, historian Paul Toews cites the affinity Mennonites found in the peace theology of Martin Luther King Jr. as a central factor that moved them to engage civil rights in general and the black freedom struggle in particular.[59]

The legislative battles for conscientious objectors in the 1940s combined with the influence of Martin Luther King Jr. have led historians to argue that white Mennonites exhibited a "quiet progressivism" with regard to race relations. But they do so without providing much evidence on how the Mennonite stance on race was different than other white Protestant groups. Placing Mennonite responses to racism in their historical context reveals that they were not any more progressive about race than other evangelical groups in the 1950s. Instead, they simply followed the broader trends set by other white churches who worried that mission programs might be hurt by the racial tension on the American home front.[60] Like many white churches in the South, the Mennonite Church entered the civil rights movement from motives that revolved around church missions. Hidden beneath the debates over cultural assimilation and the viability of the Anabaptist vision was an emerging "activist impulse" that helped forge the missionary identity of Mennonites during the second half of the twentieth century.[61]

No one espoused this view more than MBMC leader J. D. Graber, who at a conference in Chicago in 1959 gave a speech titled "Race Relations in World Evangelism" in which he urged church leaders to consider the ramifications that race problems at home could have for global missions. To drive his point home, he told the story of a remote church in Ghana where the pastor "knew about Little Rock and about Montgomery. . . . He knew about these spots in our country where this race question has flared up."[62] Graber proceeded to describe a picture that hung at the Russian information center in Ethiopia: "[It was a] huge picture, the background showing the skyline of New York City. In the foreground were white policemen on horseback with night sticks . . . the policemen were bringing the sticks down on the heads of the Negroes. Underneath the picture was a caption: 'this is the way your brothers are being persecuted and unjustly treated in capitalistic America.' The other pictures alongside this one depicted the wonderful life in Russia."[63] Graber's message was part of a broader chorus of concern coming from many evangelicals who saw church missions as a counterpoint to a supposed communist threat.[64] But that is where the similarities ended. Graber distanced himself from patriotic evangelicals who identified "Communism with the Kingdom of Satan" and equated communism with desegregation and antiracism work.

Graber was not alone in his tempered attitude toward communism. In

1952, the MCC issued a "Report on Communism" that recognized "the positive aims of communism as 'a worldwide campaign for social and economic justice to be realized in an all-embracing community of men.'"[65] Sympathetic views of communism such as the one the MCC issued often came from relief and service workers whose experience with refugee populations in places like Europe and Asia shaped their perspectives on the workings and inequalities of the capitalist system. For Graber and other Mennonite leaders the concern was not communism as much as how church missions could succeed against the backdrop of racial segregation at home. It concerned Graber so much that in the 1950s he pleaded with the MBMC to "include non-Caucasians in our foreign missionary appointments."[66]

Billboards portraying negative images of the United States and threats of communist ties did not bode well for Mennonite mission agencies. But if foreign missions worried white Mennonites, the home mission projects in which they worked with African Americans were of even greater concern. These were not communities thousands of miles and oceans away. They were close and gaining ground, with stronger churches and a rising membership.[67] While the concerns about world evangelism that Graber voiced helped thrust Mennonites into a discussion of race, sustaining that discussion in the 1960s would require a broader and more nuanced commitment that meant expanding conversations on race beyond black and white.

Latinos and the Politics of Race in the Mennonite Church

During the hot summer of 1963, Mennonite leader and peace activist Guy F. Hershberger visited Mennonite churches in the South. In one church in Gulfport, Mississippi, a woman asked, "[Will] blacks and whites be together in heaven?" Before Hershberger could answer, another church member chimed in and gave what Hershberger called the "stock answer." That is, "There will be no negroes in heaven, physical characteristics will not be present." Hershberger responded by suggesting that in heaven, "we will be recognized as negroes, whites, etc. even as Jesus was recognized in his body." Another church member then forcefully asked Hershberger, "Do you want to bring Niggers into our church? Is this what you are trying to do?"[68] As Hershberger left the church that evening, mem-

bers of the Crossroads Bible Church reminded him that they were "trying to win white persons for Christ. If negroes came to church, the non-
christian white would never be reached."[69]

Hershberger's visit to Mennonite churches in the South and his sub-
sequent report was a wake-up call to Mennonite leaders. Shortly after
Hershberger filed his report, black and white leaders met once again in
Elkhart, Indiana, where the misconceptions and stereotypes identified in
Hershberger's report filled the room. As a result, leaders expressed the
need for basic educational programs that addressed racial reconciliation.
Many of the misconceptions, theologian Norman Kraus observed, were as
simple as needing "to feel the Negroes' hair to find out if it is stiff or soft."[70]

The meeting in Elkhart was followed by gatherings in Ohio, Iowa, and
Missouri between 1965 and 1968. Leaders made it clear that each gathering was a step toward making "the church become aware of the universal
nature of the gospel and the transracial character of the believing brotherhood."[71] But even as leaders spoke of this "transracial character" of the
church, the race conferences that took place in the 1960s were limited to
only black and white participants. While Mennonite leaders like Hershberger and Vincent Harding made passing references to Mexicans and
Puerto Ricans in their sermons and lectures, the question of race relations
in the church was defined as a black-white issue. This was not unique to
Mennonites.

Even though Latino communities represented some of the strongest areas of Mennonite mission work and VS programs, they were not invited
to participate in the church-wide conversations on race. Their exclusion
was not necessarily intentional, however. During the 1950s and 1960s,
African Americans in the Mennonite Church were more vocal about issues of race relations, and they also outnumbered Latinos in the church.
Most black Mennonites also lived relatively close to where the conferences were held, in places like Ohio, Iowa, and Missouri.

But even more important than numbers and geographic proximity was
the general ambivalence over the racial status of Latinos and their collective identity as an ethnic group. In missionary reports from South Texas,
Puerto Rico, and New York, white Mennonites documented their own
misgivings about the racial makeup of Latinos. In South Texas, Mennonite
missionary Amsa Kauffman often connected the racial status of Mexican
Americans as a "brown race" with their perceived deviant behavior: "As

a class they are more or less ignorant and given to vices, shooting and cutting affairs."[72] In Puerto Rico, CPS workers often struggled with the multiracial complexions of Puerto Ricans, whom they identified as possibly "white." In one report Albert Gaeddert noted that Puerto Ricans' "physical features are very much like our own . . . except for the negro or Indian influence."[73]

These racial perceptions changed, however, once Puerto Ricans moved to New York City and other urban areas in the 1950s. For Puerto Ricans and other Latin American immigrants, migration to the United States has historically carried with it racialized consequences. This "browning tendency," as sociologist Clara Rodriguez has shown, immediately places Latino immigrants along the lower end of the racial hierarchy in the United States. As missionary efforts among Puerto Ricans expanded, missionaries struggled to understand the racial makeup of Puerto Ricans, who were a potential "white" race in Puerto Rico and an obvious "minority" in New York. In their reports to the MBMC, white Mennonites in New York City frequently noted that the skin color of Puerto Ricans and their "language handicap" relegated them to the lower end of the racial hierarchy as new arrivals in the United States.[74]

The contrasting attitudes about the racial and ethnic status of Mexican Americans and Puerto Ricans say much about the making of Latino identity. Historian David Gutiérrez has argued that before 1960 Latinos as a group were not considered "part of a discernible 'minority' population."[75] For the most part, Mexican American and Puerto Rican struggles were seen as distinct movements that had limited interaction across ethnic and regional boundaries. That Latinos were absent from the discussions on race in the church says more about how white and black Mennonites understood the boundaries of race than it does about any notion of Latino political apathy. When Latinos showed up in large numbers at one of the last race gatherings in 1968, they proved that they had paid close attention all along to the conversations on race in the Mennonite Church.

Organized at the YMCA in Chicago, the 1968 conference was the first to include a sizable Latino presence. Reports of the gathering highlight that out of 65 persons in attendance there was "a very good representation of Spanish leaders" present in Chicago. While exact numbers are not known, African American pastor John Powell did write in one memo that "when the Council was organized in 1968, there were more Spanish speaking people represented at the meeting than blacks."[76] The names that do appear in the documents include Ted Chapa, Conrado Hinojosa, and Criselda Garza (South Texas); Larry Martinez (Chicago); Sammy Santos (New York); Victor Ovando (Ohio); Mario Bustos (Wisconsin); and Lupe Gonzalez (South Bend, IN), among others. They arrived in Chicago through the organizing efforts of a Mexican American named John Ventura, who was a Mennonite pastor in Denver and first came to know Mennonites through the mission programs in Chicago.

Anything but the typical Mennonite, Ventura stood out as a politically astute pastor who was not afraid to raise his voice in the Mennonite Church. He was also one of the few Latino pastors inclined to engage both political and social concerns alongside his desire to do mission work and plant churches. "Because of his aggressiveness and outspokenness," Ted Chapa remembered, "he was labeled by some of the Mennonite big wheels as very insensitive, as a rebel [and] instigator."[77] Ventura was quite adamant about his support for what he called "Spanish" ministries in the Denver area, even if that meant competition for funds with African Americans.

Only a few years after beginning mission work in Denver, the MBMC decided to withdraw its support for Ventura. To make matters worse, Ventura quickly noticed that the monetary support that the MBMC was withdrawing from his work in Denver would be used to start churches in mostly African American communities. In a letter addressed to MBMC secretary Nelson Kauffman, Ventura expressed his frustrations over the decision to rescind funding for Latino ministries: "VS is sent to the black ghettos, very good! But in the meantime, [the MBMC] withdraws all funds from a Spanish ministry in Denver ... where we had contacts, where we had a facility, where we had personnel. It castrated a church program for the Hispano minority community, and yet was looking for some place else to become involved with the so-called minority community."[78]

Ventura's frustrations over this incident prompted a long letter of protest in which he expressed his dissatisfaction with the poor relationships the MBMC had established with Latinos in Denver. More important, however, the experience brought attention to what Ventura perceived was the low priority the MBMC placed on Latino communities in contrast to African American communities.[79] Increasing the national presence of Latinos in the Mennonite Church, Ventura believed, meant forging stronger bonds with African American leaders. Knowing that MBMC leaders had agreed to form an "interracial council" at the final race conference in Chicago in 1968, Ventura pleaded with Latino leaders from across the country to attend the gathering. The role of this new council was "to deal with the strategy related to evangelism and church development" within an increasingly visible and powerful civil rights movement.[80] His efforts worked and in the process changed how both black and white Mennonites talked about race relations within the church.

Black Power, Latino Identity, and the Urban Racial Council

Conceived as an "interracial council" to work on behalf of black and urban churches, the newly formed URC was officially organized at the Chicago gathering in 1968.[81] Organized under the auspices of the MBMC, the URC was set up to "serve as Mission Board spokesman to congregations, as mediator-counselor to urban churches, and as a liason [sic] between militant groups and the church."[82] The first committee chosen to lead the URC included three African Americans (Gerald Hughes, John Powell, Leroy Berry), one Anglo (Hubert Schwartzentruber), and one Mexican American (John Ventura).

The decision to include Ventura in the first URC committee was positive, but it also called attention to how Latinos would fit within the mostly black leadership of the URC. The issue became even more complicated when some Latino leaders at the Chicago gathering expressed their desire not to become part of the URC. In the meeting minutes, African American leader John Powell wrote that "they [Latino leadership] felt that since the Spanish people are accepted in society, and do not have the same problems as blacks, that their representation on the council should be that [of] listen[ing] and assist[ing] black members."[83]

While some Latinos at the conference did believe their struggles were different, there was also concern over how forcefully some African Americans were talking about civil rights. At issue was how black Mennonites voiced an Anabaptist theology fused with the emerging ideas of black nationalism and third-worldism. In doing so, the new black Mennonite leadership—John Powell, Hubert Brown, and to some extent Warner Jackson—expanded Vincent Harding's Anabaptist vision by infusing it with the tenets of the Black Power movement. Hoping to ignite the church, black Mennonites warned that "the consequences will be adverse to their own interests" if white Mennonites did not change course and more aggressively engage civil rights.[84]

The new black leadership was also clear that they were ready to "revolutionize the gospel." They called on the church to accept Black Power and admit that "Black is Beautiful." The energy and passion that came from black Mennonite leaders was part of a broader movement that intensified the civil rights movement in the late 1960s. Historian Jeffrey Ogbar has explained the brazen radicalism that emerged as a response to the supposed failures of some civil rights leaders to organize change in urban black communities. This in addition to the assassination of Martin Luther King in 1968 raised the level of dissatisfaction among young black activists who pushed for "a popular celebration of black historical accomplishment, reclamation of Africa, and the importance of self-determination."[85]

With racial tensions peaking across the country in 1968, the Chicago gathering put on display the frustrations of black Mennonite leaders as they raised the pressure on white Mennonites. But questions of black identity and power also captured the attention, if not the ire, of Latinos, who questioned the nationalist politics of black leaders. For Mario Bustos and Lupe Gonzalez, talk of black nationalism and black theology had no place in the church and much less in the nonresistant Mennonite church. Ted Chapa, Criselda Garza, and John Ventura, on the other hand, experienced the meeting quite differently. Instead of pushing them away, the words and passion of John Powell, Curtis Burrell, and others only confirmed the need for them to think more deeply about Mexican American civil rights.[86]

Although divided, Latinos believed the URC was ill-suited to represent their concerns equally with those of African Americans. In particular, Latino leaders feared that the focus of the council was mostly on politics that concerned mostly black and urban communities at the expense of rural communities or issues that mattered to Latinos such as immigration and farmworker rights. Not fully convinced of the viability of the URC, Latinos organized a parallel organization called the Latin Concilio a year after the Chicago gathering. Opinion about the Latin Concilio was mixed. Some Latinos believed in the idea, while others believed they should align their ideas and goals with African Americans and the URC. In the end, they organized the Latin Concilio but not without concern from some leaders, especially John Ventura, that the Concilio would undermine their role as members of the URC.[87]

Ventura feared that unless Latinos joined their cause with African Americans, Mennonite Church leaders would never seriously consider their concerns and that the only way to bring national attention to Latino issues was to align with black leaders. As the first Latino to be on a leadership committee at the national level, Ventura was placed in the odd position of having to represent the mixed feelings of Latino leaders who did not believe joining the URC was a necessary step. On the other hand, his presence solidified the representation of Latino Mennonites and symbolized a significant shift in the racial conversation within the Mennonite Church.

Ventura's appointment had also opened greater possibilities for organizing an antiracism movement in the Mennonite Church. Even if the nationalist politics exhibited at the Chicago gathering was an honest attempt to shake things up, black leaders like John Powell understood that nationalist politics would only alienate potential allies in the church. With the work and legacy of Martin Luther King stretching into interracial organizing, antiwar, and antipoverty campaigns, Powell and others understood that a new politics was needed in order to bring about change in the church. This meant forging a coalition to address African American and Latino concerns together in the church. This explains why a few months after the Chicago gathering Powell made a visit to South Texas to build support for relationships with Mexican American Mennonites. While some Latino leaders stopped short of fully supporting the URC, the momentum was in place for both African Americans and Latinos who knew that if they were to make any progress in the Mennonite Church they needed to do it together.

Race beyond Black and White

The emergence of the URC came on the heels of Stokely Carmichael's call for Black Power in 1966, which raised the level of black consciousness across the country. African American Mennonites such as Hubert Brown remember that "the Council [URC] was started in the hell of 1968, after the death of Martin Luther King . . . and also it was formed in the heat of one of America's most violent summers."[88] For white Mennonites, the formation and politics of the URC in 1968 ended the decades of struggle of the 1950s and 1960s. Continually criticized for their quiet approach to race relations, white Mennonites had finally walked the walk. As African American Curtis Burrell made quite clear, the move was a break from the past decades in which the Mennonite Church had talked about race relations "without any results."[89] The URC would work to keep tabs on white Mennonite leadership, assure that nonwhite churches had the resources they need, and begin the process of removing white pastors from churches that were predominantly nonwhite.

But the emergence of the URC also symbolized the expanded terrain of racial dialog in the Mennonite Church. In the interest of building a more equitable church, black and brown leaders joined together to speak with moral authority to demand the church move beyond its cultural narrowness and open its leadership positions to nonwhite candidates. The interethnic collaboration of the URC made it a significant movement in the Mennonite Church and across the American religious landscape, where interethnic coalitions were rare. Interestingly, the young people who once attended fresh-air programs and vacation Bible schools were the ones who helped define the agenda of the URC in the late 1960s and early 1970s.

If the 1950s and 1960s were about how the Mennonite Church would involve itself in the civil rights movement, the late 1960s and 1970s would be defined by how the church would sustain that engagement. No longer merely sustaining a conversation between black and white Mennonites, the URC stressed the possibilities of interethnic politics as the conversation shifted to talking about how African Americans and Latinos could work together. Driving these politics early on were the examples of other interethnic movements like the Poor People's Campaign in 1968 that modeled a new politics for change in the church. The merger between black and brown concerns was something that Vincent Harding had already hinted at as early as 1959 when he spoke about white Mennonite missionaries who worked in communities "where Negroes (and Mexicans and Puerto Ricans) are not far away."[90]

For Latino Mennonites, it was clear that after not participating in the race conferences of the 1950s and 1960s, they would play a major role in defining the future direction of the Mennonite Church. A major reason for that was the 1968 appointment of John Ventura to the URC, which immediately increased the visibility of Latinos within the church. Ventura's appointment to the URC is but one example of the significance of the 1960s and 1970s for Latinos across the United States. The rise of civil rights leaders like Cesar Chavez and Dolores Huerta in the fields of central California, the literary themes of Puerto Rican life as expressed by writer Piri Thomas, and the reforms instituted by the Catholic Church as a result of Vatican II all caught the attention of a nation much too accustomed to talking about race in terms of black and white.

But more important, in the 1950s and 1960s the United States was on the cusp of a demographic shift as new waves of immigrants from Latin America swept across the border in the mid-twentieth century. This surge in immigration, as historian Jesse Hoffnung-Garskof has argued, resulted from a mix of US corporate and military involvement and revolutionary movements in Latin America. In 1965 the Immigration Reform Act facilitated established patterns of immigration from Latin America and the Caribbean by granting limited "immigrant visas to the Eastern and Western Hemispheres, without discriminatory national quotas."[91] The annual limits on visas, however, did not apply to immediate family members of immigrants already in the United States. This exemption addressed the presence of family networks of immigrants that led to increased populations of Latinos in both rural and urban settings, where a mix of print culture, films, magazines, food, and music would later fuel a collective sense of Latino identity in the late 1960s and 1970s.[92] Riding this wave, Latino Mennonites challenged URC leaders to move beyond its focus on African Americans in urban communities to one that also acknowledged the Latino experience in both urban and rural areas.

In the months following the Chicago gathering in 1968, Latinos demanded a stronger link between social justice and evangelism, connections with churches in Latin America, and a focus on both an urban and rural concerns. As a result, a dynamic discussion ensued between Latinos and African Americans on the political possibilities of building and sustaining an interethnic coalition in the Mennonite Church. But even with the hope that the black and brown coalition promised, interethnic politics came riddled with struggles as URC leaders had to contend with varying political visions, pressure from white Mennonites who had grown weary of race conferences, and of course the need for funding.

As the following chapter demonstrates, financial concerns consumed much of the early work of URC leaders, who also had to contend with white Mennonites who were suspicious of the intentions and politics of this new group. There was also a sense that in a church dominated by people with surnames like Yoder and Miller, the new and unfamiliar crop of leadership posed a threat to this tightly knit ethno-religious community. With funding battles on the horizon—especially with the introduction of the Black Manifesto—black and brown leaders fashioned a movement they called a "multiethnic brotherhood." The move was applauded by some, as church newspapers boldly proclaimed: "Differences de-emphasized . . . Church Becoming Multiethnic Brotherhood."[93]

Part II

BLACK, BROWN, AND MENNONITE

CHAPTER 3

The Fight over Money

Latinos and the Black Manifesto

Where there was one primary concern of focus—Black—we now are having to look seriously at the Mexican-American and Puerto Rican—American concerns.
—JOHN POWELL, Mennonite pastor, 1970

Interethnic Alliances

Freshly appointed as executive secretary of the Urban Racial Council in 1969, John Powell found himself at the Bethel Mennonite Church in Chicago face to face with "Squeaky," the leader of the Black P. Stone Nation. Powell was there to try to regain control of the church that a week earlier had been taken over by leaders of this activist group.[1] Their demands were simple: first, that Mennonites replace images of a white Jesus and white dolls with ones that reflected the black children who lived in the neighborhood and attended the day care center and, second, that Mennonites make a financial contribution to local organizations opening day care centers throughout the neighborhood.

After a week of negotiations between Powell and the activists, things seemed to be going nowhere—that is, until Squeaky became fed up with Powell's lack of power to actually implement the proposed changes and shouted: "I don't want to talk to you, I wanna talk to the head of the Yoder family!" Squeaky's demand caught Powell off guard. "What do you mean?" he responded. Squeaky then pulled out a Mennonite Church directory where he identified leaders of church committees who all shared the last name Yoder. "With all of these Yoders here," Squeaky shouted, "you're gonna tell me there is no such thing as the head of the Yoder family in the Mennonite Church?" Powell now understood Squeaky's request. After a brief laugh and explaining to Squeaky that the Yoder family did not run the church, the two sat down to settle the dispute at Bethel Mennonite Church. When it was all over, the Black P Stone Nation relinquished control when they learned that the white pastor at the church was stepping down and being replaced by African American pastor Leamon Sowell.[2]

It is easy to understand Squeaky's confusion. For most of the twentieth century, the surname Yoder was one of the most common in the Mennonite Church, second only to Miller.[3] That ethnicity and religion were so closely tied for most white Mennonites was no surprise to African American leaders like Vincent Harding and John Powell, who often touched on Mennonite history to gather support for the civil rights struggle. African Americans understood that if they wanted to find any traction in the Mennonite Church, they had to acknowledge the legacy and history of the church.

The case was similar for Latinos, who since the era of missionary activity had become quite familiar with the ethnic surnames of Mennonites. Speaking to a group of Mennonite volunteers preparing to work in Mathis in 1970, Lupe De León reminded the group why Mexican Americans were not considered "real" Mennonites. "When people in Mathis think about Mennonites," De León told the group, "do they think about Lupe De Leon or Mr. Paiz or Mr. Longoria, Mr. Lozano, Mr. Cavazos[?] . . . No. I believe . . . people outside the Mennonite church think about the Swartzes, the Reists, the Hostetlers, the Millers. . . . We Latins are thought of as converts."[4] Challenging that perception mobilized the URC in the late 1960s and early 1970s as they worked to change the notion that to be Mennonite was to be of German or Swiss descent. In doing so, they reminded white Mennonites that they no longer had a monopoly on Mennonite identity.

This chapter explores the political and ethnic realignments of the URC from an organization that began as a resource for addressing white racism to one that became a vehicle for exploring the meanings of race and ethnicity in a multiethnic context. The move to include and expand the conversation on race in the church was not a given, however. Latinos questioned whether the URC was a good fit for them given the organization's focus on urban and black communities. But that sentiment quickly changed when Latinos realized that their credibility and national recognition depended on how closely they worked with African Americans. At the center of these political and ethnic realignments was the fight over money.

In 1969 John Powell introduced a funding model for the URC at the biennial Mennonite Church convention in Turner, Oregon. Inspired by James Forman's Black Manifesto, Powell's plan called for a "Compassion Fund" that called upon white Mennonite constituents to help sustain the work of the URC. But while the idea initially received support, growing anxiety over how the church used its resources and fears that it would help fund racial militancy or, worse, a communist conspiracy led to the Compassion Fund's demise as the 1970s began. But instead of damaging their movement, the fight over money led the URC to place a greater emphasis on building an interethnic movement with leadership coming from both African Americans and Latinos. They hoped this would have broader appeal and strengthen two emerging movements within the church.

This was a move that already had some support from African American leaders like John Powell, who believed that it was "much better to have a unified, workable body than several groups trying unsuccessfully or competitively to do their own thing."[5] But how and to what degree Latino involvement would shape the URC remained a contentious point. African American Mennonites initially viewed Latino involvement as an important step in helping the URC reach its funding goals, but that changed once Latino Mennonites made clear that they were not satisfied with a peripheral role. Latinos wanted to be equal partners with African Americans in the work of the URC and in the Mennonite Church.

This chapter also repositions the role of religion and interethnic politics within Chicano and Latino civil rights scholarship.[6] If the 1970s constituted a "Latino religious resurgence," then it was also a time when movement politics "took over" the sacred spaces of Latino churches. As the Reverend Jorge Lara-Braud wrote in 1971, "The road to renaissance [for Latino evangelicals and Catholics] lies unmistakably in their willingness and ability to insist on indigenous leadership and to make their forms of church life consonant with the spirit of self-assertion sweeping through the entire ethnic community."[7]

Lara-Braud's phrase "spirit of self-assertion" was a nod to Chicano struggles in the Southwest but also to the black freedom struggle and its influence among other movements for social change. The relation to the black civil rights movement is often overlooked in examinations of the rise of Latino religious activism in the 1960s and 1970s. While religious studies scholars have highlighted the role of Latin American liberation theology in shaping Latina and Latino religious activism, the important role of the black freedom movement has received less attention.[8] Even as Latino evangelicals sympathized with liberation theology and the inspirational movements in Latin America, they resonated even more with the religious and Protestant underpinnings of the black freedom movement and preachers like Martin Luther King Jr.

The appeal of the black freedom struggle placed Latino evangelicals in the middle of some of the most important civil rights struggles. In organizations like the National Farm Worker Ministry Board, which was made up of religious leaders, Latinos stood on the picket lines and worked within their own religious bodies to garner support for the farmworker movement. A host of groups within Latino evangelical and Catholic churches also worked to bring about institutional change: groups like Católicos por la Raza, Las Hermanas, PADRES (Padres Asociados para Derechos Religiosos, Educativos y Sociales, or Priests Associated for Religious, Educational, and Social Rights), and the Latin American Methodist Action group all came on the scene during this time. These were groups that like the URC pressed white church leaders to be more attentive to the needs of Spanish-speaking communities. More important, they challenged the secular origins of the Chicano movement by infusing it with a religious and moral fortitude that it sorely lacked. The legacy of these movements resulted in the development of Latino leadership that emerged in Protestant and Catholic groups well into the 1970s and 1980s.

As important as these movements were, however, they were for the most part made up of Latinos who focused primarily on the needs and struggles of Latino communities. What made the URC significant and unique was that it was one of the few religious groups that merged the concerns of Latinos and African Americans and to a lesser extent Native Americans. It provided a multiethnic context that worked to balance multiple concerns and struggles while maintaining a semblance of unity. The irony, of course, was that the multiethnic context of the URC was under the auspices of one of the whitest denominational groups in the country, the Mennonite Church. This is a point that surprisingly even Mennonite historians have overlooked. While Mennonite historians have addressed the struggles of African Americans in the church, they have ignored the important role that Latinos played in forging an interethnic movement with African Americans during the civil rights era.[9]

This chapter traces the ways in which these groups worked collaboratively but also investigates how the tricky politics of interethnic alliances led to battles over funding, radical politics, and ultimately how to define each group's identity. With the national prominence of the farmworker movement and the growing chorus of Brown Power across the country, Latino involvement in the URC was more important than ever. As African American leaders captured the attention of white Mennonites in the 1950s and 1960s, it was clear that Latinos had now become a political force in the Mennonite Church and the civil rights movement.

Race, Class, and the Black Manifesto

From the beginning, it was clear that African American Mennonites were asking not only for racial justice but for economic justice as well. URC leaders believed that the Mennonite Church bore a responsibility not only to plant churches in urban communities but also to help launch social programs that benefited the entire community.[10] The focus on economic justice also reflected how civil rights activists forged a link between colonialism, slavery, and the dire economic situation of many African Americans in the 1960s and 1970s. In other words, the slogan "Black Is Beautiful" was tinged with the belief that race and class are not mutually exclusive realities. In fact, when the URC first came together in Chicago in 1968, some observers labeled it a type of "labor union for the Mennonite church."[11]

The focus on poverty reemerged in the mid-1960s with the help of young black activists and President Johnson's War on Poverty. In 1964 the Civil Rights Act joined the Economic Opportunity Act in reshaping the political landscape of the United States. For the first time, two important pieces of legislation aimed to end racial segregation and poverty by promising to provide federal dollars to organize antipoverty programs nationwide.[12]

Recently, scholars have paired the notion of a "long War on Poverty" with Jacquelyn Dowd Hall's notion of the "long civil rights movement." At the heart of these studies are the organizations, activists, and religious leaders who maintained antipoverty programs in the years before and long after the federal programs ended. These studies demonstrate how the War on Poverty was tightly connected to civil rights struggles and gave rise to organizations that have remained committed to fighting poverty in urban communities.[13]

One of the most vivid examples of the connection between poverty and civil rights took place in 1968 with the Poor People's Campaign (PPC). Organized as a movement "of the nation's poor and disinherited ... to secure at least jobs or income for all," the PPC attracted the attention of civil rights leaders from multiple racial and ethnic groups.[14] The planning and organizing of the PPC, however, go back much further. According to historian Gordon Mantler, as early as 1964 Martin Luther King Jr. and organizations such as the Student Nonviolent Coordinating Committee (SNCC) and the Congress of Racial Equality were fully engaged with a campaign to address economic injustice.

That same year SNCC and the Congress of Racial Equality both lent their support to the emerging farmworker movement led by Cesar Chavez in central California.[15] By 1967 King and the Southern Christian Leadership Council were organizing what they hoped would be the largest multiethnic gathering of activists focused on alleviating poverty in minority communities. Sadly, King was assassinated only weeks before the PPC began in May 1968. But even without King's leadership, the PPC moved forward and brought together working people, religious leaders, and activists in Washington, DC, where they assembled tent cities and camped out in the rain and mud near the Lincoln Memorial.

The PPC did not live up to the hype and failed to launch an interethnic movement on behalf of poor and working people, but it nonetheless ignited a debate about the legacy of slavery, colonialism, and racism on people's quality of life. At the center of this debate was the one institution deemed to be abetting the oppression of nonwhite people in the United States—the Christian church. Charging the church with being the strong arm of colonialism in the Americas, defending slavery, and handsomely benefiting from both endeavors, black activists such as James Forman demanded the church pay back its share of the profits. A former SNCC activist and member of the League of Revolutionary Black Workers, Forman presented what he called the Black Manifesto at the National Black Economic Development conference in Detroit in 1969. He demanded that white Christian churches and Jewish synagogues pay reparations for the historic role of religious institutions in the enslavement of black people. The Black Manifesto declared: "We are therefore demanding of the white Christian churches and Jewish synagogues which are part and parcel of the system of capitalism, that they begin to pay reparations to black people in this country. We are demanding $500,000,000 from the Christian white churches and Jewish synagogues."[16] Committed to building a socialist society, Forman outlined a radical vision that moved beyond the politics of black nationalism and those eager to "jump on the bandwagon of black capitalism."[17] The Black Manifesto was the first public demand for reparations from white religious institutions and showcased the "thirdspace" politics of black activists who merged their racialized and materialist critiques of American society.[18]

More important, however, the Black Manifesto placed white churches on alert by thrusting religion and Black Power into an inseparable relationship. If churches did not pay up, Forman warned, church services would be disrupted. Indeed many were.[19] Shortly after presenting the Black Manifesto in Detroit, Forman's group interrupted a service at Riverside Church in New York City, put their demands on the doors of the New York headquarters of the Lutheran Church in America, and interrupted other church conferences from Texas to Washington.[20] Even groups not directly linked with the Black Manifesto went after churches for their silence on matters of civil rights and their lack of community involvement. Following the Black P. Stone Nation's takeover of a Mennonite Church in Chicago and the takeover of the Spanish Methodist Church by the Puerto Rican Young Lords in East Harlem, churches across the country were on alert in the late 1960s.

Mennonite churches feared they would be next unless they acted quickly. Their fears were not unfounded. Months after Forman presented his plan, Powell and other URC leaders proposed using the Manifesto as a model for developing a definitive and autonomous funding structure for the URC.[21] Suddenly, being "the quiet in the land" no longer provided cover for white Mennonites. During the summer of 1969, the church was not only a place for reconciliation but also the site of a much-contested battle over the legacy of slavery, racism, and the fortunes these tragedies amassed.

While Forman's group did not visit or disrupt Mennonite churches, the Black Manifesto entered center stage at the biennial Mennonite Church conference during the summer of 1969 in Turner, Oregon. The conference in Oregon left no doubt that the freedom movements of the 1960s had taken over the Mennonite Church. In addition to Powell giving a talk on the Black Manifesto, women such as Eleanor High were there to push for the inclusion of women in leadership positions in the church beyond their participation in the Women's Missionary and Service Auxiliary (WMSA). High received a standing ovation when she expressed her belief that women were more than ready to serve on the Mennonite Church boards.

She also urged delegates not to mix the issues Mennonite women face with issues affecting minority groups. Her comment "brought a laugh" from the delegate body. Although she claimed not to be at the conference "to champion women's rights," High's comments were interpreted by some as suggesting that the WMSA needed to be phased out. High later clarified that she meant no such thing but argued instead "that there will always be a place for WMSA if the men would just not relegate us to that organization entirely."[22]

Powell and High were joined by a group of white peace activists who had camped outside the conference grounds. They were there to demand that the Mennonite Church discontinue its relationship with Selective Service, a relationship formed during World War I, and instead encourage young men and women to become draft resistors.[23] Each of these groups demanded church reform, but none created the buzz that Powell did, as word had quickly spread that the URC leader was going to speak on race and economic justice, a topic that some deemed too polarizing for the majority of white delegates.

When Powell finally did address the delegates, he appealed to Mennonite history. In the tradition of Vincent Harding, who only a few years earlier had also summoned the ghosts of Mennonite history, Powell appealed to delegates by calling white Mennonites a "religious minority" who must commit themselves to stand in solidarity with racial minority groups. Solidarity in this case meant that the Mennonite Church needed to "immediately respond with one-half million dollars for the purpose of developing and expanding ways of serving the urban poor and minorities in new and more meaningful ways."[24]

Outlining a seventeen-point plan, Powell insisted that the money be used for college scholarships, programs to help build racially integrated neighborhoods, programs for minority youth, and an ambitious plan to help start small businesses in minority communities.[25] In addition to calling for an autonomous funding structure, Powell also called into question the role of the white pastor in urban and black communities—specifically, the fact that many Latino and black Mennonite churches had white pastors as their leaders. In the tense discussions that followed Powell's critique, a white pastor stood up and declared, "Why, if we do what John Powell is asking us to do, the next thing you know, they'll have me out of my pulpit and a nigger in there."[26] The statement shocked Powell and exposed the deepest anxieties of white Mennonites who feared black Mennonites would push them out of their pastoral roles.

In general, however, Powell's ideas and funding structure gained the necessary approval from the delegates in Oregon. The seventeen-point funding plan was called the Compassion Fund, and delegates agreed to call on all members of the Mennonite Church to "respond with a minimum of $6 per member per year . . . above the $33 per member per year needed for current ministries."[27] But while the Compassion Fund held out the best possibility for the URC to remain a somewhat autonomous organization, raising the necessary funds would force black leaders to think more intentionally about the group's future and its identity. One month after Powell's impassioned speech in Oregon, the URC began reorganizing to reflect a broader purpose by expanding the dialogue between black and white and moving beyond race as the organization's single concern.

The Politics of Interethnic Alliances

Expanding the conversation on race in the Mennonite Church would not be easy. Even after helping to organize the URC, Latinos remained skeptical about the relevance of the organization for their own community. Minutes from URC meetings in 1969 reveal "lively discussions" about whether or not Latinos should join the URC or maintain a separate organization as the Latin Concilio.[28] Pressure came from different directions, as even some white Mennonites pushed for Latinos to join the URC. During the summer of 1969, Dan Miller, a high school teacher in South Texas, wrote a letter asking Powell: "What is the possibility of enlarging that council (URC) to give the browns the same representation that the blacks have?"[29] While the possibilities of an interethnic movement were enticing, a year after the URC was organized Latinos were still debating whether or not they would join.[30]

At the heart of this debate was Latino leaders' concern that even as the URC promised national exposure and leadership positions within the church, it remained largely focused on African American concerns and the hot urban politics of the late 1960s. That, along with the specter of interethnic conflict, made the decision to join the URC difficult for Latino Mennonites. Latinos believed their concerns were reflected in the name of the organization. For some Latinos, the name "Urban Racial Council" signified a black and urban focus and neglect of the Latino rural experience, particularly that of Mexican Americans in South Texas and the Midwest. If Latinos were to join the organization, the name would need to be changed to better reflect the diverse experiences of Latinos. Moreover, Latinos were also concerned about the fact that the URC was made up primarily of black leadership. Except for Latino John Ventura and Hubert Schwartzentruber, the lone white representative, all URC leaders on the executive committee were African American.

Even with theses concerns, Latinos did highlight the potential benefits of joining the URC. High on the list was the possibility that joining the URC would improve the political position of Latinos within the church. Latinos understood that African American Mennonites in church leadership were better educated, spoke "the language of the church," and had a long history of civic activism in Protestant churches. Conversely, some Latino Mennonites were monolingual Spanish speakers, had a history of membership in the Catholic Church, and were not accustomed to challenging the authority of religious leaders. In other words, the activist politics of the URC required Latino Mennonites to take some risks by going against much of what they knew about religion and politics. But they were not completely oblivious to how church politics worked. As one of the requisites to join the URC, Latinos proposed that the leadership be shared with a co–executive secretary of Mexican or Puerto Rican descent to work alongside John Powell.

The ideas of having a Latino co–executive secretary and renaming the URC were presented at a meeting of URC leaders in Chicago in 1969. After intense discussion—and a decision to change the name to the Minority Ministries Council—Latinos agreed to join the newly renamed MMC believing that it was best to "correlate Black and Brown concerns" in order to bring better and more national representation to Latinos. Two things about this new name appealed to Latino leadership. First, most on the Latin Concilio believed that the term "minority" served as an umbrella term for African Americans and Latinos. Second, "ministries" situated the group first and foremost as an advocacy group within the church and not a political organization. This latter point was important given the uneasiness that some Latino leaders had about becoming too involved in political activities.[31]

That uneasiness translated into a desire to keep the Latin Concilio active as a way to organize their base across the country. While the MMC worked on issues relevant to both African Americans and Latinos, the Latin Concilio, made up of John Ventura (Colorado), Ted Chapa (South Texas), Mac Bustos (Illinois), and Sammy Santos (New York City), worked to promote Mennonite curriculum in Spanish, provide pathways for Latino youth to attend Mennonite colleges, and provide theological training for pastors. But more important, the Concilio also began to serve as a bridge with Mennonites in Latin America. One of the earliest manifestations of work in Latin America was the joint development of the Junta Ejecutiva Latino Americana de Audiciones Menonitas (Latin American Executive Council for Mennonite Broadcasts). Known simply as JELAM, the organization appealed to leaders of the Latin Concilio because it helped build broad connections in Latin America and capitalized on Mennonite connections in the region.

By 1969 it was clear that Latinos were on board and ready to work at building an interethnic movement within the MMC. Mexican American leaders like Mac Bustos, for example, believed an interethnic movement would help Latinos receive equal and fair representation among the broader denomination in the United States. Sammy Santos, a Puerto Rican church leader from New York City, strongly believed that "the Latin and Negro should work in unity and Christian respect." Santos's words were reassuring to Powell, who a month after the decision was final reported to the Mennonite Board of Missions and Charities (MBMC) leaders: "The Spanish churches have decided on a unified approach by Blacks and Browns; therefore at present the council is representing both black and brown concerns to the church."[32] This sentiment was realized with the appointment of Lupe De León, a Mexican American pastor from South Texas, as co−executive secretary of the MMC in the spring of 1971.

From Mennonite Pastor to Chicano Activist

Becoming a Mennonite "via the Kool-Aid and cookies route," De León grew up with white Mennonite volunteers in his hometown of Mathis, Texas, and was no stranger to the belief system and politics of the Mennonite Church.[33] His first forays into the Mennonite Church were after a missionary named Weldon Martin stopped by to visit his family. Along with the plan of salvation and an invitation to church, Martin offered the family a bag of groceries. Soon after, De León began attending services of the church that offered not only groceries but year-round access to the basketball courts that VSers had erected nearby. His most vivid memories on those basketball courts were the debates he had with white Mennonites about their positions on peace and nonviolence. He often asked the VSers pointed questions like "What would you do if somebody attacked your family?" The responses never quite satisfied him.

In the years leading up to his move to Indiana to help lead the MMC, De León was a pastor of a small Mennonite church in Premont, Texas, and a student at Hesston College. Despite being away from the centers of Mexican American activism while at Hesston in 1966, De León found himself being drawn more and more to the emerging politics of young Mexican Americans across the Southwest.[34] Much of the attraction stemmed from his frustration over what he saw as the indifference of many white Mennonite students at Hesston over the war in Vietnam. "Many of the Mennonite boys were driving around in hemi-charged cars, living like the devil and hiding behind the skirt of the church," De León remembered. "If I have friends dying in Vietnam, then why are these Mennonite boys having such a good time?"[35] This became even more personal when he received word that two boys from Mathis were killed in combat while he was studying at Hesston.

Growing up as the son of a World War II veteran and in the vacation Bible schools of VSers in South Texas, De León struggled with often contradictory views on war and military service. At issue was the respect he had for his father's military service and that of other young veterans of his father's generation. But his desire to join the military was tempered by his own father, who often reminded him that he "didn't know the real army."[36] De León eventually qualified as a conscientious objector because of his position as minister of a Mennonite church. While some of his closest friends and family left to fight in Vietnam, De León made his way to the prairies of Kansas to study at Hesston College.

While De León's story is unique, his critical view of the war in Vietnam was not. Much of what distinguished the Chicano movement in the late 1960s from the Mexican American generation of the 1950s was its opposition to the war in Vietnam. As historian Lorena Oropeza has argued, for many young Mexican Americans the "opposition to the war accelerated the transition from the politics of supplication to the politics of confrontation."[37] It galvanized the Chicano movement in urban communities across the country and helped reframe Chicano politics. Instead of citing the large numbers of Mexican Americans fighting and dying in Vietnam as a sign of patriotism, activists argued that it was representative of the continued oppression of Mexican Americans by US society.[38] De León shared this sentiment, and it had a galvanizing effect on him. But an even more important factor on his views was what he saw as the gross indifference of privileged white Mennonites who "preached peace" but directly benefited from the sacrifice of American soldiers, many of whom were from South Texas. In short, being at Hesston College during the Vietnam War radicalized De León, who only two years before had been much better at reciting Bible verses than condemning the oppression of Chicanos in South Texas.

When De León left Hesston College and returned to South Texas, he did so as a minister of the Gospel and as a Chicano activist who embodied the new assertive and militant political ethos of young people across the Southwest.[39] In South Texas Mennonite churches, he was joined by other young Mexican Americans who were also beginning to raise important questions about their roles in the church. At one committee meeting, young Mexican Americans—Chuy Navarro, Ted Chapa, Criselda Garza, and Lupe De León—gathered with MBMC leaders to address their desire to take on greater leadership roles within the churches. Arguing that "the Anglo person tends to bring a problem into the Latin community," this new and bold leadership cadre believed that their time had come.[40] Their concerns caught the attention of white Mennonite leaders. In 1966 the general secretary for the South Central Mennonite Conference, Howard J. Zehr, wrote in one report: "Personally I have been deeply concerned for the indigenous church in Texas. Lupe De León definitely feels that the church is too much Anglo."[41] As in the early 1950s when the missionary strategy changed to incorporate social services and establish programs such as VS, the late 1960s brought out a critique against VSers, who some believed operated in paternalistic ways and often failed to help develop Mexican American leadership. The criticism came from the same kids who had played basketball on VS courts and attended countless vacation Bible schools during those hot summer months in Mathis. But by the late 1960s, the children who had grown up in the mission and had taken on Mennonite religious identities were now talking back to their spiritual fathers and mothers.

As the political terrain shifted in South Texas churches, De León's work gained notoriety in the Mennonite Church and caught the attention of MMC leaders. That new attention brought Powell to South Texas to try to recruit De León to move to northern Indiana and work as co—executive secretary of the MMC. Despite De León's lack of knowledge about the MMC or the long history of race struggles in the Mennonite Church, Powell's visit proved quite fortuitous. A year later De León agreed to join Powell and the MMC, and in the spring of 1971 he became the first Mexican American to hold a national position of paid leadership within the Mennonite Church.[42]

With black and brown leadership in place, the MMC became a small part of the larger push to forge interethnic movements in the late 1960s and early 1970s. Significantly, much of the push came from the antiwar activities organized by black and brown activists. One of the largest took place on August 29, 1970, when thousands of Mexican Americans gathered in Los Angeles to protest the Vietnam War. Two years after the optimistic spirit of the Poor People's Campaign fizzled, the gathering in Los Angeles—organized by the leaders of the National Chicano Moratorium Committee—was not only the largest assembled group of Mexican American activists ever but also a multiethnic group that included white and black activists, Native Americans from Alcatraz, and Puerto Ricans from New York. It was a show of solidarity that energized the Chicano movement and helped connect activists of color in the United States to the cause of Third World people and global movements for social change. As Oropeza argues, "Chicanos and the Vietnamese were both members of the Third World in that both were a non-white people suffering from the exploitative nature of U.S. imperialism and capitalism."[43]

That the antiwar movement was increasingly multiethnic did not escape the eye of peace-loving Mennonites. In the late 1960s the civil rights movement reflected a growing political and ethnic diversity, and the MMC was on the cusp of a radical transformation in American politics.[44] With it came an increasingly strong voice from Latino leaders in the church, many of whom as children had shared in the "Kool-Aid and cookies" of the white Mennonite church but now had caught wind of the new ethnic politics of confrontation. Almost immediately after moving to Indiana to take up his position with the MMC in 1971, De León wrote an article in the Mennonite periodical *Gospel Herald*, insisting that "Chicanos want to make decisions in the church. We want to have a say in everyday affairs of the church. We want to be leaders."[45] Their first chance to make this push came at the third annual gathering of the MMC in Detroit in 1971. But before Latinos could make their case, conference participants were forced to deal with the rising controversy that surrounded the Compassion Fund.

Race and Money

By the time MMC leaders gathered in Detroit, it was clear that the Compassion Fund had not lived up to expectations. In a 1971 report that detailed Compassion Fund income, Powell reported a deficit of $104,549. Final figures vary, but it is safe to say that between the summer of 1969 (when it was first implemented) and the fall of 1971, the MMC had collected less than $160,000, well short of the $250,000 needed to fund its numerous projects, ranging from church programs to support of activist organizations.[46] Much of the shortfall was the result of white Mennonites' misconceptions about the Compassion Fund and the MMC. Many of the same white Mennonites who helped fund the program also worried about who controlled the money and whether the Compassion Fund was tied to some communist conspiracy. The angst over the Compassion Fund coincided with a broader frustration among whites over President Johnson's War on Poverty in the late 1960s. Channeling money from government and churches to black and brown activists had become unpopular by the time President Richard Nixon came into office in 1969. At the heart of this frustration was the link between War on Poverty funds and widespread "racial militancy and urban violence." The logic behind such sentiment, historian William Clayson explains, was that "if the War on Poverty did not exist . . . the militants would not have the resources to organize."[47]

Soon after coming into office, Nixon worked to shrink the Office of Economic Opportunity, the administrative arm of the War on Poverty, by eliminating the power of activists or poor people themselves to develop new programs.[48] The attempt to discontinue the War on Poverty was a shift in policy at the highest levels of the government, signaling a growing backlash against civil rights activists. In the Mennonite Church, the anxiety over funding a program that some believed led to heightened racial antagonism and disunity was enough to bring harsh criticism. In one article, Powell wrote about the prominent rumors in the church that accused the Compassion Fund of being nothing more than "the Mission Board collecting money to give to the niggers."[49] With new and more powerful attacks against the Compassion Fund, MMC leaders were compelled to counter the rumors and negative press with reports that showed where and how the Compassion Fund was being used.

Beginning in 1970, MMC leaders gave Compassion Fund grants to churches across the country with strict guidelines as to who would get the money and how much. The guidelines allowed funding of programs for evangelism in minority communities, leadership training, programs that helped minorities feel better about their racial image, economic justice, and in general any project that had a faith and social justice basis.

In 1970, for example, MMC leaders allocated $10,000 to Project MAME (Medical Aid to Migrant Employees) in South Bend, Indiana. The funds were used to help the organization provide medical care for migrant farmworkers in a six-county area in northern Indiana. That same year $5,000 was given to the Rancho Alegre Youth Center in Alice, Texas, to help provide leadership training for Mexican American youth in South Texas. Another $10,000 was allocated for the Jeff-Vander-Lou housing program in St. Louis. This was a project that brought together the Bethesda Mennonite Church and the Jeff-Vander-Lou housing program to help renovate homes and provide resources for African American families who wanted to purchase their own homes. But the largest contribution, about $20,000, was allocated for black and Latino churches across the United States for programs in cultural enrichment, summer Bible schools, camping weekends, organized softball and baseball teams, tutorial programs, and arts and crafts. At its height in the early 1970s, Compassion Fund monies helped support programs in minority congregations with more than $94,000 to fund programs in their communities.[50]

But even with a strong record of careful distribution of Compassion Fund monies, white Mennonites were not convinced. For many, the Compassion Fund lacked transparency and resembled too closely the rhetoric of "reparations" in the Black Manifesto. To be fair, white Mennonites were not the only ones who struggled with supporting the Black Manifesto or programs like the Compassion Fund. Historian Clayborne Carson has pointed out that advocates of the Black Manifesto struggled because of a "lack of black support" exhibited best by the fact that "SNCC itself refused to adopt [it] as a project."[51] Part of the problem, as Carson noted, was that Black Manifesto advocates failed to map out a long-term strategy or clearly articulate how the funds would be used for black liberation. Even as the Black Manifesto did encourage white churches to increase the amount of money they gave to minority-led projects, suspicions remained. In the end, the Compassion Fund was never able to fully shake its association with the Black Manifesto and its goal of monetary reparations.

But there was something more at play in the Mennonite Church. The paltry sums that came into the Compassion Fund reflected a larger problem that had to do with Mennonites being unaccustomed to talking openly about race and money.[52] While white Mennonites supported the work of the MMC in theory, funding a program led by racial and ethnic outsiders was a stretch for many. The financial shortfall forced the MMC to explore other funding options, but more important, it required the MMC to think more clearly about its emerging multiethnic group identity. In the middle of a deep struggle over money, the emergence of the MMC as a collaborative movement between Latinos and African Americans gave it a renewed purpose. In other words, sorting out questions of group identity was integrally tied to the MMC's financial future.

"We Are Not Communists. We Are Deacons."

Even as MMC leaders worried about the future of the Compassion Fund, the real buzz in Detroit revolved around forging a multiethnic group identity.[53] In attempting to better identify MMC leadership, African American pastor Warner Jackson emphasized that the MMC was a group of "honest men, men of good report, and men full of the Holy Ghost . . . rectifying and ameliorating inequities within the church in areas of conflict and tension between black, brown, and white."[54] Challenging any notion of an MMC communist conspiracy, Jackson added that MMC leaders were not "communists" but "deacons" of a new religious movement within the Mennonite Church, one in which Latinos and African Americans were working to bridge divides along the lines of race and class to redefine the Mennonite faith tradition and make the Mennonite Church a more inclusive institution. "Spanish-speaking and black Mennonites," African American leader Tony Brown added, "[must] work together in an effort to liberate themselves."[55]

A big part of forging this new group identity was placing a larger emphasis on the experiences of Mexican Americans and Puerto Ricans within the church. Latinos saw the Detroit conference as an opportunity to insert their version of civil rights politics into the Mennonite Church. Among the speakers in Detroit was Tomás Chávez, director of American Hispanic Ministries, whose talk focused on *La Nueva Raza* (The New Race) and called on black and brown communities of faith to join together in a movement that sought "freedom and justice for all."[56] Chávez's speech at the conference resonated with many and was indicative of the increasingly important role religion played in the Chicano movement for civil rights.[57]

Unlike the black freedom struggle and its close connection to the church, pockets of the Chicano movement adhered to a secularized belief system that characterized religion as part of the system that was oppressing people of Mexican descent. At the heart of this belief was the notion that Anglo church leaders, both Catholic and Protestant, cared little about the social realities of Latinos. Latino Catholics and Protestants had to contend with a mostly white church leadership that rarely provided resources in Spanish, rarely understood the social and political problems of Latinos in the United States, and preached more about salvation than social change.

But while there was antireligious sentiment among some Chicano ac-

MINORITY MINISTRIES COUNCILS

happenings

Vol. I No. 1
Elkhart, Indiana
November 19, 1971

Raise your arms high and wide.
Feel the breeze of FREEDOM on your
uplifted face.
Breathe the freshness of NEW being.
Experience the joy of RELEASE.
SHOUT - for you are at the threshold
of a NEW THING.

—Shirley J. Powell

John Powell, executive secretary for the Minority Ministries Council.

Minorities Get Together In Detroit

By Dan Shenk

"It is my understanding that this is the only organization in the United States that has Blacks and Spanish-speaking Americans working together as a team."

This statement was made by John Powell, executive secretary of the Minority Ministries Council, in his keynote address at the Minority Ministries Council Annual Assembly held October 15 and 16 in Detroit, Michigan.

Powell went on to say that "we are here to discover and to strategize what we have to contribute to the Mennonite Church. And I think that's a great deal."

Helping to focus the purposes and goals of the annual assembly, Lupe De Leon, Jr., associate executive secretary of Minority Ministries Council, said, "As executives we are responsible to

only at the outset, but during and after the sessions. In his devotions at the Friday evening meeting, vice chairman of the Minority Ministries Council executive committee, Hubert Brown, Elkhart, Ind., stated the importance of being unified in the Spirit. "We must be one, we cannot be divided," he exclaimed. "Let us go from this place affirming our oneness under the Lordship of Jesus Christ."

Others also kept sight of the larger picture, the forest, and did not become lost in the trees of divisive conflict. "The body of Christ must have peace," said Charles McDowell, Youngstown, Ohio. "If we can't have peace, who can?" Echoing the basic precepts of unity was Indian-American Daniel Schirmer,

changes and ratified. Announced were details of the Cross-Cultural Youth Convention to be held in August 1972 and coordinated by Ted Chapa, Corpus Christi, Texas, assisted by Art Smoker, Scottdale, Pa. Also presented was the list of delegates to World Conference in Curitiba, Brazil, next year. Representing the Council will be John Powell, Lupe De Leon, Hubert Brown and Sammy Santos, this year's executive committee chairman from Brooklyn, New York. Spanish-speaking congregations will attempt to send one to three more delegates if possible.

Elected to serve as chairman and vice chairman, respectively, of next year's assembly were Warner Jackson, Cleveland, Ohio, and Ruperto Guedea, Denver, Colorado. Black caucus

Minority Ministries Council leadership, 1972. *From left to right*: Eugene Norris, Lawrence Hart, John Powell, Lupe De León, Ted Chapa, and Hubert Brown. (Courtesy of Mennonite Church USA Archives, Goshen, Indiana)

tivists, there was a profoundly religious influence that shaped the Chicano movement, especially in the fields of central California. When Cesar Chavez published his influential essay "The Mexican American and the Church" in 1968, it served as a rallying call for many religious leaders who were hesitant to join the "Chicano cultural renaissance."[58] One leader who was anything but hesitant was the Reverend Leo Nieto. In 1968 Nieto led a South Texas delegation to Washington, DC, to join in the PPC. Considered one of the most influential Latino religious leaders of his time, Nieto was quick to remind Chicano movement leaders that Reies López Tijerina (the fiery land-grant activist) and Rodolfo "Corky" Gonzáles (a Chicano activist leader in Denver) were both deeply influenced by their religious backgrounds.

The Chicano movement forced Latino church leaders to rethink their roles in society and their relationship to Anglo missionaries the late 1960s and early 1970s.[59] Tomás Chávez's words at the MMC gathering in Detroit captured much of the spirit that permeated Latino churches at the time. Speaking of the way some white church leaders equated a Christian life with Anglo-American ideals, Chávez argued, "Why must we become an Anglo? I heard Christ say that He was the Christ of all nations—not just one."[60] For Latino religious communities, this was a moment when their cultural understandings began to blend with their religious understandings.

In San Antonio, for example, Bishop Patricio Flores (the first Mexican American bishop in the US Catholic Church) instituted "Mariachi Masses" where musicians played culturally relevant—and religiously appropriate—music during Mass. In short, Latino Christians were no longer interested in simply being a reflection of Anglo Christianity. But for Latino Mennonites it went one step further. They believed that in order to make the Mennonite Church more inclusive, forging an interethnic coalition with black Mennonites was the best option.

The energy and momentum of the Detroit conference drowned out many of the fears surrounding the Compassion Fund. A major reason for this was the new strategy devised by MMC leaders. First, they approved a motion to incorporate the Compassion Fund, which had been a stand-alone funding project, into the broader funding programs of the church. This move ended the debate over the Compassion Fund and the resentment that had built among MMC leaders who saw the failure of the Compassion Fund as a vote of disapproval by the white Mennonite constituency. MMC leaders hoped that this new relationship would enhance their financial lifeline without hindering their autonomy.

The decision came even as some Latino leaders disagreed over the real necessity of the Compassion Fund. De León believed the Compassion Fund was a distraction that reflected the desires of African Americans who, according to De León, "cared more about economic development." Conversely, De León commented that among Latinos there was a desire "to build churches . . . [and address] issues like migrant farmworkers and bilingual education. . . . We just came at it from different perspectives."[61] But differing perspectives aside, Latino leaders simply were not as invested in keeping the Compassion Fund. They were more interested in forging a strong alliance with African Americans as a springboard to help promote issues they cared about like planting Latino churches, a Spanish-language church curriculum, and supporting the farmworker movement led by Cesar Chavez. Doing these things, Latinos believed, would sustain the Compassion Fund well into the future.

But that would not be the case. As 1972 came to a close, so did the Compassion Fund. The budget line for the MMC was moved under the administrative authority of the Mission Board with an annual budget of $200,000.[62] For MMC leaders the end of the Compassion Fund was an opportunity to raise the moral stakes of their newly formed interethnic movement. While this was seen as a positive development, it did not erase the negative image that some had of the MMC. Leaders like De León reminded white Mennonites that despite the end of the Compassion Fund "a lot of things are happening in minority churches," and he cautioned against being "afraid of us because of national TV."[63]

Reactions to the Detroit conference reflected not only a new unity between black and brown Mennonites but also a sense that they were embroiled in a cosmic struggle between the depravity of racism and the possibilities of an interethnic movement for social and economic justice. One participant, Mario Bustos (a Mexican American pastor from Indiana) commented, "Satan tries to divide us, and if we don't recognize this, we'll sink, brother!" Another participant, Sammy Santos (a Puerto Rican from New York City) added, "When it comes to dealing with the problems faced by our Council, I feel like present-day Samaritans must make their decisions here and now."[64]

For MMC leaders, politics and faith were inseparable. Forging an interethnic movement represented more than savvy politics; it was an understanding that their movement—the MMC—was a social movement informed and guided by their religious faith. Instead of diminishing the influence of the MMC and threatening to end the conversation on race in the church, as some feared, the end of the Compassion Fund ignited a new and intense desire to build an interethnic movement and "bring new life and birth into the Mennonite church."[65] But even as a sense of hope spread among MMC leaders after the Detroit conference, building an interethnic movement required the grassroots support of African American and Latino churches across the country.

While black and brown leaders believed in the moral underpinnings of the civil rights movement, their feelings were often not shared by some of their own constituents. John Powell and Lupe De León often worried about how "we have been misunderstood by our constituency and mis-understood by some of the people we have tried to help."[66] Some Latinos associated Lupe De León with "un espiritu malo" (bad spirit) and often called for prayer to deal with his bad spirits and his greater passion for politics than faith in the church.[67] A similar divide existed among African Americans, which Powell described as grounded in generational differ-ences. "In the MMC there were two camps," Powell argued, "the ones who would see themselves as Negro or colored and the camp that would call themselves black. The younger folk saw themselves as black, and the older folk saw themselves as colored."[68]

As a means to ease the tension between a progressive and civil rights–minded leadership and the people in the pews they purported to repre-sent, leaders planned a Cross-Cultural Youth Convention.[69] Planned for August 1972, the themes of the conference, "Who Am I?" and "Who Are We?," signaled the first real attempt by MMC leaders to forge an inter-ethnic movement that was inclusive of both MMC leadership and brown and black people in the pews across the country. In the end, what mat-tered—and what the struggle became about—was cultural identity and the possibility of building a coherent and strong interethnic movement. The struggle for identity became a rallying cry of black and brown Men-nonites as they sought to create a space for themselves within a white Mennonite community that was growing increasingly tired of talking about race.

CHAPTER 4

"Jesus Christ Made a Macho Outta Me!"

The 1972 Cross-Cultural Youth Convention

You worry about the preaching and I'll worry about the politics.
—LUPE DE LEÓN, MMC leader, 1972

A Youth Movement

In 1972 the Minority Ministries Council printed a brochure that read: "If you're Mennonite chances are better than 9 out of 10 that you are white, affluent and will ask . . . the minority what?"[1] The brochure caught people's attention, but it also raised an important point: just who are these "minorities" in the Mennonite Church? Even as black and brown leaders rose to prominence through their work in the MMC, to most Mennonites they remained largely unknown. One reason for this was the demographics of the church.

In the early 1970s only 6 percent of people in the Mennonite Church were considered minorities. Three percent were African American, 2 percent Latino, and 1 percent Native American. There were a total of 75 nonwhite churches across the United States, where approximately 3,100 members attended.[2] This relatively small constituent base posed several problems for MMC leaders. For the most part, African American and Latino churches carried little clout in the everyday business of the Mennonite Church, and many people in the pews of minority congregations were just as clueless as whites about the role and work of the MMC. Much of the work of the MMC came out of the church offices in Elkhart, Indiana, and despite their best efforts, they had not been able to tap into Latino and African American churches beyond their own leadership base.

That all changed the week of August 20–27, 1972, as nonwhite youth from across the country gathered for the first Cross-Cultural Youth Convention (CCYC). Described as an event to inspire "minority youth to gain a sense of identity and help young people be proud to stick with the church," the CCYC was the first convention of its kind in the Mennonite Church.[3] Organizers hoped to grab the attention of a broad Mennonite constituency, but they also saw the CCYC as an opportunity to spread their ideas about culture, race, and identity to a new generation of black and brown Mennonites.

The weeklong convention was held on the campgrounds of Epworth Forest Park in northern Indiana and attracted nearly 300 Latino, African American, Native American, and white youth. With the goal of "analyz[ing] the whole issue of identity," youth groups came from as far away as Los Angeles, Florida, South Texas, New York, Puerto Rico, Oklahoma, and Canada. The youth who attended were treated to a litany of speakers who lauded the benefits of interethnic collaboration and raised important questions about how the politics of gender and race permeated the MMC's new mantra of a "multiethnic brotherhood."[4]

With an eye toward understanding the complex intersections of race, gender, and religion, this chapter pays particular attention to the complex politics that flourished at the CCYC in 1972. On one hand, the CCYC provided a space for black and brown youth to talk about their lives as young people, as racial minorities, and as evangelicals. Youth at the convention came away with a strong desire to work across racial and ethnic lines, they agreed to abstain from military service, and they offered their support for the United Farm Workers movement. But the swell of ethnic pride was tempered by black and brown youth's resistance to the notion that ethnic identity trumped religious identity. Youth at the convention, along with some of the harshest critics of the event, complained that too much emphasis was placed on interethnic and civil rights politics. While youth were captivated by the stories of racism and oppression that the speakers shared, they were troubled by the few opportunities they had to focus on issues of faith or living a Christian life.

Even so, the CCYC was a galvanizing event for interethnic solidarity.

For the first time in the church's history, nonwhite youth came together to learn about each other's experiences and movements. For a group of leaders who felt like outsiders in a majority white church, the CCYC opened an important space to share common experiences and where black and brown Mennonite youth could get to know each other. But its significance goes much deeper than that. The CCYC was a watershed moment because it showcased the variety of political perspectives that thrived in nonwhite churches in relation to civil rights, Chicano and Puerto Rican politics, and ethnic identity. In some respects, the CCYC reflected the polarities and complexities so evident in Latino religious life. In the end, the convention revealed that if MMC leaders were going to build a successful interethnic movement, they needed to pay closer attention to the nuances and political realities of the people they purported to represent.

But whether or not the attempt to build an interethnic movement was a mere flash in the pan is not the focus of this chapter. Instead, this chapter is about the struggle itself and how, as historian George Lipsitz argues, it also "involved a radical reconstruction of both individuals and society."[5] That is the intrinsic power of social movements. As Michael Omi and Howard Winant argue, social movements offer "their adherents a different view of themselves and their world; different, that is, from the worldview and self-concepts offered by the established social order."[6] Through sermons, workshops, and informal conversations, MMC leaders delineated a direction and method for talking about race, identity, and faith. However limited they were, these discourses show how interethnic politics both challenged and inspired black and brown youth in the 1970s.

From *la Iglesita* to the Cross-Cultural Youth Convention

Ted Chapa grew up attending the Mennonite Church in the small South Texas town of Premont. For Chapa and other neighborhood kids, the Mennonite mission, or *la Iglesita* (the little church) as they called it, helped offset the harsh realities of working in the fields and the racism of the public schools. "Vamos a ir a la Iglesita hoy" (We are going to the little church today), Chapa remembered saying, "because they are going to show us films, or they are going to give us candy, or they are going to have a presentation of some sort."[7] Like many Mexican American children in Premont,

Chapa grew up working in the fields; he started working in the watermelon patches at the age of 13 for 50 cents an hour.

Following the example of the VSers he met in Premont and nearby Mathis, Chapa became a conscientious objector in the 1960s and later became a VSer himself, working in a boys' home in Denver between 1968 and 1970. His years in Denver proved to be transformative. He aligned himself with Chicano movement activities in Denver and admired the work of its most visible and charismatic leader, Rodolfo "Corky" Gonzáles. In 1968 he traveled with John Ventura to the Urban Racial Council meeting in Chicago and went on to became an integral part of the MMC. So when he was invited to organize the CCYC, he agreed and immediately went to work raising money and visiting churches trying to convince youth groups to attend the convention. On more than one occasion, Chapa hitchhiked across South Texas visiting Mennonite churches and trying to drum up enthusiasm and money for the CCYC.[8]

The site of the convention at Epworth Forest Park in Indiana, a short drive west of Fort Wayne, was a campground retreat with a nearby lake, recreational activities, swimming pool, and plenty of space for youth to run around. Aside from attending morning and evening church services, youth spent much of their afternoon time in workshops, hanging out, and enjoying the recreational activities offered at Epworth Forest. The goals and objectives of the convention were clearly outlined by Chapa and convention planners, who hoped "minority youth would interact with minority youth," and would gather to search for "personal identity and self-awareness" and "grapple with what it means to be part of a non-violent church."[9] The goals of the CCYC were important for Mennonite leaders, who understood that "minority youth were questioning the relevancy of the church. Particularly a church that is dominantly white."[10]

But as the convention date neared, two concerns worried planners. First, as word spread of the "cross-cultural" convention, reports surfaced of threats coming in from nearby chapters of the Ku Klux Klan. While the threats proved harmless, they were enough to put convention planners on alert as youth began to arrive at Epworth Forest.[11] They were also concerned about the *White Christ* statue that stood prominently on the campgrounds. Chapa and other convention planners feared the statue would be damaged by convention youth who might see it as yet another symbol of white supremacy. Convention planners considered insuring the White Christ for $3,000 to $4,000 in case youth vandalized it, but after some discussion they agreed to ignore the statue.[12] In the end, so did the youth.

From the beginning it was clear that this was no ordinary Mennonite convention. For starters, African American, Mexican American, Puerto Rican, and Native American youth outnumbered white youth by a large margin. This was no coincidence. Limiting the number of white youth, organizers believed, was one way to ensure that nonwhite youth were the majority at the convention. In fact, before they could attend, white youth were screened "in order to get those there who really need interaction with minority youth."[13] Convention planners also extended invitations to a small number of white Mennonite leaders, with two conditions: first, they could not take credit for planning the convention; second, they were required to clear any articles written about the convention with MMC staff members before publication. These conditions might seem minor, but in a church where Latinos and African Americans had little administrative power, they signaled the rise of the new leadership in the Mennonite Church.

At the convention itself, the scheduled workshops pointed to the ways in which black and brown leaders were invested in reaching across established cultural boundaries. Workshops like "techniques for organizing minority youth," "Afro-Mexicano styling," "Jazzing up hymns and choruses," and "How to make a piñata, cook ethnic foods, arts and crafts, and tie-dying" were among the most popular events scheduled. Leaders tried to remain true to the conservative traditions of the broader Mennonite Church in planning these workshops. For example, they invited five different church choirs from Mennonite and other Protestant churches in Ohio, Illinois, and Indiana to come and sing hymns and songs that appealed to nonwhite youth.[14]

From the first evening it was clear that the youth were excited to be at Epworth Forest. Every morning and evening of the six-day convention youth gathered in a large auditorium to sing popular gospel songs in both English and Spanish such as "Oh Happy Day," "Steal Away to Jesus," and "Alabaré" (I will Worship). Each gospel song was carefully selected to highlight the unity that organizers tried to promote. When African American leader John Powell took the stage, he emphasized the commonalities nonwhite groups share: "You represent the poor, you represent the

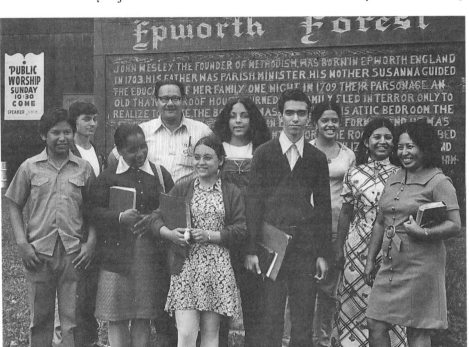

Youth pose for a picture at Epworth Forest, site of the CCYC, 1972. (Courtesy of Mennonite Church USA Archives, Goshen, Indiana)

have-nots. . . . We are in this together by history and we gotta get out of it together."[15] Powell reminded the group that they were present to raise questions about their faith and identity but most of all to send a clear message to white Mennonites that black and brown youth were the future leaders of the church.

The call to interethnic solidarity was reflected in the litany of speakers that were scheduled to address the youth. John Powell, Hubert Brown, Native American Peace Chief Lawrence Hart, Neftali Torres, and Lupe De León framed their talks as personal explorations of cultural identity for a generation in search of a collective identity. The talks deviated from the traditional script that each of these men had followed as preachers in their own right. They rarely asked youth to open their Bibles, and they avoided "altar calls" for youth to accept Jesus Christ as Lord and Savior. Instead,

African American youth group sings in church service at the CCYC, 1972. Both
Latino and African American youth group choirs performed at the CCYC. (Courtesy
of Mennonite Church USA Archives, Goshen, Indiana)

each talk was a direct call to action for youth to join the MMC in its quest
to reform the church from its German and Swiss origins into a multiethnic
space where all are welcome.

But while this message of unity certainly came across, the references to
the power of gender, religion, and race in shaping the young people's own
identities resonated most strongly. The Latino speakers, especially, shared
not merely about their personal struggles but about the larger dilemmas
around Latino religious, racial, and ethnic identities. For a diverse group
of Puerto Rican, Mexican American, Native American, African American, and white youth, the talks given by two Latino leaders—Neftali Torres and Lupe De León—revealed the deep anxieties over race and gender
Mexican Americans and Puerto Ricans faced in their struggles to define
the multiple meanings of Latino identity.

"If Christ Was Alive Today, He Would Have Been a Young Lord"

To understand how Neftali Torres, a Nuyorican Pentecostal from East Harlem, became a pastor in the Mennonite Church and one of the featured speakers at the CCYC, it is important to start in the final weeks of 1969 when Puerto Rican activism clashed with the mission of the church. On a Sunday morning in December Puerto Rican activists known as the Young Lords took over the First Spanish Methodist Church (FSMC) in East Harlem. The occupation was almost three months in the making. Beginning in October of 1969, members of the Young Lords began attending church services at the FSMC. They were not there for their spiritual well-being; instead they were there to ask the church for space to run a breakfast program for Puerto Rican children in the neighborhood. After weeks of being ignored by church members, the activists raised the ante by occupying the church and refusing to leave until church members agreed to provide space for community programs. As the 80 or so parishioners exited the church on that cold December morning, members of the Young Lords shut the doors with six-inch railroad spikes and occupied the church.[16]

For members of the Young Lords, whose "revolutionary nationalist" politics were modeled after the Black Panther Party and other revolutionary groups, the takeover of the church was an obvious move.[17] Not only was the church located "right smack dead in the center of the barrio," it was used only a few hours a week, and the rest of the time it "turned into one big brick that sits on the corner of 111th and Lexington."[18] The indifference of the FSMC seemed even more pronounced when compared to the work of Catholic churches in the neighborhood, all of which operated some kind of antipoverty program.

During the 11-day occupation of the church, the Young Lords were busy organizing "free clothing drives, breakfast programs, liberation schools, political education classes, a day care center, free health programs, and nightly entertainment." Inside the church, the group hung a white sheet with a painted message that read, "Bienvenidos a la Iglesia del Pueblo" (Welcome to the Church of the People). What became known as the People's Church Offensive attracted large crowds and helped increase the group's membership. They received letters of support like the one that came from the antipoverty activist Reverend David Kirk of Emmaus

House that read: "If Christ was alive today, he would have been a Young Lord."[19] Kirk's expression of solidarity strengthened the movement and, as Darrel Enck-Wanzer points out, reinforced the larger goal of holding accountable those "institutions they perceived to be advancing dominant interests and failing to serve their community."[20]

But while occupying the church was seen as an important moment for the Young Lords, the reactions that came from Latinos who attended the church were not positive. "They did not ask, they demanded," pastor Humberto Carranza told the *New York Times*. He went on to note that the group had no intention of joining the church: judging by "the way they dress, their insignia," Carranza said, "it is obvious that they are not bona fide worshippers."[21] On the morning of the occupation church members did not fight back or ask for police help; instead they lined up on one side of the church and sang hymns in Spanish.[22]

During the 11-day takeover of the FSMC, other Puerto Rican churches in the neighborhood were on alert. Neftali Torres recalled that at the Pentecostal church he attended, "the pastor organized all the men and tried to coordinate this effort so that at the moment that strangers came in to takeover the men would stand and take charge."[23] The concerns of area churches were not unfounded. Only a few days after ending the takeover of the FSMC, small groups of Young Lords visited half a dozen churches in the area with the hope of garnering support for their breakfast program.

In most cases the groups left without major incident, but at the FSMC an interesting discussion broke out over the goals of the Young Lords and the role of the church in the Puerto Rican community. In the aftermath, it was clear that the Young Lords had captured the attention of religious communities across New York and the nation. Supporters of the group, including many white progressives, organized press conferences that stressed how these actions served "to challenge the racist Methodist hierarchy."[24] For Torres the Young Lords' occupation of the FSMC raised important questions about how to think about faith in ways that blended his Puerto Rican identity and his emerging ideas about progressive politics. "I saw the Young Lords modeling what I was reading in the Gospels," Torres admitted, "and I gravitated toward that."[25]

Interestingly, it was the politics of the Young Lords that eventually attracted Torres to the Mennonite Church, where he met VSers in New York City who "wore coveralls and carried hammers" to work every day.

The fight for political space between Puerto Rican activists and church institutions in East Harlem was a microcosm of the larger battles for the soul of Latino evangelical churches in the United States. The tension revealed the strained position of the church in relation to civil rights and community activism, but it also showed how important activists considered the space of the church. The Young Lords saw in the church an untapped space where people naturally gathered and where political gains could be achieved. While the response of FSMC members was mixed at best, it nonetheless thrust other Latino churches into a larger conversation about the role of activism, faith, and civil rights. For Torres, his journey into the Mennonite Church also raised new questions about Puerto Rican identity and Latino racial politics.[26]

Puerto Rican Is My Race

On his way to the CCYC in 1972, Neftali Torres was asked whether he was black or Puerto Rican. "In the car there were some white guys, some black guys, some Puerto Ricans, and an Indian," Torres recalled. "In the course of our conversation this black guy said to me, 'Hey Neftali, are you black? Look at your hair!'" Torres responded, "Shoot man . . . yes, my grandmother was black in Puerto Rico. Not that I didn't want to associate with blackness but . . . I was going through a process of change again. . . . This is where that pursuit for personal identity began in a real way."[27] For Torres, what it meant to be Puerto Rican stretched beyond national longing or cultural traditions to a focus on his own racial makeup as a Puerto Rican of African descent. Torres discussed the dilemma of race for many Puerto Ricans in his talk at the CCYC:

> There are some things that distinguish me from other Puerto Ricans, like the texture of my hair. It is very evident that some of those guys and girls brought from Africa came into the family and in a way, as a Puerto Rican, I'm part of you blacks. There are Puerto Ricans that would shoot me for saying that because some Puerto Ricans are fair-skinned, straight hair, and they would not allow themselves to be identified with blacks. We have Puerto Ricans that are black, Puerto Ricans that are fair, and I was telling some friends that I have some uncles with green eyes and then me with my kinky hair.[28]

Torres's talk marked the first time that Latino youth were confronted directly about race and its relationship to ethnicity at the CCYC. But it was something that also came up as Puerto Rican youth gathered at the "Puerto Rican caucus" during one of the afternoon workshops. Here, Puerto Rican youth Sis-Obed Torres noted, "There was a point in my life where I thought I was black, my mind was black. . . . Growing up I didn't know what it was to be Puerto Rican because our people lived so close to the blacks, [and] we've picked up a lot from the black movement in terms of being aware."[29] For both men, the convention became a place to begin a dialogue around the connections and complexities of race and ethnicity. For Torres, it was certainly something that he had often shied away from as a young boy.

As a Nuyorican who grew up in East Harlem, Torres rarely had to address questions regarding his racial identity. And although he knew he was not like the Polish, Irish, and Italian children he remembered, East Harlem provided a sense of place that sheltered him from having to address his racial identity. But as references to race increased and African Americans and Latinos in the MMC questioned his racial loyalties, Torres reminded everyone at the CCYC, "This is me, a combination of black, a combination of white and Indian, that's me, Puerto Rican."[30]

Torres's self-discovery of his black Puerto Rican identity characterizes the complex racial identities of Puerto Ricans as descendants of African, Spanish, and indigenous peoples.[31] Since their mass migration to New York City in the 1950s, Puerto Ricans have rejected neatly defined racial categories and insisted on calling themselves Puerto Ricans.[32] Sociologist Clara Rodriguez has argued that "the imposition of a purely racial identity—whether white or black—on Puerto Ricans tends to deny, ignore, or alter the more important cultural identification of Puerto Ricans."[33] This, according to historian Jorge Duany, underscores the importance of national origins "and their adamant rejection of a hyphenated ethnicity."[34]

In the 1960s when Puerto Rican activists in New York and Chicago launched their own movement for social change, what Puerto Rican scholars call a *Nuevo Despertar* (New Awakening), they did so along the lines of nationalism and race.[35] Puerto Rican activists faced dual dilemmas tied to their experience as racial minorities in the United States and as colonial subjects of US expansion at the end of the nineteenth century.[36] The struggle for independence influenced an entire second generation of

Puerto Ricans who like Torres were raised in El Barrio but were born in Puerto Rico. Many grew up facing discrimination and social and political isolation as they struggled to stake out an identity beyond the black-white racial paradigm. But even with this isolation, factors like the back-and-forth migration of people returning to the island and many islanders coming to East Harlem helped maintain what historian Andrés Torres has called a "vibrant nationhood" in the 1960s and 1970s.[37]

The back-and-forth migration patterns helped maintain an emotional attachment to the island while also forging a firewall against the exclusion they experienced on the mainland. As a result, second-generation Puerto Ricans like Torres struggled with the dual loyalties of "nation" versus "national minority." Both positions led to different political strategies for those who identified as a "national minority" or with the "nation" and the independence movements on the island. Those arguing for the nation felt that the struggle revolved around national independence for the island. Those who sympathized with the struggle for civil rights and saw Puerto Ricans as a national minority believed instead that they should work for reform on the mainland.[38] For Torres the questions "Am I an American? Or am I Puerto Rican having been born in Puerto Rico?" lingered throughout the 1970s.[39]

Even so, Torres came to terms with the complexities of Puerto Rican identity through his own religious discoveries. He ended his talk by stating that "I discovered in here [the Bible] that I was a son of God. Puerto Rican and all."[40] Torres's comment points to the religious undertones of his racial and ethnic identity but also suggests how questions of Puerto Rican identity went beyond the "nation" versus "national minority" debate that sociologists and historians have highlighted. In other words, religion has played an equally important role in shaping how people perceive their relationship to the nation, their place as citizens, and their understandings of racial and ethnic identity. This is why Young Lords' occupation of the FSMC was such a galvanizing event for Torres.

A few years later, at a cross-cultural seminar in Chicago, Torres admitted that his experience with the MMC changed his political and religious direction. "I'm not charismatic any more, I don't get behind the pulpits the way I did in the past. . . . I'm beginning to talk about issues that pertain to blackness, to Puerto Ricanness."[41] If Torres's struggle with the dichotomization of race and ethnicity revealed the complex contours of Latino identity, the talk by Lupe De León affirmed that gender holds an equally powerful place in how the discourses on race helped shape religious identity and politics in the early 1970s.[42]

Reforming Machismo

When Lupe De León took the stage he immediately captured the attention of the youth present: "First of all, I am no longer an all-American boy. I found out that I belong to the Third World because of my mestizo background. As a mestizo, I'm an hombre, a macho, a father, a husband, a brother, a son . . . and the B-i-b-l-e tells me that I was created in God's image."[43] While De León stresses a variety of identities in this quotation, it was his "macho" identity that he chose to elaborate upon in his effort to describe what it meant for him to be a Chicano activist in a religious context like the Mennonite Church. Becoming an *aleluya* (hallelujah), as De León referred to himself, meant a departure from his "pachuco" days when he sported "tangerine Stacy Adams [shoes], the khakis, and the dove tail."[44] He admitted to the youth that becoming a Mennonite had taken him from the pool halls of Mathis to the quiet pulpit in the Mennonite Church in Premont and eventually to a Mennonite college in Kansas.

For De León, with religious conversion came a redefinition of his own masculinity, or what historian Elizabeth Brusco has called the "reformation of machismo."[45] Based on ethnographic research in Colombia, Brusco examined the manner in which religious conversion reformed both the public and private lives of men and in the process helped improve the material condition of the home. This process, as Brusco observed, often elevated the female role within the home and reattached the male to domestic life. But reforming machismo was also closely associated with the flowering of ethnic consciousness that De León and many other Chicano leaders experienced during the heyday of the Chicano movement. In the 1960s and 1970s, Chicano movement men looked to history as inspiration for countering the stereotypical images of Mexicans in the United States as lazy and sexually deviant. Imagining a mythical past, or what Lee Bebout calls "mythohistorical interventions," that included Aztec men, heroes of the Mexican revolution, and social bandits in Texas and California "allowed Chicanos to see themselves as a united front."[46]

But looking to history also revealed hidden histories of resistance for

Mexican American women who were fighting the sexism they encountered in the Chicano movement. The united front of the movement was mostly a spectacle of male leadership. Chicanas within the movement also looked to the history of women in labor movements, community kinships, women in the Mexican revolution, and the strength of their mothers and *tias* (aunts). In her book ¡*Chicana Power!* Maylei Blackwell argues that "reclaiming an alternative tradition of women's resistance . . . shifted the gendered political terrain as well as the historical imaginary of the Chicano movement."[47] Indeed the politics of what historian Ignacio García has called "Chicanismo"—the political and cultural ideology undergirding a sense of community, brotherhood, and activism in the 1960s and 1970s— were inextricably linked to the politics of gender.[48]

But for religious leaders like De León, talking up the merits of manhood was not only about challenging Anglo racism but also about defining a religious politics that proved Mexican American evangelicals were not "pawns for the maintenance of the status quo":[49]

> I'm between becoming a dis-anglicized Chicano and a left-wing Chicano and everybody says, Lupe, 'we're gonna pray for you.' . . . The fact is that I am who I am because Jesus Christ made a macho outta me. . . . Just because I'm a Christian doesn't mean that I'm a patsy and don't you forget it. It is my duty as a Christian, to speak against the establishment that keeps the campesinos down; inclusive in this group are the blacks, the Filipinos, Jamaicans, Chicano, Indian, and all the other people who work the land.[50]

De León wanted to make it clear that to be a Mennonite did not automatically make him a "patsy," especially given the Mennonite stance on pacifism and nonviolence. Nothing bothered him more than the perception that Mexican American evangelicals had sold out their culture and thus were at a "social disadvantage" in relation to Catholics.[51] His concerns were legitimate. In the 1960s, three prominent sociologists—Leo Grebler, Joan Moore, and Ralph Guzman—conducted a study of 56 Catholic priests in Los Angeles and San Antonio and found that "no pastor interviewed seemed to take Protestant proselytizing seriously."

Those who did acknowledge it said it did not worry them much because those who do leave do so because of the "material benefits offered . . . [to

them as] 'rice Christians.'" The study also found that while Catholics admired the devotion of Protestants, they believed that Mexican American
Protestants deliberately desecrated the Virgin of Guadalupe.[52] Making a
case for the "machismo" of not only Mexican American Mennonites but all
evangelical men was for De León a critical step if they were to be considered culturally relevant.

It was also evident that De León had come to take the low status as-
cribed to Mexican American evangelicals quite personally. Regardless
of the fact that he associated with groups like Movimiento Estudiantil
Chicano de Aztlán and the Midwest Council of La Raza and had helped
found a chapter of La Raza Unida Party and the League of United Latin
American Citizens in Indiana, his street credentials among Chicano activists remained in question. The memory came back when in the 1980s he
bumped into Chicano movement leader José Angel Gutiérrez at the airport in Corpus Christi. As De León remembered it, Gutiérrez recognized
him and asked, "Hey aren't you the preacher?" De León responded, "No,
I was an activist during those days." For all his activism, De León never
shook his status as a preacher.[53]

But it was how he ended his talk at the CCYC that left the biggest
impression. In a room full of black and brown youth who had learned the
virtues of nonviolence, De León admitted that he had come to reject the
very pacifism that kept him out of Vietnam and asserted "machismo" as the
only way to be a Latino evangelical:

> I know that most of you think that to be a Christian is to cop out, but to be
> a Christian is to be gung-ho on culture, and on the machismo that we have
> in different cultures. And I don't dig this jive that the meek and the hum-
> ble shall inherit the earth. . . . I don't dig that we're supposed to pray and
> wait until *mañana* and things will take care of themselves. . . . And I'm
> gonna say something very radical here: I'm not a pacifist, but I'm a Chris-
> tian. Can you dig that? For too long we minorities have had to be pacifists
> to be Christians. I'll tell you what, down here and up here, I know I am
> a Christian. And down here and up here I know I'm not a pacifist. I'm a
> Christian and I'm your man because I'm your brother. God bless you.[54]

After only a year working with the MMC, it became clear to De León
that countering Mennonite peace traditions by emphasizing the virtues of

manhood might help to rescue the MMC from being perceived as political wimps in the era of heightened ethnic nationalism. It was also a way to show that being a Christian did not automatically correlate with being a sissy.[55]

Mujeres Evangélicas and Feminist Politics

As De León lauded the virtues of machismo, he found unlikely allies in the Latinas at the CCYC, most notably Manuela García, a Mexican American woman from South Texas who had organized a workshop around what she called "Latin Machismo." While García challenged some of De León's ideas, for the most part she praised "machismo" against the backdrop of a white feminist movement that she believed had attacked Latino men. García opened her comments at the workshop by defining the differences between "machismo" and what she called "white woman's lib":

Some of you might say what's the difference between machismo and white woman's lib? The main thing that we should look at is that we are poor, our struggle to survive is much harder. . . . White woman's lib is where the woman wants to go out and be a professional and make her money and exploit just as much as her male counterparts . . . if you notice in white woman's lib they don't want to do dishes, they don't want to do housework, they want to get a maid, and most of the time that maid is nonwhite.[56]

García's position highlights what sociologist Benita Roth has identified as "the separate roads to feminism" for multiple racial/ethnic groups.[57] Like black feminists, Chicanas thought about gender oppression as interconnected with questions of race and class. But García's critique was only one side of the feminist debate. To the contrary, many Chicana feminists also believed that "machismo" was a systematic form of white oppression that placed power in the hands of men in order to keep entire families marginalized. Machismo, Chicana feminists argued, kept women out of the public sphere, marginalized their involvement in the Chicano movement, and was an "obstacle to revolutionary struggle." So-called loyalists like García, on the other hand, believed race trumped gender oppression and saw machismo as a way to maintain the family structure, keep alive traditional Mexican values, and stem the tide of an increasingly powerful and visible white feminist movement.[58]

In the end, García's critique reveals more about the shortcomings of white feminism in terms of race and class than it defends Latin machismo. But there was another difference here. Women like García were Latina evangelicals, or *mujeres evangélicas*, who for the most part have rarely been considered integral to the larger women's movement of the 1970s. Be that as it may, the emerging conversations of Latinas at the CCYC points to a fresh narrative that shows how engaged some Latinas were with the feminist movement. While most Latina evangelicals stayed away from the ideals of secular feminism that were advocated in the 1970s, they did agree that the movement was not only irrelevant to their context but also denigrated the role of men in both public and private spaces.

García makes little mention of religion and its role in defining or contributing to these debates. While De León makes a case for how "Jesus Christ made a macho outta me," García's workshop highlighted many of the debates happening in Chicana feminist circles in 1972. More important, García's work would serve as a precursor of sorts. As chapter 6 of this book shows, Latina Mennonites went on to organize their own conference the following year and invited Latinas from all over the country to attend. Steeped in the religious traditions with which they were most familiar, Latinas articulated a loose form of feminism that argued for gender equality without dismissing their understanding of the gender hierarchy within the Christian tradition. The movement of Latina Mennonites, and other Latina evangelicals for that matter, must be considered part of the second wave of feminism that Roth asserts "were articulated in diverse political communities."[59]

What about Jesus Power?

While the speakers and workshops consumed much of their time, the times when all the youth gathered gave everyone a space to talk back to the leaders of the convention. One of the highlights was when the youth unanimously agreed to add their names to the long list of religious groups that supported Cesar Chavez and the farmworker movement. The gesture was important given that the Mennonite Church has long warned parishioners of the dangers of union involvement. Nevertheless, the youth agreed to the following:

- That all participants . . . abstain from eating lettuce that is not harvested by workers protected under contract under the banner of United Farm Workers
- That we ask our savior Jesus Christ to be with Cesar Chavez as he and the farm workers with him struggle for justice non-violently
- That we ask Minority Ministries to endorse the lettuce boycott
- That we further ask Minority Ministries to ask the General Assembly to endorse the lettuce boycott thereby supporting their brothers in Christ
- That the Mennonite Church as a Christian body be present with the farm worker as he struggles for dignity and justice through the National Farm Worker Ministry[60]

As the resolution was being debated, a young African American woman named Sherri Jones pleaded with black youth at the convention to fully support the resolution. "I'm here to make an appeal to the black brothers and sisters to sign this petition," she said, addressing the entire group, "and to go into it fully, no jive you know, unite with the brown brothers to help them."[61]

Following Jones's plea for support, the resolution was overwhelmingly approved and followed by loud cheers and clapping from the youth at the convention. Immediately after the approval, African American leader Hubert Brown shouted, "Right on! Right on! The resolution is adopted!"[62] Here, Latino Mennonites brought the politics of the Chicano movement into the church and challenged white and black Mennonites to stand in solidarity with "La Causa." Not surprisingly, the youth at the convention were the only group within the Mennonite Church to openly support the farmworker movement.

But the enthusiasm and interethnic solidarity that emerged from the pledge to support the farmworker movement was short lived. It started soon after several Puerto Rican youth, led by Sis-Obed Torres, claimed that their food had been "butchered" and instituted a hunger strike in order to protest the way the food was being cooked. "Tomorrow," shouted

Torres to the packed auditorium, "we are boycotting the breakfast, the lunch, and the dinner."[63] For some of the youth, a poor attempt to cook Puerto Rican food undermined the entire message of the convention. The situation worsened when some of the black youth were overheard making comments about the Puerto Rican food being served. With word of a hunger strike looming, one black youth stood up to apologize: "I know I represent the black people . . . [and] I'm gonna ask all my black brothers and sisters who may or may not have made a comment about the food who wish to, [to] apologize to our Puerto Rican brothers and sisters."[64] Following the apology, the hunger strike ended as most youth gave in to their hunger. By the end of the day, bad Puerto Rican food was better than nothing at all.

The hunger strike was only one indication that the youth were not buying into all the political rhetoric being swung around. Some youth wanted more of an emphasis on God and Jesus Christ and less racial/ethnic cheerleading. At the open-microphone session toward the end of the convention, youth responded to the talks by articulating a variety of theological and political beliefs. Most shared the sentiment of a young Mexican American woman who approached the microphone to say: "I learned a lot of things . . . I learned that this is Black power, and Chicano power, Red power, and any kind [of] power, but [that] the best kind is Jesus power," to which the audience responded with raucous applause.[65] Youth also expressed that the focus on culture and identity helped them to think about their place in the world. One of the few white youth at the convention confessed, "I think it's good for whites to feel some of the things minority people have felt for a long time. I hope the convention will make us better able to comprehend and deal with the problem of racism—and help bring us together."[66]

One of the more positive notes came when the leader of the hunger strike, Sis-Obed Torres, attested to the fact that the focus on racial/ethnic identity had helped them once again trust the church:

Because of the same jive Mennonites, and the same jive church that pulled some very wrong stuff in God's name, I cut God loose and I cut the church loose. . . . I wanted to come and give Christ one more chance to see if there was a Christ among Third World people, to see if there was a possibility for Christ to work for us as oppressed people. . . . As much

Two Latinas admire a poster supporting Chicana power. Civil rights movement
testimonies, photos, and posters were ubiquitous at the CCYC. (Courtesy of
Mennonite Church USA Archives, Goshen, Indiana)

as I hate to admit it, I guess I found the answer. The Mennonite Church
threw me out once before, and this time I ain't running.[67]

Another went on to say that "out of the turbulence and struggle of this
convention, God is calling and he's breaking through."[68] The optimism
that flowed among some youth came out of the ways in which the speakers at the CCYC linked the common struggle and experiences of Puerto
Ricans, Mexican Americans, and African Americans while also affirming
the complexities of their own identities.

Disrupting the "Pure" Mennonite Kinship

Certainly many white Mennonites struggled with the highly politicized
work of the MMC, especially much of what came out of the CCYC. In

Worship service at the CCYC, 1972. (Courtesy of Mennonite Church USA Archives, Goshen, Indiana)

1972 Paul Nolt, a Mennonite from Pennsylvania, wrote about his disgust with the CCYC. Nolt accused MMC leaders of organizing a convention where there were "violent outbursts, admitted revolutionarys [sic], racism opposed, more mixing, interaction, infiltrat[ing] institutions for control, boycotts, and other doings representing a mixture of Christianity and Communism." Nolt was especially frustrated by the support black and brown youth openly offered to Cesar Chavez and the farmworker movement. "Apparently Communism won the victory," Nolt wrote, "because the conference went all out to support César Chávez. . . . God bless those few that did not stand up in obeisance to that alleged dictator."[69] While MMC leaders mostly ignored Nolt's tirade, they could not afford to ignore the dissent that was coming from some within their own ranks.

As early as 1971, African American leader Leamon Sowell wanted to do away with the MMC. In a letter addressed to the MMC executive committee, Sowell demanded the disintegration of the exclusive MMC for a more "integrated" approach. Sowell argued that the dissolution of the MMC would give minority churches more control.[70] Sowell's demand received a swift response from MMC leaders, who stated that integration was a "fallacy" and that by "integrating with MBM [Mennonite Board of Missions] we actually lose support and respect."[71]

The appeal of an "integrated" approach is what kept Puerto Rican churches in New York City from becoming involved with the MMC. For a number of reasons, the involvement of Latinos in New York City within the MMC never quite materialized in the ways that Sammy Santos and Neftali Torres had hoped. Under the direction of the mostly conservative Lancaster Mennonite Conference, the majority of Puerto Rican congregations in New York were openly discouraged from working with or joining the MMC. In 1970, Latino churches in Pennsylvania and New York organized a counter to the MMC called the Council of Spanish Mennonite Churches.[72] One of the most outspoken critics, José Santiago, claimed that the MMC was "too far away to be of any help."[73] Even the Mennonite conference in Puerto Rico was invited but had too many of its own pressing concerns to involve itself much with the work of the MMC.

Instead Lancaster Mennonite Conference leaders advocated a separate Hispanic Concilio on the East Coast whose focus would be evangelism and church planting, not political and church reform. The effort to stay away from the politics of the MMC first began at a July 1971 MMC executive committee meeting, at which missionary John Smucker and MMC representative Sammy Santos both expressed their frustration over the advocated formation of a separate Hispanic Concilio on the East Coast. Both believed such a move could hurt the broader ideas of Latino unity within the MMC. Just two months later Smucker resigned as vice chairman of the Council of Mennonite Churches in New York. Both Smucker and Santos suggested that the problems among congregations in New York were worse than first thought.[74]

But by far the most scathing critique of both the CCYC and the MMC came from Chuy Navarro, a Mexican American from South Texas and the chairman of the South Texas Mennonite Church Council. Navarro asserted that the youth convention had "turned into a fiasco." He cited the absence of youth at many of the worship services and workshops, the claims that there was "erotic dancing," and the "drug paraphernalia" found in the cabins where youth were staying as evidence of a youth convention that cared more about politics than faith. But Navarro's critique was also directed at MMC leaders who he believed were only seeking attention for themselves and not being evangelical enough.[75] He chastised them for substituting the evangelical message of the Gospel with new and emerging terms like "minority ministries," "cross-culture," and "race relations," which according to Navarro had very little to do with the core of Christianity. He added "that with these new additions the emphasis of basic bible doctrine has moved to a more lax approach." But perhaps the strongest blow came when Navarro charged MMC leaders with troubling ethnic Mennonite connections. "Where once this closely knit family of Yoders, Millers, Kauffmans, and Kraybills existed," Navarro wrote, "names like Jackson, Brown, Torres, and García have suddenly disrupted the 'pure' Mennonite kinship."[76] That one of the most pointed critiques came from a Mexican American was surprising to many. But it highlighted some of the internal divisions that were brewing around mixing politics and faith.

Navarro, while concerned about the supposed "'pure' kinship" of Mennonites, was actually voicing his disapproval of mixing the politics of protest with issues that needed to remain strictly faith based. He ended his letter by making this point and threatening to keep South Texas youth from attending future youth conventions "unless there is a minimal degree of certainty that such actions will not occur in a Christian youth convention."[77] Other Latino and African American leaders agreed, and by the time the planning began for a future youth convention, leaders were adamant that the "activities should be spiritual and should avoid opportunities to instigate activities that do not edify youth."[78] Indeed, the youth conventions that were held in 1975 and 1979 were stripped of all political overtones and any calls for interethnic collaboration. The work to build an interethnic movement in the early 1970s began to fade as Latinos and African Americans began to once again rethink their place in the church.

∽

By the end of the week, youth had heard from most of the MMC leaders, each of whom spoke from his own cultural point of view and provided clues about how to build a multiethnic movement in the Mennonite Church. The 1972 convention was significant in representing the first time that MMC leaders showcased themselves to a broad audience within the Mennonite Church. It was one of the first attempts to redefine their movement as a "multiethnic brotherhood." By 1972 the MMC had morphed into an interethnic movement with a sophisticated sense of its own identity. The change was as swift as it was necessary. The failure of the Compassion Fund forced African American MMC leaders to seriously consider the place of Latinos, a name change, and a political philosophy that believed in the power of multiethnic coalitions.

While support for the MMC was often mixed, with critiques and disagreements coming from black and brown Mennonites, there was no doubt that the CCYC in 1972 had solidified the group once again. After a tumultuous few years during which the Compassion Fund failed to produce the financial support it required, MMC leaders reinvented themselves as a cohesive group not advocating "Black concerns" or "Latin concerns" but "black and brown concerns together."[79] The change reflected broader trends in the late 1960s and 1970s, when minority groups shifted much of their focus to the intersections of poverty, race, and especially war. But while the potential of an interethnic movement held out promise, it raised important questions about how to prioritize specific needs, which movements to involve themselves in, and how best to portray a united front for white Mennonite Church leaders. There was also the added fear that, as the Mennonite Church considered restructuring itself, the fate of the MMC would be in jeopardy.

Even so, Latinos took center stage when the farmworker movement led by Cesar Chavez hit close to home for many Mennonite farmers in central California. Even while the MMC focused on becoming an interethnic movement in 1972, it quickly shifted to a major cause of civil rights activism for Latinos—the farmworker movement. And while white Mennonites had been willing to take risks in combating the "race problem," the ambivalence of many Mennonites with regard to the farmworker movement shifted the debate once again. But this time, it signaled the rise of Latinos within the Mennonite Church and foreshadowed the rise of Latino religious identity politics that emerged in the late 1970s.

CHAPTER 5

Social Movement or Labor Union?

Mennonites and the Farmworker Movement

It seems reasonable to take the view that while Chávez is a sincere idealist,
with the welfare of farm workers at heart, he also seems unable to achieve
these goals. . . . Mennonites ought not to participate in boycotts promoted
by either of the unions in dispute.

—GUY F. HERSHBERGER, "Mr. Peace," Mennonite historian and ethicist, 1974

On the Migrant Trail

Most summers in the 1950s, Paul and Ann Conrad followed Mexican American families to the cotton fields of West Texas. Loaded with Bibles and other Christian literature in their van—literally a church on wheels—they traveled 500 miles to minister to the 18 or so Mexican American families who made the trip from Mathis, Texas, to the cotton fields around Lubbock. The families, many of whom worked long hours to save enough money to get through the winter, were also faithful members of the Mennonite Church in Mathis (Iglesia Menonita del Calvario), where Paul and Ann ministered. With more than half of their congregation gone for most of the summer and early fall, the Conrads believed that following the families was imperative to maintaining strong relationships.[1]

Once the Conrads arrived at their West Texas destination, they stayed with Mexican American families in "their little rooms," shared meals, and every morning went out to pick cotton. In the afternoons, they parked

Mennonite missionary Paul Conrad handing out Christian literature to migrant farmworkers in Lubbock, Texas, 1950s. (Courtesy of Paul and Ann Conrad)

the church on wheels near the cotton fields and prayed for the workers, handed out Bibles, and offered farmworkers the opportunity to accept Jesus Christ as their Lord and Savior.[2] Church leaders' trips to the cotton fields of West Texas were often seen as a sign of real solidarity by Mexican American families, who upon their return to South Texas felt an even stronger commitment to the Mennonite Church.

Following workers to the cotton fields also spoke of the close relationships that white Mennonites had with Mexican American families in South Texas in the 1950s. But that feeling of closeness soon changed when some began to view those relationships as paternalistic. The sentiment was shared by Ted Chapa and Lupe De León, both of whom had toiled in the fields of West Texas earning little more that 40 cents an hour, when they became leaders in the Minority Ministries Council (MMC) in the early 1970s. While they admired the work of the Mennonite volunteers, the emergence of the Chicano movement had raised their political consciousness just as they were thrust into leadership positions within the church.

For many Latino evangelicals and Catholics the Chicano movement served as a political and theological turning point.[3] As new groups of Latino leaders emerged in evangelical and Catholic churches in the 1960s and 1970s, the farmworker movement was a source of inspiration and a model for the connections between social justice and faith. In the Mennonite Church it was no different. The politics of Cesar Chavez and the farmworker movement created deep political reverberations for Mennonites that stretched from a poultry plant in Indiana to the produce fields of central California.

While individually many Mennonites sided with the farmworkers in their struggles with growers, leaders of the various Mennonites institutions involved decided instead to appease Mennonite growers and not take sides. The decision was surprising to many Latino leaders. Even though white Mennonites worked alongside farmworkers in West Texas in the 1950s, supporting a national movement for farmworkers' rights was another matter entirely. Mennonites were anxious about supporting a movement they saw as incompatible with their beliefs of peace and justice.

The ambivalence over the farmworkers' struggle resembled the uncertainties many Mennonite leaders had concerning the politics and theological positions of Martin Luther King Jr. and the black freedom movement. While Mennonite leaders appreciated King's stance on nonviolence, his theological understanding of "coercive" nonviolence and his associations with liberal theology worried some Mennonites and limited their involvement in the black freedom movement.[4] Central to the Mennonite position against coercive nonviolence were the writings of peace activist and Mennonite leader Guy F. Hershberger, who in 1939 wrote, "There is no difference in principle between so-called non-violent coercion and actual violence."[5]

That philosophy was a central marker of Mennonite peace identity in the mid-twentieth century. Regardless of the concerns some had about political activism, the black freedom movement captured the hearts and minds of Mennonites, and in 1960 King was invited to speak at two Mennonite colleges.[6] But while Mennonites viewed the black freedom movement as a social movement, they were not as clear about the place of the farmworker movement. Was it a labor union or a social movement?

The inability of Mennonite leaders to reach consensus on this question, this chapter argues, led to their decision to remain neutral. Siding with the farmworkers would have alienated a small but wealthy segment of

Mennonite growers, who often gave large donations to the work of church missions and service work through such parachurch organizations as the Mennonite Central Committee (MCC). The decision caused a great deal of tension between Latinos and white Mennonites and was a great setback to the progress that had been made on racism within the church since the early 1950s.

This chapter also rethinks the role of the church in the farmworker movement. The past ten years have seen an increased focus by scholars on the role of Protestant and Catholic leaders in the farmworker movement. Indeed religious leaders and Cesar Chavez himself raised the moral stakes of the movement by infusing every aspect of the movement—from marches to boycotts—with religious symbolism and practices. But few scholars have examined how the debate over whether the farmworker cause was a labor union or a social movement shaped religious responses and participation. Some religious groups were not willing to join Chavez in his crusade to help farmworkers precisely because it was unclear whether they would be supporting a labor union or a social movement.[7]

Supporting the farmworker movement placed many churches and religious organizations at risk of losing financial support from wealthy growers in central California. This was especially true for churches and religious organizations whose constituents were largely growers and who stood to lose a great deal from the success of the farmworker movement. As historian Dennis Valdés has pointedly explained, Protestant churches "depended more than Catholics on local support and consequently stayed farther away from issues considered controversial."[8] Even so, Protestants have a long history of service among migrant farmworkers that dates back to the 1920s and 1930s with the work of migrant ministries first in California and later in Texas.[9]

This legacy of support made liberal Protestants key players in the farmworker movement in the late 1960s and 1970s. In this regard Mennonites were behind the curve. Their silence on farmworker rights bothered Latino Mennonites. Latinos later learned that the silence of the Mennonite Church was due in part to concerns over offending wealthy Mennonite growers in central California.

Debate over this issue was not unique to the Mennonites, but it did contradict how the church had engaged other civil rights movements. Historian Joseph S. Miller argues that Mennonite leaders chose not to take sides in the farmworker movement because Mennonites did not have the tools to "become involved in mediation and conciliation."[10] But only a few paragraphs later, Miller shows that in the 1960s white Mennonites "defied their local draft boards" during the Vietnam War and that the black civil rights movement had drawn white Mennonites to "the picket lines of the freedom marches."[11] The farmworker movement, however, was different. Its organizational ties as a "union" troubled some Mennonites who believed its "coercive" tactics went against some of the most deeply held pacifist Mennonite beliefs. Nevertheless, the farmworker movement instigated a national conversation about farm labor, social movements, and the place of Latinos in the Mennonite Church.

Crowded Chicken Houses

Mennonite involvement with the farmworker movement began in their own backyard. In 1969, Mennonite businessman Annas Miller of Goshen, Indiana, was accused of providing poor housing for large numbers of Mexican Americans who traveled from South Texas to work in his poultry plant. Accusations had begun a year earlier when the Migrant Service Committee (MSC) of Elkhart and Kosciusko Counties commissioned a report to take a closer look at the relationship between farmers and farmworkers. Since at least the late 1950s, Mexican American families had flocked to Indiana to harvest tomatoes, seed corn, and apples. Migrant workers, mostly Mexican Americans from Texas, were attracted largely to the tomato cannery in Milford and to the tomato fields in southern Elkhart and northern Kosciusko Counties in northwestern Indiana. In 1970 the Annual Report on Farm Labor in Indiana also counted around 100 Puerto Rican migrants from Florida who came to Indiana to work in the fields or in turkey or poultry processing plants.[12]

In its weak labor laws for agricultural workers, low wages, and racial discrimination, Indiana was no different than other migrant destinations. In central Indiana, a region known for growing tomatoes, residents of the town of Elwood worried when a self-help housing program proposed a plan to help build permanent homes for Mexican American migrant workers. Anglo residents of Elwood, which had "never had a nonwhite resident," made threatening phone calls to self-help housing employees and eventually forced three to resign their positions.[13] Situations like the one in Elwood are why migrant workers believed the working and living conditions in Indiana were especially bad. In the MSC report, one migrant worker commented in frustration about working conditions in northwestern Indiana, "From Utah to Wyoming, and Idaho to Kentucky, Virginia, and Alabama, THIS is the worst place.... I'm sick of it here—I'll never come back!"[14]

But while the MSC report did raise significant questions, it took the death of a migrant worker to shift community attention to the living and working conditions of farmworkers. In 1969 Ignacio Blanco was found dead on the grounds of the Pine Manor turkey processing plant in Goshen. He was killed by a single gunshot wound, and authorities ruled his death a suicide. Blanco, who made the annual trip to northwest Indiana with his wife and nine children from Mission, Texas, was only 46 years old at the time of his death.[15] For many in the community, Blanco's death served as a call to action against what many perceived as the crowded and unsanitary living conditions of Mexican American workers at the Pine Manor plant.

Almost immediately, the living conditions at Pine Manor became the center of attention in the small town of Goshen. Don Klaasen, the local chairman of the MSC, wrote an editorial a few days after Blanco's death in which he described the housing facilities at Pine Manor as consisting of "a tar-paper shack hidden behind tall corn or over the hill . . . or a room 10 by 20 with two or three beds where three to five children sleep in the same bed."[16] But while no one believed the living conditions of workers and their families were ideal, some disagreed with Klaasen's descriptions. "It was crowded and it was a chicken house and it wasn't the nicest place to live," Mennonite pastor Moses Beachy remembered, "but it was temporary."[17] But the concerns raised by Klaasen were legitimate. Reports noted that workers often felt that at Pine Manor they "lived like pigs," with no adequate trash disposal, no indoor plumbing, and increasing concern about the odor coming from a nearby pond where children often played.[18]

Unfortunately, cases like the one at Pine Manor were all too common across the Midwest and the nation. In 1968, Puerto Rican migrant workers reported in federal court that they were subject to death threats and "machete beatings" if they tried to leave or quit their jobs at the South Florida farm of K. D. Eatmon.[19] Mexican Americans who settled in the South Bend, Indiana, area in the 1970s often struggled to find employment and many—nearly 40 percent—lived below the poverty line.[20] Less than a year after the Pine Manor case, orchard owner O. M. Tompkins was arrested in Traverse City, Michigan, after he ignored a mandate by the Michigan Health Department to remove workers form the unsanitary labor camps he provided.[21]

The Michigan Department of Health found 20 Mexican American families, all of whom were from Texas, living in decrepit conditions with "children sleeping within a few feet of a manure-littered cow barn."[22] Tompkins's arrest was the first of its kind in Michigan, and it came on the heels of a report citing poor living conditions, low wages, and high rates of disease in labor camps in Texas and Florida.[23] Even as farmers claimed these reports were "biased," they were enough to capture the attention of religious leaders who decided to build a cause around the needs of migrant laborers.

In northern Indiana, members of the First Unitarian Church and El Centro Cristiano de la Comunidad, known as "El Centro," in nearby South Bend exposed the living conditions at the Pine Manor workers' camp. Latinos and Anglos from the Unitarian Church and El Centro came together for what they called a "Chicano-Anglo" fiesta, where they watched the film *Harvest of Shame* and launched an official boycott of Pine Manor products to begin on November 14, 1971. Boycotters demanded that Pine Manor fence in the "open cesspool," relocate housing, and provide indoor plumbing for farmworkers and their families. Sandra Powell of the First Unitarian Church threatened to expand the boycott "through Christmas and expand to a wider area" if their demands were not met.[24]

Essentially because the case involved one of their own prominent Mennonite businessmen, Mennonite churches and organizations remained conflicted about responding to the issue. The first Mennonite group to speak out was the Spanish American Committee, a program of the Peace and Social Concerns Committee of the Indiana-Michigan Mennonite Conference, but they refused to join the boycott and instead sided with the owner, Annas Miller. Their refusal surprised boycotters, who could not understand how a "Spanish American" group would not support the boycott.[25] But aside from Mennonite conflicts with boycotts and what they deemed "coercive" tactics, the Spanish American Committee sided with Miller and played down any indication that migrants were treated badly at Pine Manor.

Knowing that Mennonite involvement would be critical to changing the conditions at Pine Manor, local activists from El Centro in South Bend urged leaders of the MMC to help bring about a resolution. It helped that only a few months earlier Lupe De León had joined the MMC as an associate secretary and that in 1970 the MMC had provided a grant to local farmworker organizations. As part of the very first disbursement of the controversial Compassion Fund, MMC leaders granted $10,000 to Project MAME (Medical Aid to Migrant Employees) in the South Bend area. The funds were given to help Project MAME provide medical and prenatal care for migrant farmworkers in a six-county area in northern Indiana.[26]

The familiarity of the MMC and the fact that De León had been a farmworker himself placed the MMC in a good position to help mediate the conflict and bring changes to Pine Manor. They did both. In an attempt to end the boycott, De León attended a series of meetings with all interested parties in late November 1971 to discuss the concerns over the housing at Pine Manor and to settle immediate differences.[27] Less than a week later, the boycott was called off. In the end, leaders of the Mennonite Board of Missions and Charities (MBMC) agreed to help fund a 15-unit housing project for farmworkers that would force Pine Manor and its owner, Annas Miller, to close its inadequate living quarters. Despite a lack of support from Miller, who did not object to the plan but said he did not wish to be involved, the MBMC pursued the agreement they had established with the groups that organized the boycott.[28]

The boycott lasted a little over a month and ended abruptly, but it helped steer Mennonite leaders into a much larger discussion about the farmworker movement in California. In California, however, the stakes were much higher, as the situation there involved a number of Mennonite growers who represented two distinct Mennonite groups: the Mennonite Brethren and the General Conference. But the case at Pine Manor demonstrated that the farmworker movement was not simply a West Coast issue. What Cesar Chavez started in California spread throughout the country and helped strengthen a movement started in the small town of Delano, California. In fact, much of the support for the National Farm Worker Ministry (NFWM), the organization of religious leaders who supported La Causa, came from religious communities in the Midwest and on the East Coast—from Sandusky, Ohio, to New York City.[29] More important, Pine Manor showed that taking sides by joining a boycott would not be easy for Mennonites, especially when it was their own who were being confronted.

Mennonites, Unions, and the Politics of Engagement

During the late nineteenth and early twentieth centuries, Mennonites moved to California from the Midwest and settled in the small agricultural towns of the San Joaquin valley of central California.[30] They moved for a variety of reasons, but mainly to leave behind areas in the central plains affected by drought and to take advantage of California's rich agricultural possibilities.[31] While they arrived with a shared ethno-religious heritage as Mennonites, they varied in denominational loyalty. Many of the Mennonites who settled in central and Southern California were part of the Mennonite Brethren or General Conference Mennonite denominations. They held varying theological and political views, views that differed somewhat from those of the "Old" Mennonite Church, with which the MMC was affiliated and which is the focus of much of this book.

Religious schisms in North America and south Russia (Ukraine) during the latter part of the nineteenth century gave birth to the Mennonite Brethren, General Council, and Old Mennonite Church as separate denominational groups, but they nonetheless share a long history of cooperation.[32] Since the 1920s the one organization with ties to each of these groups, the MCC, has served as the relief and development organization for all three groups. But in 1973 that collaboration was called into question when the MCC stepped in to ascertain how Mennonite growers—most of whom belonged to the Mennonite Brethren or General Council Mennonite Church—were responding to the farmworker movement and its leader, Cesar Chavez. What resulted was a significant moment that redefined the relationships among Latinos, the Mennonite Church, and the MMC. While there remained broad but sometimes uneven support from each denomination for Martin Luther King and the black freedom movement, the issues raised around Mexican American farmworkers, Cesar Chavez, and the Chicano movement failed to garner the same type of broad support from white Mennonite leaders.[33] At the center of this debate was a long and uneasy relationship between Mennonites and labor unions.

In 1973 Jocele T. Meyer, a member of the Women's Missionary and

Service Commission (WMSC), formerly the Women's Missionary and Service Auxiliary, was excited about the possibilities of supporting the work of the NFWM. Her midweek Bible study group at Lee Heights Mennonite Church in Cleveland had started discussing the plight of farmworkers. Along with other Mennonite women, she subscribed to the NFWM mailing list and received publications from Church Women United that covered farmworker issues.[34] In December 1973 the NFWM met in Cleveland to garner support, speak to the issues of farmworkers in the Midwest, and advocate a boycott of Fisher-Fazio supermarkets, northeastern Ohio's largest grocery chain.

At the request of Lupe De León, Meyer was in Cleveland to represent the WMSC and support the farmworker cause. But when Meyer learned that part of the meeting's agenda involved picketing and leafleting, she became nervous. She was familiar with the boycott of Fisher-Fazio and had stopped shopping in its stores, even though "they have some of the best specials in the city." She was learning to avoid non–United Farm Workers (UFW) lettuce and grapes but still struggled and admitted that she "unthinkingly ate a lettuce salad at a restaurant last week."[35]

Picketing was not easy, and Meyer admitted in a letter to the WMSC leadership committee that "had this been a supermarket in my neighborhood, I am not sure I would have joined them [the protestors]." Disregarding her fears, Meyer passed out leaflets and spoke to customers as they entered the grocery store. Knowing that Mennonites "have shied away from union participation," she nonetheless believed that "the plight of these workers who supply most of the fresh fruits and vegetables we buy at the super market is something we dare not be blind to."[36]

Meyer's decision to picket one of Ohio's largest grocery store chains was not easy. Aside from her own anxieties, she was also aware that throughout much of their history Mennonites balked at union participation. As early as 1937 the Mennonite Church passed a resolution that prohibited union membership because "the coercive nature of strikes and the adversarialism of collective bargaining were incompatible with Christian values."[37] According to historian Janis Thiessen, "union membership was rejected in part because the threat of strike action was considered an exercise of force on the part of labor." For Mennonites, "killing someone as a soldier in wartime was morally equivalent to walking a picket line in peacetime." No one espoused these views more than the executive secretary of the Committee of Economic and Social Concerns, Guy F. Hershberger. Hershberger regarded labor unions as "power organizations" and believed that strikes violated the principle of nonresistance so important to Mennonites.[38]

The hard line against union participation eased after World War II as Mennonites stopped short of prohibiting membership but not without stern warnings about the coercive politics of labor unions.[39] But even with the change, Mennonites remained conflicted about how to engage labor unions without it "conflicting with their Christian testimony." This ambiguity played a large role in how Mennonite leaders responded to the farmworker movement in California. For Mennonites, especially Guy Hershberger (or "Mr. Peace" as some Latinos called him), the union tactics of Cesar Chavez and the UFW were too coercive for comfort.

Building a Farmworker Movement

In the 1950s Cesar Chavez worked as an organizer with the Community Service Organization (CSO) in California under the leadership and direction of Fred Ross. In 1962, in frustration over the hesitancy of the CSO to organize farmworkers, Chavez left the CSO and moved his family to Delano, California, to organize farmworkers there.[40] This was not the first time Mexican farmworkers had organized against low wages and poor working conditions. As historian Zaragosa Vargas has shown, since Roosevelt's New Deal farmworkers have slowly and steadily organized for their social and political rights. These movements set the stage for the modern Chicano movement and provided the historical waypoints that marked Mexican American labor, political, and social activism in the mid-twentieth century. In the years prior to World War II, "the labor movement remained the central organizing base out of which Mexican American protest activity emerged."[41] Especially in California the CSO was a major factor in organizing Mexican Americans.

When Chavez began visiting farmworkers, literally going door to door in towns across the San Joaquin valley, he worked to forge relationships with families and convince them that their working conditions could indeed change. But with no labor organizing or collective bargaining rights, farmworkers had little faith in the possibility of change. In the fields where they worked, they lacked drinking water, restroom facilities, and lunch or rest breaks. To make matters worse, their jobs did not fall under minimum wage requirements or qualify them for unemployment insurance.[42] Organizing farmworkers, who lacked rights and received little public attention, was a tremendous gamble.

With a slow but steady flow of support, Chavez and his good friend from his CSO days, Dolores Huerta, together launched the National Farm Workers Association (NFWA) in 1962 and two years later started publishing the newspaper El Malcriado. From 1964 to 1965 the newspaper was published entirely in Spanish and reached a circulation of nearly 1,000. More important, the newspaper, along with the development of a credit union and a death benefit program, helped the NFWA build a strong support network among Mexican farmworkers during the first few years of the movement.[43]

The game changer for the NFWA, however, came on Mexican Independence Day (September 16) in 1965, when nearly 1,200 members agreed to join the strike against Delano grape growers. Organized by Filipino American members of the Agricultural Workers Organizing Committee, the strike lasted five years and helped spread support for the farmworker movement across the country as millions of Americans caught wind of La Causa. The grape strike helped establish Chavez as a leader whose quiet and unassuming manner won the support of people from across the country. Nowhere was this clearer than in the growth of the small newspaper El Malcriado, whose circulation had increased to over 6,500 in English and Spanish editions by the end of 1965, reaching places as far away as Texas, Oregon, Washington, Wisconsin, Ohio, and Florida.[44] When the strike ended in 1970, the entire table grape industry was under contract.

But the movement had only just begun. According to movement organizer and scholar Marshall Ganz, by the late 1970s "the UFW had successfully negotiated more than 100 union contracts, recruited a dues paying membership of more than 50,000, and secured enactment of the California Agricultural Labor Relations Act, the only legislative guarantee of farm workers' collective bargaining rights in the US."[45] The farmworker movement also provided the broader Chicano movement a national audience—beyond the stronghold of the Southwest—leading white liberals, students, and African American activists to see the Chicano movement as a national movement. By the mid-1970s it was clear that the gamble had paid off and that Chavez and his supporters had built the most successful agricultural worker movement in the history of the United States.

From the very beginning Chavez's organizing philosophy revolved around social movement ideology. The farmworker movement was, as one scholar put it, a "transcending mission" whose practical politics reflected union tactics but whose performance and discourses reflected a larger social and political movement.[46] Chavez understood the limitations of traditional unions and knew that without the broad support of diverse constituencies, organizing farmworkers would be impossible. What made the union different was Chavez's ability to bring national attention to a regional problem. He drew the attention of white liberals, radical students, and leaders of the Chicano movement, and the boycotts captured national and global attention.

Scholars who have studied the success of the UFW movement generally agree that it was more than a traditional union. Sociologist Craig Jenkins has observed that the UFW "exemplified the basic goals and strategies of the social movements of the stormy sixties."[47] Looking at the labor movement among Mexican Americans in general, historian Zaragosa Vargas has shown that the "labor struggles of Mexicans were inseparable from the issue of civil rights. . . . Just as racial discrimination led Mexicans to pursue the righteous path to unionism, it pushed them into the struggle for social justice."[48] Even those who criticized the UFW saw it as "a civil rights movement."[49]

In reality, however, the UFW struck a delicate balance between a traditional union and a social movement. It could not authentically address labor concerns without also raising concerns of racial discrimination and social marginalization. This inevitably led to further speculation that, as Cletus Daniel has argued, revealed Chavez's "personal ambivalence toward both the ultimate purpose of worker organization and the fundamental objective of his prolonged activism."[50] But despite his ambivalence, Chavez was able to transform the 1965 grape boycott into a civil rights struggle that invited teachers, students, religious leaders, white liberals, and sympathizers from across the country to think for the first time about who picked the fruits and vegetables they enjoyed.

According to Ganz, it was these associations with groups across the country that catapulted the farmworker movement from a regional struggle to a national movement on par with the black freedom struggle in the South. As Ganz asserts, UFW members "identified themselves as a union that cared about racial self-determination in relation to the evil white oppressors. . . . The movement drew on churches, liberals, students, civil rights groups as it framed its struggle as a farm worker civil rights movement."[51] Mennonites, however, did not see the farmworker movement as a civil rights struggle. For many, especially Mennonite growers in central California, it was seen as a threat to their livelihood.

Mennonites with Guns

From the time Cesar Chavez launched the NFWA in 1962 to the major grape strike victory in 1970, the Mennonite Church refused to involve itself with the emerging movement. But what began at Pine Manor in Indiana in 1971 continued through 1974 as Mennonites from across the country weighed in on how best to resolve the ongoing tensions in the fields. Mennonites were latecomers to the movement, and their hesitation was evident in how members of churches throughout California and the rest of the country worried about the consequences of siding with the farmworkers. Protestant groups in California varied in their support, from both the northern and southern conferences of the United Church of Christ, who supported the grape boycott, to the Fresno Area Council of Churches and the Presbytery of San Joaquin, who remained uncertain about the strike and often criticized the farmworker advocacy of the pan-Protestant group the California Migrant Ministry.[52]

But while religious groups were divided in their support, both Catholic and Protestant Latinos showed strong support for Chavez and the farmworker movement in both Texas and California. In fact, as historian Paul Barton has argued, the Chicano movement was a game changer for Latino Protestants and Catholics, as many of them began to openly support social movement causes.[53] Their support was often so widespread that disgruntled growers frequently denounced religious leaders for "using the Roman collar to act as labor organizers."[54] Many of these religious activists brought the Chicano and farmworker movements into their churches in ways never seen before. The same was true in the Mennonite Church. Nowhere was this more evident than in the Cross-Cultural Youth Convention in 1972 when black and brown youth showed unanimous support for the farmworker movement. As it turned out, they would be the only Mennonites to offer official support to La Causa.

But only a year later the support of black and brown youth was a distant memory as rumors spread that Mennonite growers were carrying guns to patrol their fields against striking workers. There were also growing concerns about worker discontent at some of the farms owned by Mennonites in the small towns of Reedley and Dinuba in central California. While many Mennonite growers were known as "kind and compassionate" employers, they also had the reputation of being "some of the hardest-driving and miserly employers in California farming."[55]

In 1974 representatives of the three largest Mennonite groups (Mennonite Brethren, General Conference, and Mennonite Church) and members of the Peace Section of the MCC engaged in a series of meetings with Mennonite growers in central California.[56] The meetings were part of a process to appease the fears of Mennonite growers who were beginning to believe that their respective church bodies were sympathetic to the UFW cause. Mennonite growers who belonged to the General Conference denomination were especially concerned.

They raised questions about articles in the church press that were supposedly supportive of Cesar Chavez and about a game that appeared in church educational curriculum that asked students, "You got a bellyache from eating too much non-union lettuce? Lose one turn until your stomach compassion improves." Fearful that some Mennonite schools were sympathetic to the UFW, growers warned church leaders, "Schools need to be careful not to jump on the bandwagon of [just] anyone who calls for peace!"[57]

But aside from wanting to better understand the perspective of the Mennonite growers, church leaders were especially concerned about growing suspicions that some Mennonites were carrying guns in the fields to protect themselves from UFW strikers. Some Mennonite growers maintained that they only carried guns to "shoot jack rabbits," while others admitted only to taking a gun into the fields at night. There were also reports circulating that Mennonite "farmers have picked up sticks to make sure that the striking farm workers knew they meant business."[58]

One of the more bizarre stories had to do with a Mennonite woman and picketing farmworkers. According to Mennonite growers, "picketing farm workers who were chasing a young boy . . . were scared off when a

Mennonite woman picked up a large stick and threatened them with it."[59] It was not uncommon for growers to carry a weapon when they patrolled their fields, but for Mennonite growers to carry a weapon betrayed the core Mennonite values of peace and nonresistance. While not all Mennonites carried guns or big sticks, the reports were enough to alert Mennonite Church leaders to the seriousness of the situation in California.[60]

Concerned about possible violence, the team of Ted Koontz (MCC), Harold Regier (General Conference), Phil Hofer (Mennonite Brethren), and Guy Hershberger (Old Mennonite Church) arrived in central California for a weeklong meeting in March 1974. They were welcomed in California only after "it was clear that MCC had not taken an official pro-Chávez position." The MCC agreed to the stipulation. Only a day before the team arrived, the MCC executive committee passed a resolution promising Mennonite growers that the "primary concern for the situation be carried by the churches in the California area."[61] To be clear, the Mennonite growers that church leaders were scheduled to meet were not a major concern for UFW organizers. Mennonite farms were generally smaller and not as important to UFW organizers. The issue for Mennonite growers, however, was that once other sectors of the farm industry unionized, the higher costs would be passed along to them in some form or fashion. Whether or not UFW organizers were targeting Mennonite farms, Mennonites were feeling the repercussions where they mattered most—in their pocketbooks.[62]

Fact-finding missions of this sort were nothing new. In 1972 the Arizona Ecumenical Council, which represented mainline Protestant and Catholic groups, initiated its own investigation of farm labor issues in Arizona. Their report aroused the ire of a UFW organizer in Arizona who said that the "committee's report did an injustice to the farm worker."[63] But as important as religion was to the farmworker movement, for both political and moral support, religious groups were often torn between appeasing their grower support base and the movement some believed represented biblical calls for justice. The turmoil often pushed Protestant groups "to reexamine the ethical role of organized religion during times of social unrest."[64] In other words, the farmworker movement raised important questions for church groups who believed they should side with the workers but who also feared the backlash of the powerful growers.

Mennonite Growers and La Causa

No one was more vocal in the crusade to share the "grower perspective" than Mennonite grower Alvin Peters. In the early 1970s Peters was at the center of the farmworker debate within the Mennonite Church. When Peters extended an invitation to church leaders, he did so assuming that Mennonites on the East Coast did not understand the dynamics of farm labor disputes in California. He also feared that growers were being demonized by Mennonites who sided with Chavez.[65] Taking matters into his own hands, Peters made personal visits to Mennonite colleges in Indiana and Ohio, where he defended his fellow growers. During one visit to Bluffton College in Ohio, Peters's contempt for the UFW and Chavez was so persuasive that students halted their support of the boycotts and the UFW altogether. In addition to making his own trips east, he often invited people to California on fact-finding tours that allowed middle-of-the-road Mennonites to come and learn about the supposed struggles of the growers.[66]

Soon after the Koontz, Regier, and Hershberger visit, a group from Goshen, Indiana (Dan Hertzler, Beth Sutter, and Ruth Sutter), made the trip west. With an invitation from Peters, the group had access to other Mennonite growers and even spoke with some of the Mexican American farmworkers on Peters's farm. With no Mennonite institutional connection this time, the notes about this visit revealed more clearly the hostile attitudes of many of the Mennonite growers. In one meeting, Beth Sutter described the awkwardness of meeting with Peters and some of the Mexican American farmworkers who worked on his farm:

> Passing by on a pick up was a load of workers. Alvin hailed them, and they pulled in the driveway. They got off the truck and moved toward us. Then Alvin said, "Ok, here I've got any type of Mexican you'd want—wetbacks, green carders, any type you'd want. Ask 'em if they want to join the Union!" Then Alvin told the foreman (these people all worked on Peters' farm) to interpret for us and to ask them if they wanted to join the union. . . . No one asked anything, so Peters repeated the union question. It was so embarrassing for us and humiliating for them. Peters was getting nervous because they wouldn't answer. The men just kept staring at us. Then Alvin said it was because the "boys" thought we were from

the union that they wouldn't talk. "You see, they're scared." After more awkward moments he "shooed them away."[67]

In another interview, Mennonite grower Ray Ewy complained that Mexican American farmworkers "are violent . . . [and] carry knives. The flags have razor blades in them where they are attached to the pole, the poles have lead pipes on them." Sutter noted that Ewy "made it a point to say that he 'definitely did not like Gracie and Neftali [Torres] or Lupe De León . . . [and] went on to say that 'the Mexicans should be able to laugh at themselves like the Japs did about their internment.'"[68]

While Koontz, Regier, and Hershberger met with two UFW representatives, their report mostly sympathized with the growers. They stood by grower claims that farmworker wages were some of the highest in the nation, and they left unchallenged the claim that poverty among farmworkers was more the "result of mismanaging money or unwillingness to work when work is available" than low pay. When Koontz, Regier, and Hershberger shared the latter statement with Mexican American Mennonites, they "laughed at the suggestion."[69] Growers also painted a rosy picture of relationships with their workers. They claimed that workers "are generally satisfied . . . [and] would leave if the farmer would join the UFW." Another Mennonite grower, Richard Hofer, did not understand why activists were clamoring for better housing, since "that kind of people do not want nice houses. They're not like us." Mennonite growers were also unanimous in their belief that the church should not side with the UFW and "should rather preach the gospel."[70]

In their reports, the MCC officials noted that on several occasions they had heard Mennonite growers blatantly admit that they "hate Mexicans," while at least one person admitted that "it would not hurt her conscience to shoot troublemakers."[71] The usually quiet Mennonites took a stance against what they perceived as a serious threat to their businesses and livelihoods. Based on this perceived threat, Mennonite growers blamed the UFW for a poor harvest season and for agitating an otherwise content worker base. Moreover, Mennonite growers bought into the hysteria about the UFW movement really being a communist conspiracy that sought "to reclaim the Southwest for Mexico or to form a new nation."[72] At the end of their report, church leaders continued to ask, "What is the United Farm Workers and what are their purposes?"

If church leaders were confused about the goals of the farmworker movement, they were just as lost about the role the church should play in labor disputes. While the report did acknowledge that the "Christian faith is relevant to this problem," they admitted not knowing exactly what role the church should play.[73] The report was heavily geared to understanding the grower perspective and gave little clarity about the issues that the farmworkers faced or the purpose of the UFW. This was intentional. In addition to concerns about the UFW as a union, MCC leaders worried that siding with the farmworkers would alienate wealthy Mennonite growers whose financial donations at the annual MCC "Relief Sale" fundraiser helped raise thousands of dollars for the work of the MCC.[74] So much was riding on the Koontz, Regier, and Hershberger reports that the MCC executive director at the time, Bill Snyder, was warned that if the MCC did side with the farmworkers, Mennonite growers would end their financial contributions to the MCC.[75]

Withdrawal of support from Mennonite growers was something MCC leaders were not willing to risk. So whether or not the team who visited Mennonite growers in California actually supported a neutral decision, in reality they had little choice but to acknowledge that growers were also being victimized by the strikes. In his own report, Regier noted that the UFW had plenty of resources to tell its side of the story and that "our visit to California will not accomplish anything unless we tell the grower side of the story in our reporting."[76] In the end, church leadership and members of the MCC Peace Section followed the suggestion of Guy Hershberger, who asserted that joining a labor union was "a questionable procedure in any case, and in the case of the UFW it would be promoting a lost cause. Such participation will have a divisive effect within the Mennonite brotherhood, with much to lose and little to gain."[77] Koontz agreed and in his report recommended that the churches in central California and the MCC not get involved or choose sides. The meetings had gone so well for Peters and other Mennonite growers that Peters suggested having more.[78]

Soon after their trip west, the MCC tried to distance itself as much as possible from any notion that they had provided official support for the UFW. A month after his visit to California, Koontz received a threatening phone call from Jack Angell of the American Farm Bureau. At that time, the Farm Bureau was the nation's strongest ally for growers. It "opposed civil rights advances" and from the beginning had "launched a full-

scale attack on César Chávez and the United Farm Workers."[79] Angell was about to publish a list of churches and organizations that had contributed to the NFWM as a type of exposé for a "farm bureau publication."

In the phone call, Koontz explained that it was the MMC and not the MCC that was sympathetic to the farmworker cause. In a note explaining his position, Koontz wrote that "the minority council does not represent the views of all Mennonites and that Mennonite Central Committee is made up largely of Mennonite groups which have no organizational tie to the body sponsoring the Minority Ministries Council." Koontz tried to be as clear as possible "that Mennonite support for the National Farm worker Ministry was from the Mennonite Minority Ministries Council."[80]

The Political Is Personal

Shortly after the Koontz, Hershberger, and Regier report was released, the trio of Ted Chapa, Lupe De León, and Neftali Torres took a West Coast trip of their own. The trip was organized to challenge the assumptions made by the previous reports and to gain firsthand knowledge of the tense relations between Mennonite growers, Chavez, and the UFW. For Latinos, the hangups that Hershberger and others noted in their reports did not go over well. Since the Minority Ministries Council had given its support to the farmworkers movement in 1972, Latino leaders had become integrally involved in a movement that they saw as more than simply a cause for justice. For Latinos, the cause of the farmworkers was a personal struggle. Many had worked in fields as children and teenagers under the scorching heat with poor wages and no restroom breaks. In a letter to Voluntary Service worker Dan Clark, De León explained why the farmworker cause had taken on such importance in his life: "It is no longer an intellectual awareness that I have gotten through reading books, but it is now a personal awareness ... [of the] freedom for which my ancestors fought and died on foreign fields so that we could have freedom.... They fought and died for freedom and the campesinos have no freedom."[81]

After their trip, De León, Chapa, and Torres released their own report, in which they voiced their support for the farmworkers and concluded that financial motives were behind the decision of the MCC and white Mennonite leaders not to take sides in the struggle. "Obviously MCC suffers economically," the trio reported, "if it aligns itself with those who do not agree with the growers. This assumption is made recognizing that a great many supporters of MCC are Mennonite growers in California who are opposed to César Chávez and the UFW."[82] For Latino leaders the financial motives seemed obvious, but they did not expect the comments that came from Guy Hershberger. In a separate report, Hershberger outlined his own views on the farmworker movement and made it clear that the MCC Peace Section would not support the UFW. Hershberger took this position without saying a word about where the MCC Peace Section stood in relation to the growers.

If Hershberger was out to protect the MCC and its valuable donors, he was also acting on his belief that union tactics and principles presented real contradictions for people who believed in peaceful nonresistance. The problem, however, was that Hershberger's views on unions and union activities were ambiguous at best. Hershberger encouraged Mennonites to work with unions only as the "Christian conscience permits." This meant that Christians could not join unions to "simply join the struggle for power, even if the goal was justice." But Hershberger was not as clear in outlining when union membership was justified. When Hershberger did support union membership, as he did in 1962 when he supported Mennonite teachers joining the American Federation of Teachers, he ignored the "outright union tactics" and claimed only that this was "another matter."[83]

In another case, Hershberger supported African American leaders when they organized the Montgomery bus boycott in 1955 but called it a "movement" instead of a "boycott," which in his view entailed a demand and a threat.[84] But with regard to the UFW, he made clear the distinction that most Mennonite leaders understood—that the UFW was a union first. Hershberger encouraged Mennonites to involve themselves in "social programs for the promotion of justice and equity for farm workers rather than supporting union activity." But perhaps what upset Latino leaders the most was Hershberger's comment that "what's needed is some talk—and a little humor."[85] Torres, Chapa, and De León responded by noting that "Guy's report shows us that he obviously does not have the insight on this particular issue that he needs. His suggestions smell of 'gringoismo.'"[86] Unfortunately, Hershberger's position on the UFW weakened any credibility he had earned with Latinos and undermined much of his ability to speak on issues of racial justice.[87]

One month later Torres, Chapa, and De León presented recommendations to take an official position in support of the farmworkers at a meeting of the Mennonite Board of Congregational Ministries (MBCM). The push from Latino leaders came as a call for the church to raise its voice, as it had been silent for too long. The report made the case that an agency that works closely with churches and evangelism should care about the farmworkers' struggle by asserting that the movement was not limited to the Chicano struggle but raised issues of justice for all minority groups.

Neftali Torres highlighted the threats he received from Mennonite growers, who warned him that "we're the supporters, we'll cut your funds if you say things about us, things that will hurt the farmers and protect the workers." But after an impassioned presentation that was followed by intense discussions, the MBCM refused to accept the report. "You talk about anger and what it does to you inside," Torres remembered. "My upper lip began to twitch. I was so angry, let down, and my lip began to quiver. . . . I couldn't express myself outright because I'm Christian, I'm not supposed to do that, I'm a minister, I'm not supposed to express hostility."[88]

With the MCC Peace Section, the Mennonite Brethren, and General Conference Mennonite groups taking no official stand on the farmworker issue, the MBCM had been the last hope for Latino leaders.[89] But here again, the center of the discussions was the "union" question. One of the participants, John A. Lapp, pointedly asked the group if "the issue is the United Farm workers as a labor union or are we dealing with a social movement?" Lapp answered his own question by noting that the movement "is an ethnic identity and Chicano movement rather than just a union. . . . The UFW becomes a vehicle like the SCLC [Southern Christian Leadership Conference] for the black movement." Lapp was right, but it was too late. While many white Mennonites sympathized with the farmworker cause, alienating wealthy growers and disagreements over the "union" question prohibited the church from taking an official position. Aside from proposing programs to help farmworkers, the MBCM and the church at large stepped aside and remained neutral.[90]

⁓

When Mennonite church groups decided to remain on the sidelines of the farmworker movement, they were not alone. Growers' interests, the fear of losing significant financial contributions from wealthy growers, and the sense that this was a West Coast issue caused a great deal of anxiety for both Protestants and Catholics. Yet the UFW counted on a heavy dose of Protestant and Catholic support throughout its movement as bishops and pastors agreed to formally support the boycotts. Historian Alan Watt goes so far as to argue that without the actions of religious communities and without Chavez's spiritual leadership, the UFW would have failed to bring the grape industry under contract.[91] While Watt's point is questionable, the important roles that religious leaders and religious symbolism played within the farmworker movement cannot be denied. Equally important, however, were the internal dilemmas it raised for supposedly progressive churches like the Mennonite Church.

In the end, Mennonite Church leaders failed to recognize something that even Mennonite growers knew quite well, namely, that the UFW was more than a labor union; it was a social movement working for justice and the dignity of Mexican Americans and all farmworkers.[92] Even after many conversations with growers and farmworkers highlighted the need for labor reforms, reports aimed more for "reconciliation" and "dialogue" between workers and growers than for actual reforms. Chris Hartmire, the leader of the NFWM, criticized the Mennonite approach as "hardly fair play. This is the powerful talking to the powerless," he said in one report. Focusing on growers and dialoging with them was something Hartmire considered a "waste of time."[93]

But this was only part of the story. The Mennonite push to "dialogue" with growers was mostly an attempt to appease its own wealthy constituents who threatened to pull their financial support if any Mennonite group gave official support to Chavez and the movement. To be sure, the UFW succeeded without support of the Mennonites. But for Latinos within the church who had witnessed firsthand the church's commitment to black civil rights and antiracism, the symbolic denial of support hit home. For Latino Mennonites, this was a golden opportunity for white Mennonites to prove their commitment to issues that mattered most to Latinos while also validating their struggles as a racial minority. The issue was compounded by the fact that the Chapa, Torres, and De León report and its recommendations were rejected in favor of the recommendations of white Mennonite leaders. Frustrated, Latinos began to search out other avenues to bring attention to the concerns within the church in beyond.

As white Mennonites wavered on an important political cause, Latinos started to reassess their relationship to the MMC and interethnic politics.

The farmworker movement debacle had only reinforced notions of cultural nationalism, best expressed in the popular Chicano movement poster that proclaimed "Mi Raza Primero" (My People First), as Latinos once again shifted the terrain of identity politics.[94] But instead of a narrow view of cultural nationalism, one that trumped Chicano concerns over all else, the struggles around the farmworker movement shaped how Latinos began to think about a shared sense of Latino identity, or "Latinidad."[95] For Latino Mennonites, the farmworker movement was not only a Mexican American struggle, but one that affected a multitude of minorities who worked the land. As a Puerto Rican migrant himself, Neftali Torres understood the connection to the land, the struggle for fair wages, and the search for home. His own Puerto Rican migrant experience and what he saw in the fields of California solidified for him the notion that "somos Latinos [we are Latinos]. . . . I cannot be solely Puerto Rican and not be connected to the Hispanic world."[96]

The interactions and relationships between Mexican Americans and Puerto Ricans were solidified and strengthened through their mutual struggles in the church. But as the following chapters show, the battles for self-representation are continually problematic and contested. Forging Latinidad, in other words, raised a new set of struggles that both challenged and strengthened Latinos within the Mennonite Church. Nowhere was this more visible than in the very public politics of Latinas in the church. In 1973 Latinas moved away from the male-dominated politics of the MMC and began gathering to worship God and talk about issues that mattered most to them. As the following chapter shows, these conferences once again shifted the terrain of identity politics within the Mennonite Church from the interethnic politics of the MMC to Latino identity politics. The result reveals how Latino evangelicals shaped the changing religious landscapes in the United States and in the process fashioned new religious and identity politics as they rose to prominence in the 1970s.

Part III
~~~

Becoming Evangélicos

CHAPTER 6

Mujeres Evangélicas

Negotiating the Borderlands of Faith and Feminism

We should not let society make us believe that to talk about the feminist movement is taboo. Instead of reacting against such changes, we should actively involve ourselves in a process to examine the pros and cons of such changes.
—MARÍA TIJERINA, 1981

Unconventional Women

On April 14, 1973, close to 60 Latinas gathered at the Iglesia Evangélica Menonita in Moline, Illinois, for the first conference organized by and for Latinas in the Mennonite Church. Conference organizers Maria Bustos, Lupe Bustos, and Maria Rivera Snyder planned what they hoped would be "something special for Spanish-speaking women."[1] Indeed it was. Women came from as far away as Texas and New York and as close as Indiana, Chicago, and churches across Iowa. According to Maria Bustos, the women gathered "because there was a need to get to know each other and worship God together in Spanish."[2] Initially called a *servicio de inspiración* (service of inspiration), the gathering was mainly about getting women whose husbands often traveled or were involved in church work out of the home and away from chores and child care into a space where they could share a religious experience with other women. "This was a time for women to come," remembered Seferina De León, "and where the husbands could stay with the children, so we can be refreshed . . . and we would sing, pray, and share."[3]

From the early days of Latino Mennonite churches in Chicago, New York, and South Texas, women have sustained the church and in many cases were the majority of people in the pews.[4] According to theologian Loida Martell-Otero, for Latinas the Protestant church has historically been a place "of social contacts, of leadership development, of nurture and support."[5] But even as the church opened space for women, it also set clear parameters on the leadership roles women could play in the church. Though men were the numerical minority in many Latino Mennonite churches, they held the majority of the leadership positions on committees and virtually all the pastoral positions in the church. The leadership positions left to women were largely those of Sunday school teachers, song leaders, and Bible study leaders. As important as these positions were, they kept women out of the broader positions of leadership in national organizations like the Minority Ministries Council (MMC). That all changed in the 1970s when Latinas began to organize their own conferences separate from the MMC men.

This chapter highlights the complex and often untold stories of mujeres evangélicas (Latina evangelicals) and the important roles they played in the life of the church. The increased participation of Latinas in the church, this chapter argues, paralleled and eventually led the shift toward Latino religious identity politics in the 1970s. Through culturally distinct forms of music, hosting their conferences in Spanish, and promoting cultural values that also resonated with MMC men, Latinas rose to prominence at a moment when both Latino and African American men were beginning to question the viability of a multiethnic brotherhood. Their success was due in part to their broad grassroots appeal to women who until then were not involved in church leadership. Women like Gracie Torres, Seferina De León, Maria Bustos, and others created a space for mujeres evangélicas where they could "be away from the men for awhile and praise God."[6] Their movement attracted women from across the United States and Puerto Rico who longed for a space to talk about issues that mattered most to them: family, faith, and the role of women in church leadership.

Of these, it was the question of women in church leadership that sparked the most debate around faith and feminism among Latinas in the Mennonite Church. While Latina Mennonites never used the "feminist" label, they did practice their own brand of "female collective action" that asserted the leadership capabilities of women, the importance of the family, and the importance of education for women. Within the patriarchal religious tradition of the church, Latina Mennonites created their own spaces where they assumed leadership positions as preachers and encouraged Latinas to reexamine the traditional roles of women.[7] While they believed in the role of men as "spiritual leaders of the home," they also made a case for the roles that women could play in the church as preachers and prophetesses.

These seemingly contradictory positions created a contested and somewhat ambivalent juncture of faith and feminism where Latinas negotiated their place in the church and the home. It was a space where they preached female empowerment in one breath and traditional gender roles in another.[8] As this chapter demonstrates, negotiating faith and feminism did not come through loud protests or walkouts; instead it manifested itself through meetings, through group prayers, and through their belief that God had called women to use their leadership skills in the church. In the process, they changed the direction of the MMC in general and helped mark a path for the rise of Latino religious identity politics that flourished in the late 1970s.

In examining the borderlands of faith and feminism, this chapter heeds historian Maylei Blackwell's call to examine "the multiple feminist insurgencies of women of color by looking beyond 'the' women's liberation movement as the only site that produced 'real' feminisms."[9] Expanding the contours of what is considered feminist action is critical to writing history that explores the multiple and sometimes contradictory forms of women's activism that emerged in the church, on the shop floor, or in the home. Doing so not only reveals the political range of the feminist movement but also shows how women in the church debated the virtues and pitfalls of feminist thought even as they organized their own version of the movement in their churches.

This chapter also resituates the place of Latina evangelicals. While their unconventional histories are for the most part left out of traditional church history narratives, their work and leadership has left an indelible mark on the politics of race and gender within the church.[10] Their absence from the history books only confirms Minerva Garza's assertion that "church history has been essentially men's history," leaving out the important contributions of women.[11] Much of the work of Latinas in the church was done in an era when most were reminded that *las mujeres no predican* (women don't preach). But even the best efforts of white missionaries and Latino men to marginalize women could not keep them from taking the lead as preachers and missionaries in their home communities.

Following the work of Elizabeth Brusco, Anna Adams, and Lara Medina, this chapter takes seriously the perceptions women had about their own struggles while also considering how female collective action redefined notions of domesticity and faith.[12] As anthropologist Elizabeth Brusco argues, "If we are going to exclude women from feminism because they value the roles of mother and wife and because they see the family as their source of strength . . . we are committing a grave error."[13] Brusco's keen observation marks the important way that Latinas in the Mennonite Church engaged feminist politics during the turbulent 1970s. The 1970s were a decade that according to historian Edward Berkowitz produced "an amazing array of revelations and changes in social, political, and public thought and policy" for women. In other words, "women had their sixties in the seventies."[14] The case was no different for Latinas in the Mennonite Church. While they were relatively quiet in the 1960s, by the 1970s they were an integral part of forging ahead with a new Latino Mennonite agenda.

A Group of Our Own

For Maria Bustos, Lupe Bustos, and Maria Rivera Snyder the first conference of Latinas in Moline was an answer to their prayers. The group of 60 women, most of whom were Mexican American or Puerto Rican, showed up to enjoy each other's company, worship God, and meet women from across the country. Maria Bustos described it as "un programa completamente en Español para compartir, tener compañerismo, y animarnos unas a otras como damas Latinas" (a program completely in Spanish to share with one another, get to know each other, and encourage each other as Latina women).[15] For Latinas like Seferina De León it was an opportunity "to have a group of our own to listen to each other and figure out how we can help each other."[16] There was also a deep desire to reach out to women whose husbands were either pastors or church leaders and often spent more time on the road and in meetings than at home. The conference was a perfect opportunity for women to gather and sing, pray, and share with one another while "the husbands stay home with the children."[17]

Prior to meeting in Moline, Latinas had rarely held any positions of leadership within the church and for the most part remained behind the scenes. Even though women attended MMC meetings, they mostly led worship sessions, cooked the meals, and prepared the coffee. In fact, the only woman to hold a leadership position on the MMC executive committee was Criselda Garza, a Mexican American woman from South Texas. Garza was one of the few women who attended the 1968 meeting in Chicago and was a part of the first Urban Racial Council executive committee.[18]

So it is easy to understand why the first Latina conference was special to so many women. The first conference was a one-day event. The keynote speaker was Maria Rivera Snyder, a Puerto Rican woman who also taught nursing at Hesston College. But aside from the speakers and activities planned, the most memorable event was the miraculous healing of Pastor Mac Bustos.

Originally from Chicago, Mac and his wife, Maria, Bustos moved to Davenport, Iowa, in 1963 to help start the Segunda Iglesia Menonita at the request of the Iowa-Nebraska Mennonite Conference. After a few years in Davenport, the Bustos moved the church to nearby Moline, Illinois, where they refurbished an old Catholic Church to host their first services in 1970.[19] Only three years later, however, Mac Bustos was ready to step down as pastor because of health problems that made the pain in his legs unbearable. That changed when he showed up toward the end of the women's conference. As soon as he walked in, the women helped him up the stairs to the altar at the front of the church, where they gathered around him, each holding crosses tied together, and prayed for him. The MMC newspaper reported the event as women remembered it that day: "He hobbled to the front of the sanctuary, obviously in great pain, where his brother Mario and several women laid hands on him. . . . A few moments later, just after he took the communion wine, Mac said, slowly and with amazement in his voice: I have no pain! Immediately after the prayer, he got up and said, 'I have no pain' and left his medication at the altar."[20]

After the event, organizer Maria Bustos and many of the women in attendance agreed that the healing of pastor Mac Bustos was confirmation that God wanted them to plan a second conference. With the help of a

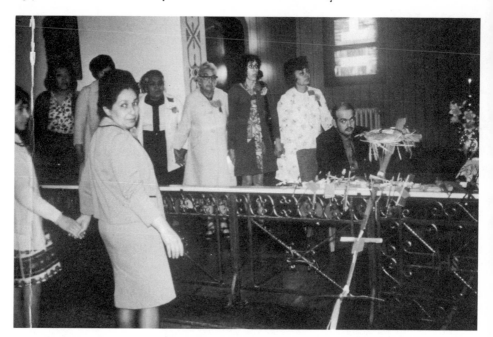

Women at the first Latina conference in Moline, Illinois, gathered around Mac Bustos as they prayed for him in 1973. Following the prayer, Mac's recovery was deemed a miracle and a sign that the women's conferences must continue.
(Courtesy of Steve Bustos)

$3,000 grant from the Women's Missionary and Service Commission (WMSC) of the Mennonite Church, a second conference was planned for 1974 in Lancaster, Pennsylvania. The decision to organize a second conference was made at the fifth annual Minority Ministries Council (MMC) conference in October 1973, where Maria Bustos was affirmed as the "planning coordinator" and where they chose the theme for the second conference: *La Mujer Decidida en un Ambiente Hostil* (The Confident Woman in a Hostile Environment).[21] They also formalized their movement by changing the name of the conference from *Servicios de Inspiración* (Services of Inspiration) to *Conferencia Femenil Hispana Menonita* (Hispanic Mennonite Women's Conference).[22]

But they did not stop there. In 1976 they organized their third conference in Corpus Christi, Texas, where over 150 Latinas converged around the theme *Embajadoras de Cristo* (Ambassadors of Christ). Celebrating what they called a "spiritual fiesta," the conference in Corpus Christi attracted women from as far away as Puerto Rico and New York City. Two years later they gathered once again in Goshen, Indiana, under the theme of *Libertad y Responsibilidad en la Familia Cristiana* (Liberty and Responsibility in the Christian Family). One of the more impressive aspects of these conferences was the fact that they were for the most part organized with funding that came from the women themselves, an accomplishment that the male leaders of the MMC never came close to matching.

Without question, fundraising efforts were helped by the fact that each conference attracted large numbers of women. While 60 women assembled at the first conference, by 1980 the conferences attracted over 200 women. More important, however, was how Latinas were able to garner the broad support of Latino churches across the country. Latino churches from New York (Brooklyn), Texas (Brownsville, Premont, Mathis, and Robstown), Chicago, and Defiance, Ohio, each contributed somewhere between $40 and over $100,000 to help organize the conferences. If the MMC struggled to reach grassroots churches with its message of racial harmony, the strong financial support that Latinas gathered from churches across the country was proof they were more successful in reaching the people in the pews. Their fundraising efforts were matched by the Mennonite Board of Missions and the WMSC, which in 1976 contributed over $3,000 to Latina leaders for the planning of their conferences.[23]

"We Were Never Invited to Join the Minority Ministries Council"

Two weeks after the first Latina conference in April 1973, women from across the Mennonite Church were invited to the first Cross-Cultural Theological Consultation in Des Plaines, Illinois. They included Manuela García (Mexican American), Helen Robinson and Barbara Sowell (African American), Gracie Torres (Puerto Rican), and Shirley Powell (white). Acknowledging the few women who participated, Shirley Powell wrote, "Comparatively, there were fewer women, of course, but at least we were represented."[24] And while gender was not a topic of discussion, Manuela García managed to sneak in a point that garnered the attention of the church press: "Polygamy is wrong," she said, "because the Bible says that no man can serve two masters." The newspaper editor recorded that Gar-

Women at the second Latina Conference in Pennsylvania in front of banner reading "Mujeres en Acción" (Women in Action), 1974. (Courtesy of Steve Bustos)

cía made the statement "with a smile," as if to prove a point about the lack of attention to gender dynamics within the room.[25]

The Cross-Cultural Theological Consultation garnered considerable attention in the church press. The MMC newspaper, *Happenings*, gave the event front-page coverage with the headline "Differences Deemphasized . . . Church Becoming Multi-Ethnic Brotherhood."[26] But as the church was celebrating "brotherhood," most of the male leadership was either unaware of or paid little attention to the conference of Latinas that only two weeks earlier had come together to "help women connect . . . [and] celebrate womanhood."[27] Prior to the women's conference the relevance of gender for MMC leaders centered mostly on the public musings of Lupe De León and his struggles with Chicano masculinity and the Mennonite Church.

The role of women within the MMC rarely came up among leaders who saw no problem with an all-male leadership council. As Puerto Rican Mennonite Gracie Torres remembered, "We were never invited to join the Minority Ministries Council."[28] Like the male leadership of the black

and Chicano civil rights movements, MMC leaders focused on racial injustice in the church and society and were not prepared to address the
marginalization of women within their own ranks.

But exceptions did exist. In 1969 the Latin Concilio debated whether
Criselda Garza, a Mexican American women from South Texas, should be
allowed to serve on the Concilio. After some debate, Latino leaders unanimously agreed she should, and she became the first Latina to serve on both
the executive committee of the Concilio and the MMC. While Criselda's
election and subsequent service was an important milestone, it would not
be until 1972 that the tone and substance of women's issues addressed
within the church changed significantly.[29] Nowhere was this more evident than at the Cross-Cultural Youth Convention in 1972. At the convention, Manuela García led a workshop on "machismo," which highlighted both the positive and negative aspects of what Alfredo Mirandé
has called "exaggerated masculinity."[30] García's workshop set the tone and
the parameters for how Latinas would talk about church leadership even
as attendees distanced themselves from the white feminist movement, or
"white woman's lib," as García called it during her workshop.

At issue for García was how questions of feminism and the emascula-
tion of men ignored the dynamics of race and threatened the gender norms
in the home. In the workshop, García lectured the group on the emerging politics of feminism among some Chicana activists. She insisted that
she "didn't like the idea of a man being less than a man. For me a man is
a provider. . . . You destroy a man's machismo, you not only destroy him,
you destroy his woman and you destroy the little ones because they have
no one to identify with."[31] She went on to note how race played into definitions of white manhood: "My little brother says it's all right for the
women and children, but I'm a man, that's not for me, those whities are not
men, those white guys help the women in the kitchen, those white guys
do what the lady says, those white guys let their ladies go to work, those
white guys change the little kids' dirty diapers, he's not a man."[32]

While firmly indicting diaper-changing fathers, García's talk also revealed the deep conflicts that Mexican American women had with white
feminist thought—mainly, that white feminism ignored how the intersections of race, gender, and class worked to marginalize women of color.
These debates took on another dimension when they were cast within the
walls of the church. While García was one of the most outspoken women

in the church, other Latinas in the church agreed with her indictment of "white woman's lib." At the center of these debates for Latinas in the church was the importance of the family in defining gender roles.

For Latinas in the church, maintaining traditional gender roles in the home was more about centering the family as the locus of power than it was about acquiescing male privilege. The belief that men were the "spiritual heads of the home," followed a biblical mandate that Latina Mennonites took quite seriously. As an important source of strength, the family unit was at the center of the politics and theology of Latina Mennonites. Placing the family as the cornerstone of their belief system placed them on similar footing with Chicana feminists who were having their own debates around the family. While the substance of the family debates among Chicana feminists differed from those of mujeres evangélicas, both managed to place the family at the center of either their faith or political activism.

For Chicana feminists who argued that the family "was a locus of resistance to 'Anglo' cultural domination," there was a belief that challenging traditional gender roles in the home did not make them cultural sellouts.[33] In 1975, Maxine Baca Zinn's article "Political Familialism" identified the family as critical in challenging both racism and patriarchy and defined "familialism" as "an activism that showed commitment to maintaining families."[34] Chicana feminists and Latinas in the Mennonite Church agreed about how the power and substance of the family was central in bringing about social change in both society and the church. But the two groups differed in very real ways as well. For example, while Chicana feminists believed that traditional gender roles in the family were "limiting," Latina Mennonites had little desire to challenge the roles in the home. They believed the Bible clearly outlined the gender hierarchy of the home. The roles of women and men outside the home in places like the church, however, were not as clear.

Latinas, Feminism, and the Church

The questions about the roles of women that emerged in the 1960s and 1970s were a continuation, not a break, from work and organizing dating back to the early twentieth century. But these questions, and the actions Latinas have taken, have varied across time and denominational affiliation. Simply to identify a singular role ignores the multiple ways in which mujeres evangélicas have served the church either as missionaries, preachers, or social justice activists since the early twentieth century. In 1917, only seven years after the Mexican Baptist Convention of Texas was founded, Mexican women formed the Union Femenil Misionera de Texas (Hispanic Women's Missionary Union of Texas) with María Hernandez as its first president.[35] According to theologian Nora Lozano, members supported a wide network of missionary programs, but they also involved themselves in social ministries that centered on working with ethnic Mexicans on both sides of the border on issues such as literacy, health care, poverty, and housing.[36]

In 1933 Mexican American Methodist women in San Antonio, Texas, organized what eventually became known as Mujeres Metodistas Unidas (United Methodist Women). According to historian Adriana Pilar Nieto, this group was the first cadre of Mexican American women to organize a separate organization from the national women's group of the United Methodist Church. While they had a focus on missionary work, they also continued a tradition of social service work with an emphasis on education and health care issues that mattered to Mexican American women.[37] Social service work was especially popular among Puerto Rican Pentecostal women in the mid-twentieth century. Women leaders like the Reverend Leoncia Rosado Rousseau (known as Mama Léo) and the Reverend Ana Villafañe helped launch drug and alcohol rehabilitation centers in the Bronx at a time when "the Bronx looked like an atomic bomb had hit it."[38]

These women were "warriors," as Elizabeth Ríos argues, because they took the ministry of the church to the streets, where they provided a level of assistance to people with drug and alcohol problems. Around the same time in the Rio Grande valley of South Texas, Yolanda Villareal worked as a missionary and Sunday school teacher for the Mennonite Brethren Church. With the comfort that "la Virgen de Guadalupe was going to be okay with this," Villareal led children's ministry programs in rural communities on both sides of the border. Her work and effort kept families coming back to the Mennonite Brethren Church week after week.[39]

Even without formal roles in the church, Latinas created their own spaces where they preached, served the community, and extended the work of the church from the pews to the streets. Latinas in the Mennonite Church were no different. Growing out of a storied tradition of organizing among Latinas in the church, their quest to organize conferences and create spaces of leadership development in the 1970s also paralleled the movement by white women in the Mennonite Church. In doing so they joined a litany of religious women's groups across the country that addressed the distinct roles of men and women in both Protestant and Catholic churches.

In many cases, these movements blended feminist thought with religious action, as the late 1960s had ushered in "the language of women's liberation" to many mainline Protestant denominations.[40] For example, both the United Presbyterian Church and the American Baptist Convention approved resolutions that required churches to work toward the equality and inclusion of women at all levels of the church. On a national level, groups like the Church Women United of the National Council of Churches involved themselves in direct-action campaigns when they supported the farmworker movement and other social movements.

According to historian Ann Braude, "The women who transformed American religion, particularly in the 1960s and 1970s . . . understood their efforts as part of the larger social movement of second-wave feminists."[41] But more important, the power of second-wave feminism in the churches extended beyond the boundaries of the United States. As the work of Elizabeth Brusco and Karen Offen has proved, in places such as Colombia and India conversion to Christianity led to the "reformation of machismo" and in other places opened spaces for women to challenge patriarchy.[42]

The tradition of second-wave feminism also undergirded many of the important strides that white Mennonite women had made by the late 1960s. In 1969 the Mennonite Conference of Ontario appointed the first woman delegate to the Mennonite General Conference session in Turner, Oregon. There was also a growing recognition among white Mennonite church leaders that "women's noninvolvement leaves men's involvement incomplete."[43] So when the Mennonite Board of Congregational Ministries in collaboration with the WMSC organized four men and four women as the Role of Women Task Force, the timing came as no surprise.

What was surprising was the important role that Latinos and Latinas played in this discussion. Ironically, in the wake of discussions of machismo, Latino men such as Neftali Torres were at the forefront of the gender debate. In the study document that went out to most Mennonite

churches, Torres's picture appeared on the front page facilitating a discussion among a group of mostly white Mennonite women.[44] But, as the
following section demonstrates, instead of choosing to align themselves
with one side of the role of women debate or the other, Latinos and Latinas believed in traditional gender roles but also in bending those roles in
ways that opened spaces for women to be equal partners with their male
counterparts.

The Borderlands of Faith and Feminism

The impetus behind organizing the Role of Women Task Force came from
the increased visibility of women in church leadership positions that tra-
ditionally were reserved for men. However, the participation of women
in various church roles predates the 1970s. As historian Beth Graybill
has argued, the growth of Mennonite missions in the years after World
War II opened opportunities for white Mennonite women who wanted
to serve as missionaries. Specifically, Graybill demonstrates that the shift
away from fundamentalism to an approach of both social service and "saving souls" in the postwar era opened spaces for women to join the growing movement of Mennonite missionaries. That trend continued into the
1970s as the number of women on church boards, in pastoral positions in
Mennonite churches, and in theological seminaries increased. But while
new opportunities opened up for women in the Mennonite Church, some
believed these appointments were "too modest" and nothing more than a
form of "tokenism."[45]

The findings of the Role of Women Task Force came as no surprise to
its organizers. The study identified at least two major themes that emerged
about the distinct roles of men and women in the church. The first theme
reflected passages in the Bible (1 Corinthians 11:1−16; 1 Corinthians
14:34, 35; Galatians 3:28) where there is a call for men and women to
share an equal relationship in Christ, but "for functioning and decision-
making, man is to be the leader (head) and woman is to be submissive to
him." The second theme was that some Mennonites believed in the "mu-
tuality of men and women in Christ necessitating equality in worth and
function as the Spirit gives gifts to the church."[46] In other words, if God
extends the gifts of preaching and church leadership to women, then they
are justified in their quest to be leaders.

No matter which side people took in the debate, the report cited the "deep emotional attitudes and feelings" that were associated with this issue.[47] But for Latinos and Latinas the issue never brought out emotions in quite the same way. In fact, they agreed with both themes that surfaced in the task force report. On one hand they agreed with the biblical role of men as the head of the household, but on the other hand they also believed that women were endowed with spiritual gifts and thus capable of church leadership. The most visible leaders during this time—Neftali Torres, Lupe De León, Maria Bustos, and Maria Rivera Snyder—all agreed that women "who have been called by God" should be allowed to serve on equal footing with men.[48]

Ironically, Maria Bustos was often quoted as saying that she struggled with whether or not women should be allowed to be pastors. Even though it was well known that Bustos believed that women who "were well prepared and had a calling from God" should be given every opportunity to be pastors of congregations, walking that fine line between the themes that emerged in the roles of women and men is what distinguished Latina Mennonites and made their movement so relevant for the growth and development of Latinos in the Mennonite Church.[49]

This apparent contradiction also set the stage for the day when women in the Mennonite Church "would take positions in the church that until [then had] been held by men."[50] But choosing to align themselves with both themes also showed the extent to which Latinas associated themselves with the broader feminist movement. While women like Gracie Torres were ridiculed by feminist friends for having "archaic" ideas about gender roles, Torres was quick to remind them that she did not consider herself "a slave to a man, but rather that [her husband] . . . depended on what I can offer him in council."[51] Latinas understood their role in the home as divinely ordered and thus holy, but they also demanded respect from men who they felt did not consider women as capable church leaders.

Herein lies the brand of feminist politics that Latina Mennonites defined in the 1970s: recognition of women as leaders who also believed that the gendered order in the home, with the husband as "spiritual leader," need not be reformed. For women like Seferina De León, creating spaces for women away from men was not about "fighting with the husbands" but about letting "them . . . know that we are not just having babies, fixing the food, or having the house clean" and that "every woman has value, the Lord has given us gifts."[52] Historian Gastón Espinosa in his work on Latina Pentecostals has called this a kind of "paradoxical domesticity whereby [women] are exhorted to be end-times prophetesses in the public sphere and devoted mothers and good wives in the private sphere."[53]

For Latina Mennonites the case was a bit different from that of Latina Pentecostals, who already had a history of serving as missionaries and evangelists; Latina Mennonites in the 1970s were only beginning to stake a claim in a predominately white church.[54] For Latina Mennonites the feminist movement of the 1960s and 1970s presented both positives and negatives. For many it paved the way for thinking about the empowerment of women in both the public and private spheres. It also opened up the possibility for talking more openly about issues around domestic life, health and well-being, and the family. In fact, many of the conferences that the women organized touched on all these issues.

Two of the organizers, Maria Rivera Snyder and Maria Bustos, valued education and were among the most vocal women on issues affecting women in leadership, education, and the church. Bustos often encouraged young Latinas: "No dejen de estudiar hasta que hallan logrado su carrera. Estudien más su idioma" (Keep studying until you have reached your career goals. Study your language").[55] Maria Rivera Snyder and other Latinas frequently contributed articles on women's health and leadership and the personal liberation of Latinas in the widely circulated *Ecos Menonitas* (the Latino Mennonite newsletter of the 1970s).[56] These women wrote about a number of issues related specifically to the shame Latinas often associated with sexuality, childbirth, health-related issues, the family, and marriage. In particular, Rivera Snyder published articles that encouraged Latinas, or "Meno-Latinas," as she called women in the church, to "liberate ourselves from false and antiquated concepts."[57] She warned Latinas of the detrimental effects of "negative concepts that institutions, the church, our communities, and television" on women's sense of self-worth.[58]

The question of how to think about and conceptualize feminism within religious contexts has produced a vibrant debate among historians and religious studies scholars. Julie Ingersoll in her work on conservative evangelical women contends that scholars have been too preoccupied with searching for "hidden forms of empowerment" in a conservative evangelical culture. Latina theologian Loida Martell-Otero has also challenged the notion that the experiences of Latina Protestants can be categorized as "feminist" and suggests instead that scholars should pay close attention to the practices and experiences of mujeres evangélicas.[59] Similarly, Gastón Espinosa cautions scholars against equating the struggles and movements of Latina Pentecostals to those of Latina feminists, noting that such a comparison would be "inaccurate."[60] This may be the case, but it leaves mujeres evangélicas in a type of theoretical limbo where their histories remain marginal to the broader story of women's rights in the United States.

The work of scholars such as Lara Medina, Sarah Hartmann, Kristy Nabhan-Warren, and Ann Braude, however, suggest another possibility. These scholars have explored how the multiple discourses of feminism have undergirded the work of religious women to make the church a more responsive and relevant place for women.[61] Yet the depth and breadth of feminist discourses varied across church groups and religious institutions. For example, the women who made up the National Council of Churches of Christ believed "sexism was a sin," and for these women "feminism became part of spreading Christ's mission in the world."[62] On the other hand, Las Hermanas—the first national religious-political organization of Chicana and Latina Roman Catholics in the United States—did not begin as an openly feminist organization when it organized in the 1970s. Nonetheless, historian Lara Medina identifies the group as a "feminist organization" because of its commitment to bettering the position of Latinas within the US Catholic Church.[63]

But it was also clear that the feminist movement often looked at religious women with disdain. When Chicana nuns of Las Hermanas made the case for the "feminist potential of Catholicism" at the 1971 Conferencia de Mujeres por la Raza, the idea was rejected in favor of characterizing "the Catholic Church as an oppressive institution."[64] Latina Protestants and Pentecostals viewed the church in entirely different ways. According to Anna Adams, women perceive the church as a place that offers the best possibilities for gender parity. The perceptions of these women, Adams argues, should be taken seriously because they "shape the way some women relate to their churches and have empowered them to reevaluate some church practices. Their perceptions matter because they have served as a force for change."[65]

That was the case for Latina Pentecostals in general and Latina Mennonites in particular. They believed in the church as a force for change in society and in their relationships with their husbands and families. Latina

Mennonites spoke of equality for women in the Mennonite Church, but they did so without dismissing how they understood the gender hierarchy within the Christian tradition. They believed that removing men from their leadership role had dire consequences for the family, as most followed a strict interpretation of the Apostle Paul's words in the New Testament. "Where I did not agree [with the feminist movement]," remembered Gracie Torres, "and I even disagreed with other Mennonite women who were very vocal in those days, was that I believed in the headship [of a man in the home]."[66] With no perceived counter to the mandates in the New Testament, Latinas were not about to go against their reading of the Bible. As theologian Loida Martell-Otero observes, "In any theological argument you may put forth in a Hispanic Protestant community, you better have a chapter and verse you can quote to back it up."[67]

Latina Mennonites demanded a shared voice with MMC men, who had dominated the discourses on race. But Latinas did more than demand a shared voice. The conversations that emerged around feminism and religious doctrine mobilized and fundamentally changed how Latinos and Latinas thought about the intersections of religious faith and Latino cultural traditions. While Latinas were some of the strongest adherents to Mennonite modes of fashion during the early years of the mission period, by the 1970s, women like Seferina De León started wearing traditional Mexican dresses to church and as a result helped usher in a new era in Latino cultural and religious revival. Nowhere was this clearer than in the conferences Latinas organized throughout the 1970s. The conferences became the place where *coritos* and other musical forms took center stage.[68] After attending the third biennial conference in Corpus Christi, Iris Navarro commented that "the great music has been amazing . . . each of these choruses inspired us with its beautiful melodies."[69] No longer hindered by the Mennonite demands of four-part harmonies and long-sleeved shirts, Gracie Torres and Seferina De León taught the church to sing Mexican *rancheras* along with the popular music of the civil rights era.

Gospel Music and Religious Identity Politics

When Altagracia A. Gonzalez Ramos ("Gracie Torres") began singing the worldly and socially progressive music of Bob Dylan and Joan Baez at the Lawndale Mennonite Church in Chicago in the early 1970s, it was a far

María Bustos, coordinator of the Conferencia Hispana Femenil, the third Latina
Mennonite conference in Corpus Christi, Texas, 1976. (Courtesy of Steve Bustos)

cry from her days as a street preacher in East Harlem. As part of a family
who had migrated from Puerto Rico to the Bronx in the late 1930s, Gracie
grew up speaking more English than Spanish and lived in a neighborhood
where most of her friends were either Polish or Jewish. Before her family
moved to the Bronx, they attended a Presbyterian church in Puerto Rico,
but once they arrived in the Bronx, they immediately joined a Pentecostal church. She grew up watching the televangelist Oral Roberts and was
impressed by his charisma, preaching, and miraculous healings. Church
was an important part of her and her sister's life. Her mother would often send them both to Sunday school classes at any number of churches
nearby, including a Disciples of Christ congregation and the Messianic
Jewish Center.

In 1956, at the age of 15, Gracie became a born-again Christian at a
revival service in nearby Queens, where she remembered being "so over-
joyed inside . . . I saw myself telling people on the street corner about Je-

sus Christ."[70] A few years later, Gracie and her good friend and room-
mate Millie were doing just that. Every Saturday night Gracie and Millie
stood on the corner of 116th Street and Lexington Avenue in East Harlem
singing gospel music and preaching to the "addicts, prostitutes, and people
from all walks of life who lived in Spanish Harlem."[71] Large crowds often
gathered to listen to and heckle the women preachers.

After a long night of preaching, Gracie and Millie would often escort
young people in need of help to the Damascus Christian Church, where the
Reverend Leoncia "Mama Léo" Rosado Rousseau ran a church-sponsored
drug rehabilitation program through the Damascus Youth Crusade.[72] Sustained almost entirely by church donations, the program was one of the
first to help rehabilitate drug abusers and was so successful that it eventually opened branches in other New York boroughs. In its time it helped
nearly 300 young people, most of whom were Latino, who struggled with
alcohol or drug addiction.[73] According to historian Virginia Sánchez Korrol, the programs started by Mama Léo helped increase the church's visibility on the streets while also serving as an example for young Puerto
Rican women who wanted to be leaders in the church and serve their
communities.[74] One such woman was Gracie Torres, who in the 1960s not
only preached on the streets but also ministered to patients at the Barry
Goldwater Hospital in Queens on Sunday afternoons. While doing her
ministry rounds at the hospital she met Mennonites who worked at the
hospital as part of the Voluntary Service program.

In the 1960s, Gracie paid little attention to the social revolution going on around her. Her main focus was her street preaching and helping
young women and men who needed rehabilitation. That changed in 1970
when she moved to Chicago with her husband, Neftali Torres, who had
accepted a position as pastor of the historically Mexican American church
Lawndale Mennonite. With the role of minister strictly reserved for men,
Gracie joined the Lawndale choir, in which she quickly became the lead
singer. The director of the choir, Arlen Hershberger, led a multiethnic
choir at Lawndale, which was one of the few Mennonite ensembles that
directly engaged civil rights, politics, and the increasing antiwar sentiment in their music.

It was there that Gracie first came across the progressive music of Joan
Baez and Bob Dylan. "I came from a background that you don't sing un-
godly songs in the church," Gracie explained, "but I was becoming politi-

cally aware about some of the issues affecting Mexican families . . . and it was music that had a message against injustice. I was awed by it and was glad that the world was writing music that was biblically inclined, things that Jesus stood against."[75]

But while it was the music of the civil rights movement that attracted Gracie, it was the accordion sounds of a new musical revolution in South Texas that captured the attention of Seferina De León. Born in the small ranching community of Argenta, Texas, Seferina was the eldest of six children. Her father tended the land of a white farmer, and her mother cleaned homes for white people in the community. From a very young age, Seferina was responsible for many of the chores at home, making sure dinner was ready for her family, and helping her younger siblings with their homework. Though she led an otherwise sheltered life and rarely left her home, she was the first one in her extended family to graduate high school. In order to marry her high school sweetheart, Lupe De León, she turned down a full scholarship to attend Durham Business School in nearby Corpus Christi.

Her love of music was fostered in the cotton fields of South Texas, where members of her father's family would sing as they worked. "We would pick cotton together," Seferina remembered. "We would get in a row and people would start singing and we would harmonize to each other . . . and that's where I started singing."[76] She started attending the Mennonite Church in Mathis at the age of 15 when one of her aunts invited Seferina and her mother to a church service. Not long after, both agreed to be baptized in the Mennonite Church. In 1962 journalist Marjorie Vandervelde visited her home and immediately noticed the 18-year-old whom she called "pretty Seferina." Vandervelde asked her what her responsibilities in church were, to which Seferina responded, "I am a chorister and a teacher in the primary department of Sunday school. . . . I love to sing."[77]

It was not long before she was leading her family in the new Christian songs she was learning as they made their way to church every Sunday. The music she was learning in church was radically different from the music she was accustomed to singing in the cotton fields with her family. In the 1950s and 1960s most Mennonite churches had nothing more than an organ and piano or simply sung their music a cappella. Even Latino

Mennonite churches in South Texas continued the tradition of quiet and well-orchestrated Mennonite music.

That changed in the 1970s. While the politics of the Chicano movement attracted her husband, Seferina remained committed to the music of her childhood. The Chicano movement brought about a cultural renaissance among young activists, but changes also brewed within Latino churches across the country. Nowhere was this more evident than among Mexican American Pentecostals like Paulino Bernal, who redefined the Mexican American conjunto scene by changing not so much its rhythms and cadences as its lyrics and its audience.[78] While Paulino Bernal was the leader of the monumentally popular Conjunto Bernal in South Texas, his conversion to Christianity helped opened the door for the solidification of Mexican American cultural themes in the Protestant and Pentecostal churches.[79] "By listening to Paulino Bernal and some of these other people, who were singing Christian music but using the contemporary style in the song, I said I guess it's okay. He used the vocals and backgrounds and how they harmonized so nicely and he is such a good accordion player. It was not a *baile*, but he did use his gifts."[80]

This shift toward culturally representative music was an outgrowth of the increasing popularity of Paulino Bernal in the late sixties and early seventies in the Tejano (Texas Mexican) Christian music scene. Bernal was already an icon in South Texas, but his switch to *música evangélica* (evangelical music) made him popular among Mexican American Pentecostals in South Texas and the Tejano diaspora. Lupe De León recalled:

I can remember listening to a radio station in South Texas that announced, 'y ahora con ustedes el hermano Paulino Bernal,' and I said my goodness, Paulino, I used to dance to his music at La Villita and he became a Christian? . . . What was lacking at that point [early 1970s] was *vida* in the churches. We were very quiet and docile, and with the coming in of Latino indigenous people in the church the guitars came out, the pianos and organs were no longer the instruments, and we started singing *himnos rancheros, boleros rancheros*, and that kind of stuff; that was the awakening of the churches to a more authentic indigenous type of worship, and people embraced it, and a lot had to do with the Pentecostal influences coming from the Latino leadership.[81]

A few years after Seferina first heard of Paulino Bernal's conversion, she met him in person when he performed at the third biennial conference of Latinas in Corpus Christi. Even though Bernal was a big name in the Texas Mexican music scene, he was relatively new to gospel music. That served the Mennonite women well, as he accepted their invitation to perform at their conference. Bernal shared with the women that after 20 years as a professional musician and leader of Conjunto Bernal, he had converted to Christianity and now "*canta para Cristo*" (sings for Christ).[82]

When Seferina moved to Elkhart, Indiana, after her husband joined the leadership of the MMC, she quickly connected with Gracie Torres in nearby Chicago. Their friendship helped launch a musical revolution of sorts by changing the rhythm and tone of Mennonite Church worship music. More important, it brought together both streams of cultural influence—from the conjunto music sounds of South Texas to the music of the civil rights movement—and changed how Latinos and Latinas worshipped in the Mennonite Church. The worship music that was first introduced at the Latina conferences quickly spread to other Latino Mennonite churches across the country as women returned to their home churches after each conference with a new set of music and rhythms. Rhythms that at one point were thought to be the "devil's music" were now revolutionizing how Latinos thought about their faith, culture, and identity.[83]

When Gracie and Seferina began to sing together in the Lawndale choir, they joined a musical tradition already strong among African Americans in the Mennonite Church. Beginning in 1970 the MMC helped sponsor four gospel music albums, which ranged from Mexican rancheras to African American gospel music. The first was an album by Barbara Sowell titled *Be a Christian*. The album by "soul Sister Sowell" was sold to raise funds for the work of the MMC. The following year the MMC sponsored an album called *Praises* by the "Mennonaires" choir of Burnside Community Mennonite Church in Columbus, Ohio. Both Sowell and the Mennonaires highlighted the "black experience in their music" while promoting the work of the MMC.[84]

The MMC followed up on those albums with one by the Lawndale Choir in Chicago called *Everything Is Beautiful*. Both Gracie and Seferina are featured on this album, but they released a separate album later that year that fused their musical interests. With the help of their choir director at Lawndale, Arlen Hershberger, Seferina and Gracie produced an

Gracie Torres (*left*) and Seferina De León (*right*) with Rick Ventura on guitar at the Cross-Cultural Youth Convention, 1972. (Courtesy of Mennonite Church USA Archives, Goshen, Indiana)

album that was promoted as "Spanish Gospel music . . . arranged in their respective Puerto Rican and Mexican folk idioms."[85] The music on this album became central to the changing musical trends among Latinos and African Americans in the Mennonite Church. The ideas of the civil rights movement converged with the musical gifts of women such as Gracie Torres, Barbara Sowell, and Seferina De León to produce music albums from their own cultural perspectives. The days of singing a cappella or using only the organ and piano in Latino Mennonite churches were long gone.

～

The music and singing of Gracie and Seferina contributed to the tone and the direction of religious identity politics among Latino Mennonites in the mid-1970s. With the wound over the church's lack of support for the farmworker movement still open, the music of Gracie and Seferina became both an inspiration and a central building block that allowed the politics of identity to flourish. Spanish-language gospel music created an atmosphere in which Latinos and Latinas felt more comfortable incorporating Latino cultural elements into their religious lives. For example, in churches where musical instruments were once prohibited, Latinos were now incorporating drum beats, bass guitars, and accordions to the gospel music they had grown accustomed to singing. Latinas who before had dressed as conservatively as white Mennonite women in the 1950s were now wearing traditional Mexican dresses to church on Sunday mornings. In short, the church atmosphere turned more festive and better resembled the energy of Pentecostal churches that many Latino Mennonites admired. This was a religious and cultural awakening that emerged out of the debates that Latinas had around the contested relationship between feminist thought and religious doctrine.

For Latina Mennonites, the intersections of faith and feminism defined the contradictory positions that they took with regard to traditional gender norms in the home and women's leadership in the church. While Latinas rarely challenged patriarchy or the machista leadership of Latino men in the church, they also did not sit idly by and accept the gendered limitations that religious doctrines placed on them. Instead of creating a movement to have more Latina preachers, they simply created their own spaces where Latinas could preach to other Latinas about issues that mattered to them most. Instead of singing music that appealed to a traditional, white Mennonite audience, they followed the lead of Latino Pentecostals like Paulino Bernal and African American gospel singers like Barbara Sowell by bringing culturally relevant and vibrant *coritos* into their worship.

As Latinas created spaces "away from the men," they inspired a growing sense of Latino pride and identity through their conferences, leadership, and music.[86] Even more important to Latinas was that the spaces where they gathered for communion and worship were all in *"nuestra idioma"* (our language).[87] The quiet movement of women that began in Moline, Illinois, linked Latino Mennonites to the broader movement of mujeres evangélicas, where the legacies of the civil rights and feminist movements opened new opportunities for Latinas in church leadership, in theological schools, and as musical leaders in a new pop-culture religious movement.

By the mid-1970s it was hard to argue that women should not preach or hold leadership positions in the church. Whereas the all-male MMC leadership struggled to build a grassroots base, Latinas were quick to organize 18 church groups with a total membership of over 300 across the country.[88] Even as Latina Mennonites created a space for faith and feminism, rejecting notions of equality in the home but pushing for women in church leadership, they succeeded in garnering the attention of MMC leaders and became important leaders in the church. One of the most important leaders was Maria Rivera Snyder, who in 1974 was chosen to colead the planning committee established to organize the new Concilio Nacional, which is covered in the following chapter. Appointments like hers signaled a shift in the roles women would play in the making of a new Latino church in the 1970s. Without question, what began as a quiet movement of 60 women in a small Latino church in the Midwest shifted the direction of Latinos in the Mennonite Church toward a new agenda that took on cultural, political, and increasingly evangelical overtones.

The music that Gracie and Seferina sang and performed became the basis for promoting a shared sense of Latino identity precisely when the politics of a "multiethnic brotherhood" were coming under increased scrutiny. In the wake of this shift, the interethnic politics of the MMC were challenged by a renewed search for African American identity on one end and Latino identity on the other. As the following chapter shows, this shift began with the fifth annual meeting of the MMC at the Camp Zephyr in Sandia, Texas, in 1973. Here church leaders put plans into place to dissolve the MMC in favor of a model that they hoped would better integrate African Americans and Latinos into the Mennonite Church. In an attempt to gain better access to institutional power within the church, black and brown leaders decided to go their separate ways.

The Sandia Model, as it came to be known, did away with the MMC and in its place created a separate office under the Mennonite Church General Board for African Americans and Latinos. The Mennonite Church General Board served as the umbrella organization for every department of the Mennonite Church. Placing a Latino and African American representative under the supervision of the highest board in the church, some leaders believed, better integrated minorities into every facet of the church. In reality, however, it spurred a heavy debate about the place of Latinos in the Mennonite Church.

CHAPTER 7

"Remember Sandia!"

Meno-Latinos and Religious Identity Politics

*In spite of all of our clashing, here and there I have seen models of reconciliation.
That's why I keep going.*
—EMMA LaROCQUE, Plains Cree métis and Mennonite, 1976

Latino Religion in the 1970s

The mid-1970s were good years for Latino Mennonites. Overall membership numbers were on the rise and the new Concilio Nacional de Iglesias Menonitas Hispanas (National Council of Spanish Mennonite Churches) replaced the Minority Ministries Council (MMC) as the leading organization for Latino Mennonites.[1] In the mid-1970s Latinos became the fastest growing segment of the Mennonite Church. Their numbers doubled in five years, from 500 members in 1970 to 1,061 by 1975, and by 1980 that number went over 1,500.[2] From Idaho to New York to Texas, leaders were organizing Spanish-speaking churches. The era of white Mennonite missionaries had come to a close, as Latino leaders declared that "the Anglo pastor needs to decrease so that God may increase."[3]

But even as Latino Mennonites grew in number and took on more visibility within the broader church, challenges remained. Most of the materials on Mennonite faith and theology were in English, the number of Latinos and Latinas on church boards and other institutions remained low, and the educational levels of Latino pastors were also quite low. Some pastors never made it past high school, some had little or no Bible training, and no pastor had studied at a Mennonite seminary.[4] As Latino Mennonites addressed these challenges, they joined a broader movement of Latino evangelicals who in the 1970s were quickly changing the American religious landscape.

When Latino and African American leaders grudgingly decided to disband the MMC in 1973, they did so with the hope that it might lead to better representation of minorities across all levels of the church. White Mennonite leaders believed it was time to fully integrate black and Latino Mennonites and do away with the specter of racial identity politics within the MMC. But at least initially, the move toward integration looked like it was only going to produce further alienation of Latinos and African Americans. For Latino Mennonites especially, the years after 1973 seemed to confirm suspicions that church membership had its benefits but full inclusion remained limited.

But it was not all bad. As this chapter argues, Latino Mennonites spent the latter part of the 1970s staking out a political space in the church by drafting policy statements, planting more than 50 congregations, publishing Mennonite literature in Spanish, and organizing a Bible school with the specific aim of training Latino and Latina leaders for church leadership. They did so by playing up religious identity politics and asserting themselves as evangélicos, or as they called themselves, "Meno-Latinos." The viability of religious identity politics came at a time in the 1970s when Mennonite leaders were calling for an end to talk of race in favor of a more palpable and integrated approach that moved beyond the politics of a "multiethnic brotherhood."

This chapter follows the recent trend among historians who are rethinking the role of radicalism and religion in the 1970s. For the most part, historians have identified the 1970s as the decade that gave rise to the conservative and politically astute Christian Coalition. According to historian Paul Harvey, the Christian Coalition "cobbled together religious folk from a variety of traditions . . . who shared a common faith in 'family values' and a political agenda of lower taxes, less government, school prayer, increased military spending, and opposition to abortion."[5] But the 1970s were defined by more than individual morality and the rise of the

religious right. As writer and activist Dan Berger argues, the 1970s represented a "deeply ambivalent and contentious moment" when multiple
ideologies were taking root in American politics and religion.[6]

The decade of "disco discrimination" (to use the title of one of Hector Galan's documentary films) became a point of critical reflection for
Latino faith communities across the country. From the conjunto rhythms
of Paulino Bernal to the Encuentros Pastorales among Latino Catholics,
the 1970s were a defining decade for Latinos, who believed the church
needed to better reflect their culture and values and took the lessons of the
Chicano and Puerto Rican social movements and mobilized to transform
their religious institutions.[7]

According to Presbyterian pastor and activist Jorge Lara-Braud, much
of this had to do with the rise in Latino and Latina religious leadership.
Nowhere was this more evident than in Latino evangelical churches.
Compared to the 200 or so Mexican American priests in the Catholic
Church, there were more than 1,000 Mexican American or Latin American pastors in Protestant congregations across the Southwest and Northeast.[8] Latino religious identity politics were in full bloom in the 1970s
as religious leaders demanded from their mostly white coreligionists that
they be attentive to the cultural and political needs of Spanish-speaking
communities.

By Latino religious identity politics I mean the ways in which Latinos joined religious and cultural practices in creating a religious space
that was relevant and responsive to their needs.[9] Looking at it in this light
moves Latino religious history to the center of the broader and transnational story of Latinos in the postwar era. Like African Americans, Latinos
merged their biblical understandings of justice to help transform religious
institutions that they believed were unresponsive to the needs of Latino
communities. In the mid-1970s, Latino religious identity politics emphasized what white Mennonites did not want to hear: that after 20 years of
discussions on race, the church had made few strides in diversifying its
leadership.

Remember Sandia! Rethinking the Place of Black and Brown Mennonites

Located about an hour northwest of Corpus Christi and only a 15-minute drive from Mathis, the small town of Sandia, Texas, is best known for watermelons and as a former stop of the Texas and New Orleans Railroad in the late 1930s. Since the 1950s it has also been a major destination for church groups and families hoping to enjoy an outdoor experience at Camp Zephyr. Established in 1957 by the Baptist Church, Camp Zephyr has provided a quiet and serene space for spiritual reflection and hiking trails for eager youth groups.

It was at Camp Zephyr in Sandia that Latino and African American Mennonites met in 1973 as part of the fifth annual conference of the MMC. The conference in Sandia marked the first time the MMC gathered as a group in South Texas, and it would be its last gathering. Five years after the MMC had organized in Chicago in 1968, it disbanded far away from the urban and rural centers in the Midwest where many of its struggles in the 1950s and 1960s were rooted. But more important, the conference gave rise to the Sandia Model as a new way for the church to organize itself in relation to Latino and African American Mennonites. In the words of the Mennonite General Board leaders, the Sandia Model opened the possibility for the "the integration of minorities into full participation of the brotherhood."[10]

The Sandia Model promised to integrate African American and Latino Mennonites into every facet of church leadership by dissolving the MMC and replacing it with the Black Council and the Concilio Nacional de Iglesias Menonitas Hispanas.[11] It was a deliberate effort to move away from the identity politics and multiethnic coalition of the MMC in order to promote an integrated church in which questions about race and identity took on less importance. Both of the newly formed councils would be under the aegis of the most powerful office in the Mennonite Church, the General Board. Leaders who supported integration believed it was the right move because it raised the level of minority involvement to the highest level of the church. It also promised to shape how all Mennonite Church boards worked to incorporate minorities into leadership positions. Instead of continuing the MMC, which enjoyed affiliated sta-

Maria Rivera Snyder prepares to speak at the fifth annual conference of the
MMC in Sandia, Texas, 1973. (Courtesy of Mennonite Church USA Archives,
Goshen, Indiana)

tus with some independence, church leaders trusted that integration was
the best model for moving toward an inclusive church.

The Sandia Model emerged out of collaboration among the MMC,
Mennonite Board of Missions (MBM), and the General Board and called
for several important changes. First, it required that Mennonite Church
boards and agencies involve minorities in their membership and that priority be given to minorities for staff positions in the church. Second, it
called for two associate secretaries, one African American and one Latino,
to help facilitate the integration of minorities into every facet of the Mennonite Church. Third, it transferred the program administration of minority churches and advocacy from the MMC to the Home Missions section
of the MBM.[12] This proved to be significant in that it transferred MMC
funds back into the hands of white Mennonite leaders. In 1974 when the
MMC officially ended its existence, it transferred a total of $214,000
back to the Home Missions office.[13]

Lupe De León and Seferina De León talk with Bishop Patricio Flores at the MMC gathering in Sandia, Texas, where Bishop Flores led a workshop for church leaders, 1973. (Courtesy of Mennonite Church USA Archives, Goshen, Indiana)

Although the Sandia Model emerged in 1973, its origins dated back to the late 1960s when African Americans debated which approach—integration or autonomy—better suited their goals to make the Mennonite Church more inclusive. Integration was never a popular idea among most MMC leaders, but it did find support among some. When African American pastor Leamon Sowell first suggested a more integrated model for relating to white Mennonites in 1970, his idea was dismissed and seen as a sign of how out of touch Sowell was with the "multiethnic brotherhood." MMC leaders believed that integrating the MMC would only result in "tokenism" and would cause black and brown Mennonites to "lose respect and support" of white Mennonites.[14] From its beginning in 1968, black and brown leaders believed the MMC should remain a semiautonomous organization with primary accountability to minority churches across the United States.

The strategic pull toward autonomy made the talks over integration tense for both Latino and African American leadership. Eight months before the meetings in Sandia, Ernest Bennett, the executive secretary for Home Missions, wrote that he "sensed a growing uncertainty as to whether this [integration] should really happen" and added that there was "growing concern among minority persons" over the possibility of ending the MMC.[15] Behind these concerns were fears that the talk of integration had more to do with calming the tensions between Latino and African American leaders, most notably the flare-ups between Lupe De León and John Powell.

A Problem between "Minorities and Minorities"

While the root of the problems between De León and Powell are not known, the conflict put in motion the plans to dissolve the MMC as suspicions grew that the two leaders would no longer be able to work together. The most damning evidence came from several memos from Dorsa Mishler (assistant to Ernest Bennett in 1972 and 1973) that showed how the internal problems of the MMC were "not only between minorities and majorities, but between minorities and minorities."[16] While Mishler did not identify a specific problem, subsequent memos pointed to the discord brewing between Powell and De León. Most of the attacks that Mishler described were directed against Powell. In one memo Mishler reported to Bennett that another staff person, Jim Kratz, met with De León in the parking lot and recounted how "Lupe talked vehemently about his feelings regarding John Powell. He talked about staying related to the Board but doesn't know how much longer he can work with John."[17] At the same time, Mishler reported to Bennett that "John [Powell] is hurting right now because he feels some staff persons are against him and also possibly some minority persons."[18]

The tensions were enough to make Ernest Bennett nervous about whether plans for integration would actually move forward in 1973. Bennett went so far as to propose a halt to all conversations about integration until everyone on the MMC executive committee felt good about moving forward. Right up to the moment the MMC kicked off its meetings in Sandia, the integration plan was a political fireball that Bennett and others recognized needed to be addressed with care.

While tensions between De León and Powell worried Bennett and others, Mishler's assertion that this was only a problem "between minorities and minorities" ignored the very real tensions and disagreements surfacing around the plans to integrate. MMC executive committee member Hubert Brown reminded Mishler that the most relevant tensions were not between minorities but between MMC staff and white Mennonites in the MBM office. Brown went as far as to accuse MBM leaders of trying to sabotage Powell's character by accusing him of incompetence and mishandling funds.[19] Brown's comments referred to accusations that Powell and other African Americans had mishandled funds while at a conference in Kenya in 1973. Powell was accused of using church money to attend theatrical shows in London, entertaining where no business was being conducted, and running up hefty bills while mixing business with pleasure.[20] None of the accusations was ever proven, but they were enough to stigmatize Powell and reduce his ability to shape how the plans to integrate might actually play out.

With accusations of internal bickering and pressure from white Mennonites mounting, the plan to integrate and do away with the MMC remained contested right up to the end. MMC leaders vacillated between rejecting the plan and giving it their full support. No group embodied this more than the executive committee of the MMC, which only five months prior to the meeting in Sandia questioned the true motives behind integration. Dorsa Mishler wrote in a memo to Ernest Bennett that she believed integration was part of a plan "for the whites to absorb Minority Ministries . . . [and] the Board of Directors blocking MMC's wishes to decentralize."[21] The decentralization plan was a last-ditch effort to block integration by moving the MMC offices to Saint Louis and Corpus Christi. In June 1973 Powell and De León believed that decentralization, not integration, was the best option for the MMC.[22] But that position would change as the Sandia gathering approached. Only a few months later the executive committee began to advocate integration:

> If we want to continue as a council composed of all minorities in the Mennonite church, then we will have to radically reorganize ourselves. For we are besieged with serious and undesired problems. We have tried taking the pulse of council members and have discovered a confused, bewildered, and at points, an apathetic majority who lacks vision and creativity

to point in a new direction. We cannot remain as is, our administrators are in a box, our programs lack imagination, and we are disconnected from each other. We need to capture a feeling of working together, struggling together; brown, black, and red together building a rich heritage of what minorities in the Mennonite church can do if they have the will to do it.[23]

As these changing positions over integration demonstrate, the feelings of MMC leaders were mixed and complex. MMC executive committee member Tito Guedea, who at first opposed integration, later commented to Paul Kraybill (general secretary of the General Board) about "the growing feeling in the brown community that the merger may be a good idea after all."[24]

The tensions brewing internally, especially among Powell and De León, convinced Latinos that integration might be the best option. It was no surprise, then, that by the time the meetings in Sandia kicked off Powell and De León viewed the benefits of integration quite differently. De León believed that integration provided the best opportunity for representation of minorities on church boards while also opening up a separate space to address Latino issues. Powell, on the other hand, believed integration undermined the semiautonomous nature of the MMC and threatened to weaken the political capital MMC leaders had worked so hard to build within the church since 1968. As it turned out, both leaders were only half right.

By the time the Sandia meetings rolled around in October 1973, the integration plan had gained traction, especially among Latinos. With an overwhelming Latino presence in Sandia, the first round of voting proved to be divided along lines of race, with African Americans rejecting the Sandia Model and Latinos supporting it almost unanimously. But later that afternoon, after a series of closed-door sessions, the Sandia Model received full support from both groups. Frustrated by the vote, Powell submitted his letter of resignation immediately.[25] When asked why he decided to resign, Powell said that his "family [had] undergone a lot of stress and strain and letters and accusations."[26]

But there were other factors. After the MBM rejected his proposal to decentralize the MMC and reject the Sandia Model, Powell believed that it was time to go, as he "did not want to get in the way of the advancement of minority people within the Mennonite church."[27] With that statement

Powell bid farewell and left the Mennonite Church. His departure left a void in leadership and left some African Americans questioning whether "the Spanish are more ready for this [merger] than the Blacks."[28] At least on the surface it appeared that Latinos were better prepared for the merger. While José Ortíz took over as associate secretary for Latin concerns in August 1974, Dwight McFadden was not appointed to his position as associate general secretary for black concerns until January 1976.[29] But before McFadden was appointed, Ortíz quickly learned that the Sandia Model created more problems than it solved.

José Ortiz and the Evangelical Shift

With a new plan in place, Latino leaders were optimistic. The energy from the Latina gatherings created new roles for women in church leadership. Latinas were no longer serving the coffee or cooking the meals. In 1974 Latinas such as Maria Bustos and Mary Valtierra were also part of the group that was responsible for shaping the Latino agenda for the latter half of the 1970s. With renewed energy, Latino leaders met in Corpus Christi early in 1974 to lay out their plans for the future. Most important was organizing a list of candidates for the new position of associate secretary for Latin concerns that the Sandia Model guaranteed. As discussions ensued, the group was split along lines of citizenship. Some believed the candidate should be a US Latino who was fluent in English and Spanish, understood the history of Latinos, and was familiar with how the Mennonite Church operated in the United States. Others believed the candidate should be from Latin America in order to establish better relations with Mennonites in that region. After some debate, a young pastor from Puerto Rico, José M. Ortíz, emerged as the obvious candidate.[30]

Originally from Coamo Arriba, a small rural community in Puerto Rico, Ortíz was a perfect fit for the position of associate secretary of Latin concerns.[31] Ortíz had become a Mennonite as a young boy and by the 1960s and early 1970s taught and pastored in Mennonite churches across Puerto Rico and the United States. By all accounts, Ortíz was a safe figure politically. While he was aware of the struggles of Puerto Ricans and other Latinos on the mainland, he was primarily concerned about issues related to the church and evangelicalism. For Latinos who were prepared to take the lessons of the MMC and the Chicano movement to the next level, Ortíz provided an opportunity for them to become integrated in the decision-making bodies of the church.

His charisma and intelligence made him an instant hit. At a church service in Chicago to inaugurate his term, Latino Mennonites came from Iowa, Wisconsin, Indiana, Illinois, and even California to the Lawndale Mennonite Church in Chicago. People believed that Ortíz was best suited to begin moving Latino Mennonite churches from mission stations to full-blown congregations with their own established programs.[32] His education, evangelical thrust, and home base in Puerto Rico made him a prime candidate to lead Latino Mennonites into a new era in which evangelism and church growth trumped political and church reform. Ortíz's inauguration service was a sign of things to come, as Latinos were reminded that identity was not found in race or politics but only "en Jesucristo quien ofrece vida eternal" (in Jesus Christ who offers eternal life).[33] With Ortíz's appointment, Latinos were optimistic that the promises of the Sandia Model would be realized.[34] But amid the buzz, Ortíz understood the challenges that were ahead of him. In his first report to Latino leaders, Ortíz described his job as a "frightening experience . . . like moving into a big house with little furniture."[35]

"Integration Should Not Be Used against Us"

Even with the positive vote for integration, the criticism of the Sandia Model maintained momentum. It was not that some MMC leaders believed in separatism. The concern revolved around whether or not black and Latino Mennonites would be able to integrate from a position of strength. Those who questioned the merits and structure of the Sandia Model did so because they believed it lacked a long-term vision for building a more integrated church. On the other side were white Mennonite leaders like Paul Kraybill who believed integration was the right move because it proved that African Americans had "little interest in pursuing their 'blackness' now that they are moving into the mainstream of the Mennonite church life."[36]

But the reality was that African Americans were not moving "into the mainstream," and many continued to look at the Sandia Model with skepticism. Some MMC leaders, like Warner Jackson, simply never came to terms with the idea that integration was the best way forward. In June

1974, two months before Ortíz began his assignment, Jackson expressed his frustrations over the Sandia Model in a letter addressed mainly to white Mennonites.[37] Jackson criticized white Mennonites for allowing an emphasis on "Christian unity" to deny black and brown Mennonites "a reasonable measure of autonomy and cultural self-expression within the structure of the church."[38] With his skills as a prosecuting attorney, Jackson made a scathing critique of the Sandia Model in which he accused white Mennonite leaders of carefully planned manipulation to dissolve the MMC.

In his letter, Jackson denounced white Mennonite leaders—most notably Paul Kraybill and Ernest Bennett—for pushing integration without first receiving full approval from MMC members. At issue for Jackson was how the Sandia Model sought to formalize and institutionalize the identity politics of the MMC. In place of a cadre of African Americans and Latinos at all levels of the church, the Sandia Model put minorities at the top level of the church structure—with the General Board—with the hope that this would have a trickle-down effect on other church agencies and boards. But most troubling for Jackson was that integration denied black and brown leaders "the right to be governed to some extent by representatives we choose. . . . Integration should not be used against us to disintegrate us in terms of ethnic distinctiveness and uniqueness." Jackson went on to write that "in fairness to themselves, minorities also need and require a measure of 'separatism' for purposes of realizing autonomy and dignity."[39]

Separating black and brown, however, became the necessary evil of the Sandia Model. Integration guaranteed a system where minorities were represented at the highest levels of the church but had little if any influence on minority representation on other church boards. The success of the Sandia Model hinged on whether white Mennonites would ensure that each church board had black and brown representation.[40] There was some success. By 1976 Latinos and African Americans could be seen on more church boards—from Home Missions to the insurance group Mennonite Mutual Aid—than had been seen previously. But representation without a group like the MMC to push policy and financial decisions had, in the words of one Mennonite leader, led to the "erosion in their [Latinos' and African Americans'] influence and visibility. . . . In the past, caucuses were attached to the most influential board in the Mennonite church—

From left to right: Lupe De León, John Powell, and Warner Jackson, speaking at the MMC annual conference, 1972. (Courtesy of Mennonite Church USA Archives, Goshen, Indiana)

MBM. Being attached to General Board has diminished caucus effectiveness."[41]

Pushing Latinos Out

Beyond the concern of diminished effectiveness, Concilio leaders worried over a host of new and unexpected problems. After a series of unsuccessful attempts to ramp up church missions among Latinos, Ortíz amped up his criticism of white Mennonite leaders for treating Latino churches like "conference pets" administered by people who have little or no understanding of the Latino experience.[42] At the root of the problem was how

Mennonites themselves organized their church institutions. The Mennonite Church differs from other denominational groups in that it does not have a structured hierarchy that is clear and well defined. There are no presbyteries, no bishops, and no authority that sets denominational mandates. As Ortíz put it in an article he wrote on the problems with Mennonite structures, "There is generally a low view of leadership figures among Mennonites."[43]

The Mennonite Church has historically placed most of the power among churches by following a decentralized style of organization and operation that for many is not only difficult to comprehend but also difficult to integrate and change.[44] Mennonites are notorious for "committee work," which seeks to build consensus at the expense of making expeditious decisions. It is, as Ortíz put it, "a fantasy island where everyone's voice is heard and the process of discerning is as important as the issue."[45] It took Mennonites nearly 16 years, from 1925 to 1941, to establish how a pastor is chosen, ordained, and installed in a church.[46] This pattern created problems for Latinos, who were often expected to "function like most Mennonites" without a clear understanding about how theology, church structures, and power functioned together in the Mennonite Church.

Not only was it difficult to comprehend Mennonite Church structures, but the Concilio was structured away from the most powerful board—the MBM—which had all the access to and knowledge of minority churches across the country. Instead the Concilio was under the aegis of the General Board, whose function was more bureaucratic than anything else. The General Board operated as an overarching group that looked over all Mennonite institutions but rarely stepped in to dictate policy or governance. It also did not help that when Ortíz took his position as associate secretary for Latin concerns, the offices were in Lombard, Illinois, 130 miles west of the MBM offices in Elkhart, Indiana.

But by far the biggest problem that emerged was a plan proposed by regional church conferences to gain administrative power over minority congregations in their regions. This only amplified the feeling of marginalization that Latino leaders already felt. If regional conferences gained new administrative powers, it would further diminish the role of the Concilio at the General Board level. In a stern memo to Ortíz, Lupe De León warned of future troubles for the Concilio if the measure for regionalization passed: "Some of the strongest conferences are toying with the idea of

taking total responsibility administratively and otherwise for their conference mission program. . . . It may be that I am over-reacting but my feelings
are that some of the conference leadership mistrust the missions program
of the total denomination being in the hands of non-ethnic sons of Menno.
God forgive me if I am wrong. God help us all if my vibes are correct."[47]

If the proposal to hand authority over church missions to regional
conferences passed, it would mean that Concilio leaders would no longer work closely with Latino congregations. In other words, Ortíz, Maria
Bustos, De León, and other Latino and Latina leaders would first have
to talk to someone in Kansas before organizing projects with Mexican
American churches in South Texas. For this reason, De León pleaded with
Ortíz: "You must carry on the struggle from now on. . . . I trust that you
and the *Concilio* realize the implications of this type of '*movida*' for your
own survival."[48] De León was right. Regionalization would eliminate any
inclination of power coming from the Concilio. By 1976 it seemed that
the Sandia honeymoon was over, as Latino leaders struggled to balance im-
pending conference regionalism, a shrinking influence, and little progress
to support any benefit of integration. The words of Concilio board member Al Valtierra, who had been a staunch supporter of the Sandia Model
and integration, best captured the sentiment of Latino leaders in 1976:

> The purpose of the reorganization, we were informed, was that instead
> of dealing with Latin interests separately, we would join with the gen-
> eral brotherhood to be of one body. This has not been achieved, since
> we need to solicit from the other agencies and their priorities are not our
> priorities. . . . In essence the General Board has not kept their promise of
> bringing us together with the brotherhood, but instead has taken away
> our funds and that way we cannot implement the programs we believe
> have priority. Personally I believe my involvement at the national level of
> the Mennonite church will be of one more year and if at that time I see
> that the church does not meet its commitment, then I will reconsider my
> commitment to a church that is so insensitive to my people and in conse-
> quence I will seriously consider leaving the church.[49]

The sense of loss that Valtierra described was rooted in the reality that the
MMC, which had allocated funds to and worked directly with churches
and programs, had been completely dissolved.[50]

But not all was lost. Amid these struggles Latinas continued to organize popular conferences across the country, and there was new energy emerging from Latinos' and Latinas' ability to sidestep the obstacles imposed by what had proven to be a chaotic church structure. They did so by committing to stronger relationships to Mennonites in Latin America and by rethinking the role of religious identity politics. For Latino Mennonites, this meant identifying as "Meno-Latinos." Where the name originated is unknown, but it did have a major impact on how Latino Mennonites carved out a space for themselves in the post-MMC Mennonite Church.

The Limits and Possibilities of a Meno-Latino Identity

When Ortíz began his position as associate secretary for Latin concerns in August 1974, he was determined to move the Concilio away from its role as a mere liaison to the white church. His goal was to work for Latino congregations, train personnel, develop policies to help Latino churches function better, explore mission possibilities, and develop leadership among youth. But it was also clear that these would not be easy tasks. For Ortíz it was quite evident that the Sandia Model had led to "insecurity, low morale, and a lack of mutual accountability" among Latino leadership.[51]

The problems stemmed from white Mennonite leadership who Ortíz believed saw Latinos as merely "cultural translators, hatchet men, and match makers. . . . Our offices are looked upon as dumping grounds for unwanted agenda."[52] Part of the problem was that a clear agenda had not yet emerged for the newly organized Concilio. The concerns about theological education, Sunday school curriculum in Spanish, pastoral guides for Latino leaders, and a national magazine were on the table but had not yet been acted upon.

That changed in 1975 when the Concilio launched the magazine *Ecos Menonitas* as the first publication to focus on Latino Mennonites. The following year the Office of Congregational Education and Literature in Spanish was established and quickly went to work translating materials, producing *Ecos Menonitas*, and investigating the possibility of developing other Mennonite literature in Spanish. The hope was to one day develop books and Sunday school materials written by US Latinos and Latin American authors for Spanish-speaking Mennonite churches.

In addition to fostering a much-needed Spanish-language print culture, another major advancement was the development of an immigration program through the auspices of the Mennonite Central Committee (MCC). As a result of one of the final administrative efforts led by Lupe De León, the MCC Peace Section accepted a proposal to host an immigration conference in 1977 that addressed the "problem of illegal aliens." The conference proved so successful that the MCC decided to open an "immigration desk" and hired Karen Ventura as the first Latina to address immigration issues at the MCC.[53] Ventura's appointment responded to a greater concern on the part of Latino Mennonites about the issue of increased immigration from Latin America. But it also helped launch a series of conversations between Latin American Mennonites and US Latino Mennonites.

One of the earliest conversations revolved around building on the relationship between the old Latin Concilio of the late 1960s and the audiovisual Latin American ministry group known as Junta Ejecutiva Latino Americana de Audiciones Menonitas (JELAM). Those conversations had essentially stalled with the advent of the MMC and its strong US focus, but Concilio members were now ready to rekindle that relationship. Part of the long history of Mennonite missions in Latin America, JELAM was the center for Mennonite radio ministries, literature development, and church missions. Mennonite missions in Latin America began in the early twentieth century but grew exponentially during the 1940s and 1950s. As historian Juan Martínez has shown, "By the middle of the twentieth century virtually every Anabaptist group in North America was sponsoring some form of mission activity somewhere in Latin America."[54]

Connecting with Mennonites in Latin America was long overdue, but it also highlighted the ways in which Latinos wrestled over questions of identity in the 1970s. In Latin America, Mennonites had no problem adding "evangelical" to church names in order to confirm that Mennonite churches were part of a broader network of Pentecostal and mainline Protestant churches in the region. Jaime Prieto Valladares's book on Mennonites in Latin America shows that most Latin American Mennonite conferences, from Mexico to Colombia, identified as "*Iglesias Evangélicas*."[55]

Joining JELAM signaled for Latino Mennonites an increased comfort level in identifying as evangélicos over the bland and often confusing "Mennonite" affiliation. But the shift was not an easy one. The moves to establish theological education and pastoral curriculum that emerged in the late 1970s showed that Latino Mennonites' religious identity fell somewhere between being evangélicos and being Mennonites. On one hand, Latinos were careful about officially identifying as evangélicos for fear of alienating white Mennonites who stressed that Mennonite theology was a viable alternative to more mainstream theological orientations. On the other hand, however, Latinos, especially those not affiliated with the Mennonite Church, welcomed the recognition that identifying as an evangélico brought. Calling themselves evangélicos was also a quick way to sidestep the obvious question that always emerged in conversations with non-Mennonites, "¿Qué es un Menonita?" (What is a Mennonite?). The problem was that many Latino Mennonite pastors could not answer the question. Some of the newer Latino pastors knew little about Mennonite theology and hadn't any clue what the central tenets of the faith actually were. As more Latino Mennonite churches were organized in the late 1970s, most of the new Latino pastors were either transplants from another denomination or did not live near any Mennonite school or seminary where they could receive training.

If membership opened the possibilities for Latinos in church leadership, many believed that full inclusion could only happen when Latinos closed the gap between identifying as evangélicos and identifying as Mennonites. For Concilio president Conrado Hinojosa this meant that Latinos would commit themselves to educating themselves in Mennonite theology and church polity. Hinojosa criticized Latinos who "often disagreed" or took theological positions that pitted them "one against the other."[56] The future leaders of the Mennonite Church, he believed, should be "trained in Mennonite schools with Mennonite teachers."[57] This was easier said than done. Mennonite seminaries tended to be located in the center of the Mennonite enclaves in Kansas, Indiana, and Virginia, far from the centers of Latino church growth in urban areas. To address this problem, Latinos needed to create something new in an area that was representative of their demographic base.

"Integrated and Separate": The Hispanic Ministries Program

The problem in the 1970s, as Mennonite historian Rafael Falcón has noted, was that the "shortage of leaders pushes congregations to hand over the flock to pastors from other denominations."[58] Providing theological education for Latinos was not only a concern for the Mennonite Church. In general, Protestant and Catholic groups worried about the lack of Latino leaders who had theological or Bible school training. In the early 1970s Latinos made up less than 1 percent of the students enrolled at seminaries accredited by the Association of Theological Schools.[59]

These low numbers reflect the limited availability of Bible training in Spanish in the United States in the 1970s. The most well-known programs included the Los Angeles Bible Institute, the Rio Grande Bible Institute in South Texas, and the Mexican Baptist Bible Institute and the Nazarene Hispanic American Seminary in San Antonio. The lack of higher education resources motivated Latino Mennonites to try to create their own seminary program.[60] In 1976, with the help of a $10,000 grant from MBM Home Missions, Concilio leaders moved forward with the creation of a Hispanic Ministries Program.

Designated as a program for "Hispanic Mennonite theological training," Concilio leaders proposed an extension program at the Instituto Bíblico Nazareno Hispano Americano (Nazarene Hispanic American Seminary) in San Antonio.[61] From there a joint relationship developed between the Concilio, Hesston College, and the Nazarene Hispanic American Seminary in 1976. Two years later the program began with a total of 10 students from places as far away as Illinois, Pennsylvania, Oregon, Guatemala, and Puerto Rico.[62] The basic objective of the program was to provide Bible training in Spanish for Latino Mennonites in order to strengthen leadership resources for Latino churches.[63] That vision was shaped by the struggles for inclusion in the Mennonite Church that Latinos had engaged in since the 1960s.

But there was also a larger vision that included contextualizing theology within Latin American culture. "For the Latin American Christian of our days," wrote Rafael Falcón, "it is about reconnecting and reconciling the gospel with our own culture."[64] The challenge for Latino Mennonites was to create a space where Latinos could study the Bible from their own cultural context and in the process move away from an irrelevant "Anglo Saxon Christ."[65] Understanding the Gospels from a Latino cultural context also presented the opportunity to help shift Mennonite theological study away from its European roots. It meant rethinking theological positions of peace and nonresistance in a context where violence, poverty, and racism were all-too-familiar realities.

At the end of academic year 1978 the Hispanic Ministries Program at the Nazarene Seminary graduated four students with associate of arts diplomas, and another six had earned enough credits to transfer to a Mennonite college of their choice. Victor Alvarez, the first director and professor of the program, wrote in one report that "this is the best opportunity to obtain theological preparation in Spanish in order to begin church ministry."[66] The partnership between the Nazarene Seminary and Hesston College lasted for one year before Goshen College administrators in Indiana invited the program to move north. Even before the program gained traction in San Antonio, the president of Goshen College at the time, J. Lawrence Burkholder, suggested that Concilio leaders consider moving the program to Goshen College, where it would be surrounded by Mennonite scholars and library resources.[67]

Access to Mennonite "theological orientation" was a major draw of Goshen College, one that outweighed the language and culture program available at the Nazarene Seminary, but student unrest also helped seal the decision to move north.[68] According to one of the students, Héctor Vázquez, "the denominational differences caused discrimination against the Mennonite students" at the Nazarene Seminary.[69] While little evidence exists about such incidents, it was enough to convince Concilio leaders to accept Burkholder's invitation. In the fall of 1979 the Department of Hispanic Ministries opened its doors at Goshen College and welcomed the first cadre of 16 students.[70]

Nearly half of the students were women, and a majority of the first class were transfer students from the program in San Antonio.[71] Some students received financial support from their home congregations, while others received funding from mission agencies like Eastern Mennonite Missions. Carmen Lourdes Miranda and Rafael Falcón, both well-known Puerto Rican scholars, helped launch the program at Goshen College.[72] The program offered courses in three important areas: theology and religion, history and culture, and Spanish-language training.

The early years were cause for much celebration. For the first time, Latino Mennonites had carved out a space for themselves within one Mennonite institution of higher education, and the move provided some assurance that future leaders would be trained in Anabaptist/Mennonite theology. One of the most promising students was the first graduate of the program, Samuel López, who graduated in 1980. Born in Tuxpán, Guerrero, México, López immigrated to the United States at the age of 17. Immediately after graduation López became a leader in the church, and his positive experience in the program was indicative of how other students felt as well.[73] For students like Ramiro and Marta Hernández the excitement was palpable. "The most exciting thing is just being here," Ramiro commented. "I have two more years and then its seminary."[74] Alfa Tijerina (Archbold, Ohio) and Miguel Cruz (Puerto Rico) were both excited that there was a place for Latino students on campus. In one interview they mentioned that "a lot of people don't know what a Latino is. . . . This program will show our point of view really well."[75] In 1979 the first Union Estudiantil Latina (Latino Student Union) was established on campus, and the number of potential students for the Hispanic Ministries Program was growing.

But while the move to Goshen College was an important step for the program, it also reaffirmed the tenuous place of Latinos in the Mennonite Church. Nowhere was this more evident than in the institutional space of the Hispanic Ministries Program. When President Burkholder made the invitation to Concilio leaders to move the program north, he also suggested that the program be "integrated and separate" within the structure of the college.[76] That institutional fit would eventually hurt the viability of the program, but in the late 1970s being at Goshen College did open doors for Concilio leaders, who worked to push forward a measure to translate into Spanish and publish Mennonite literature and Sunday school curriculum.

Through the leadership of the Office of Spanish Literature, Concilio leaders envisioned a literature program for book publications and Sunday school materials written by US Latino and Latin American authors for Spanish-speaking churches.[77] Organizing the Office of Spanish Literature was no small feat. It involved collaboration with other Mennonite groups (Mennonite Brethren, General Conference, and Brethren in Christ groups) and advocacy and support from Latin American Mennonites. The movement created a transnational and interdenominational effort that came about through the diligence of people like Ortíz and other Latino leaders such as Arnoldo Casas and Rafael Falcón, both of whom served on the Mennonite Board of Congregational Ministries. But more important, the work of translating materials initiated a new conversation with Latin American Mennonites.

From Hispanic Ministries to the Declaration of Cachipay

Though the talks and relationships between the Concilio and Latin American Mennonites were only beginning in the late 1970s, the two groups made huge strides when they met together at a conference in Cachipay, Colombia, in 1980. Here members of the Concilio and delegates from 10 Latin American countries gathered to organize the movement to translate and publish Mennonite literature in Spanish. This joint project was the first of its kind and fulfilled the early goals of the Concilio in its quest to expand its influence beyond the United States. From the meetings in Colombia, participants issued the Declaration of Cachipay, which served as the official call for all Mennonite groups in the United States and Latin America to support the Office of Spanish Literature with prayer and financial resources.[78]

The Declaration of Cachipay was a major step forward for Concilio leaders. While the Sandia Model attempted to integrate Latino Mennonites into the mainstream of the Mennonite Church, the Declaration of Cachipay sent a resounding message that Latinos were more interested in building their own institutions and collaborating with Latin American Mennonites in order to understand the Mennonite experience from their own cultural context. The Declaration of Cachipay also institutionalized Latino and Latin American identity as a core component of the Mennonite Church. For the first time Mennonite literature would incorporate Latino themes, be available to monolingual Spanish speakers, and provide yet another space for Meno-Latinos to express their understandings of Mennonite beliefs from their own perspective. Those who attended the conference understood what the declaration meant for the future of Latino Mennonites: "This consultation [is important] not only because of its continental projections for Anabaptist [Mennonite] believers of Hispanic formation and language but also for what this curriculum may signify as an Anabaptist literary and educational witness in our context."[79] The Declaration of Cachipay also helped establish the office of Currículo Anabautista de Educación Bíblica Congregacional (Anabaptist Curriculum of Congregational Biblical Education) in 1981, which helped extend the work into areas of Sunday school and Bible school curriculum.[80]

The new relationships between US Latinos and Latin American Mennonites forged at Cachipay looked promising in theory. But as leaders on both sides quickly learned, collaborating on a project to produce Menno-nite literature in Spanish came riddled with complications and disagree-ments. For starters, tensions emerged between various Latino groups over whether the Spanish-language materials would be produced in Latin America or the United States. The groups also disagreed over how to mar-ket the materials once they were produced, and there were even disagree-ments over how the nuances of the Spanish language would be addressed in the curriculum. These challenges limited the success of the connec-tions between US Latinos and Latin Americans and in the end produced a product that neither side was happy with.[81] The Cachipay meetings led to a bumpy ride into the 1980s, as visions of "Latinidad" in the Menno-nite Church would have to bridge the politics of the civil rights movement with the rise of a new era of immigration politics. In the late 1970s and early 1980s increased immigration from Latin America set a new agenda for Latino Mennonites that forced them to incorporate a new vision of Latinidad tinged with evangelicalism that moved away "from the social action concerns of the sixties and early seventies to church growth."[82]

Religious Identity Politics in the 1970s

The move to "church growth," however, was not a complete break from the civil rights politics of the Chicano and Puerto Rican movements. Even as Latino evangelical churches had a tense and uneven relationship with civil rights politics, in the late 1970s churches caught up to the reforms that changed their institutions. The struggles of the civil rights era helped build an infrastructure in the church that opened the doors to Latinos for leadership, theological education, and culturally relevant church litera-ture. In a 1977 article titled "The Melting Pot Is Not Melting," Concilio leader José Ortíz reminded white Mennonites that Latinos were not as-similating in the ways their own German and Russian ancestors had. As he explained, while "cultural pluralism" had met with "a favorable intel-lectual climate" in the church, "assimilation and amalgamation [were] hav-ing a tougher fight."[83]

The actions of Latino Mennonites provide a different way to view the mix of identity politics and religion in the late 1970s. While historians have focused on the ubiquitous rise of the religious right in the 1970s, it is easy to forget that it was also a decade when Latino religious identity politics thrived. It was a moment when, as historian Arlene M. Sánchez Walsh contends, Latinos connected with "the larger evangelical world and, within that world, . . . carved out separate social, cultural, and religious spheres for themselves."[84]

For Latino Mennonites, the 1970s were a decade that merged civil rights politics with an evangelical impulse to plant new churches. The blending of the spiritual and the political formed the backbone of religious identity politics that mobilized Latinos within the Mennonite Church. Through her work on faith-based organizations in New York City, Catherine Wilson has shown that "religious identity politics transcends the objectives of the political sphere by recognizing that such cultivation always has a supernatural force."[85] Faith, in other words, was not secondary to politics but instead an integral component of Latino evangelicals' engagement with civil rights politics and in the process changed their church institutions.

The rise of Latino Mennonites in the 1970s represents a general pattern among other Latino faith communities. From Catholic to evangelical churches, Latino religious leaders demanded that their churches recognize the contributions and needs of Spanish-speaking communities.[86] Latino and Latina religious leaders demanded religious materials in Spanish, better representation in decision-making structures, and better opportunities for theological education.[87] But perhaps the most important achievement was in Latinos' and Latinas' contributions to theological and religious studies. The 1970s saw the rise of prominent Latina and Latino theologians such as Virgilio Elizondo, Justo González, Marina Herrera, Ada María Isasi Diaz, and Allen Figueroa Deck, all of whom contributed to what Eduardo Fernández has called "the formative period of U.S. Hispanic theology."[88]

These theologians were concerned with revealing the theological particularities of the Latino reality in the United States and providing a rubric in which to better contextualize theology in Latino religious communities.[89] The rise in scholarship led to the establishment of seminary programs that adjusted their curriculum accordingly. Like Latino Mennonites who established a Bible school to address their own concerns, in 1972 the Mexican American Cultural Center opened in San Antonio, and two years later the Perkins School of Theology in Dallas established a Mexican American program.[90] These educational developments were part

Committed to merging politics and faith, Latino and African American Mennonites and members of the MCC gather in Washington, DC, to learn about immigration policy and promote immigrant rights, 1977. (Courtesy of Mennonite Church USA Archives, Goshen, Indiana)

of the legacy of the civil rights movement that saw the rise of many other programs in black, Chicano, and Puerto Rican studies in both public and religious institutions in the 1970s.[91]

The practice of Latino religious identity politics in the 1970s does more than show how active Latinos were during this period. It also stretches the timeline of Chicano movement and the civil rights movement into the late 1970s and reveals how these movements shaped religious change. Historian David Montejano makes this point clear when he describes how in the mid-1970s the Catholic Church in San Antonio used "its parish network and resources to create an urban political pressure group for community public service."[92] Churches played an increasing role in social liberation movements across the United States. Chicano and Puerto Rican social movements did not fade in the 1970s. Instead, religious Latinos and Latinas who believed the church had strayed from its mission of peace and social justice reinvented these movements. That Latinos and Latinas were busy changing their churches at a moment when most assume that Latino movements for social change had ended points to a new way to think about religion in the 1970s. That is, American religion was not simply becoming more conservative or helping make televangelists rich.[93] Rather, it was being pushed open by Latinos and Latinas who believed that their causes and concerns had been ignored long enough.

For Latino religious leaders, the civil rights movement provided the language and in many cases the political infrastructure to work at changing religious institutions. In 1972 Chicano Catholic priests helped start the Mexican American Cultural Center in San Antonio in order to train church leaders in theology and social action. That same year the First Hispano Pastoral Encounter took place in Washington, DC, as the first step toward providing pastoral resources to Latino/a Catholic leaders. A second encounter was hosted in 1977, and several regional encounters took place in Houston; Toledo, Ohio; and Dodge City, Kansas, between 1972 and 1977. The Catholic Church listened to the demands and responded by naming more Mexican American bishops at the national level. Mexican American Catholics, as historian Roberto Treviño has pointed out, "entered a changed relationship with the institutional church, especially as it affected their struggle for social equality."[94]

This changed relationship was defined as much by the discourses of Chicano and Puerto Rican politics as it was by the liberation ethics voiced by Latino and Latina theologians. This eclectic mix represents one of the most important ways in which Latino social movements were redefined and rearticulated in the late 1970s and early 1980s. The result was an effective strategy that had a lasting impact on how Latino religious communities moved from the margins of their church institutions to become central players in advocating for a place at the religious table. Most important, however, the battles within religious institutions extended the timeline of Latino civil rights efforts and put in place the necessary components for continued struggles over immigrant rights that have emerged since the 1980s.

By the beginning of the 1980s, Concilio leaders felt good about their progress. They had worked toward publishing Mennonite materials in Spanish and organized a Bible school to train Latino and Latina church leaders; Latinas continued to organize their conferences well into the 1980s and steadily began taking on more leadership roles, and they helped organize an immigration office through the MCC. In addition to these accomplishments, Ortíz worked to establish a handbook for Latino congregations to address issues of pastoral salary and Mennonite polity and theology and to provide a guide for church leadership. These resources all served to equip Latino congregations with the tools to better succeed in a predominately white church that often failed to understand Latino religious identity politics.

In August 1982 the Concilio celebrated 50 years of Latino membership in the Mennonite Church, promoting the theme "*Forjando Nuestra Historia*" ("Forging Our Story"). The celebration on the campus of Hesston College brought together Latinos from across the country and Puerto Rico and highlighted the struggle for inclusion in the Mennonite Church and the ways in which Latinos made the church more receptive to Spanish-speaking communities. While Latino Mennonites from South Texas and New York still played an important role in the church, the 50th anniversary celebration revealed that the Concilio had taken on a decidedly Latin American flavor. In fact, with the exception of Lupe De León, no one from the original Latin Concilio in 1968 was still actively involved in the Concilio in 1982.[95]

Another big change came in 1982 when José Ortíz announced that he would no longer serve as leader of the Concilio. He admitted feeling good about the increased representation of Latinos on church boards and the new programs he initiated as the church entered the 1980s and the fact that he had followed through on a promise to build bridges with Mennonites in Latin America. After his visit to El Tercer Congreso de Menonitas Latinoamericanos (the Third Congress of Latin American Mennonites) Ortíz called the meeting a "new frontier for Latinos in the North. For the first time they crossed borders and familiarized themselves with this [Latin American] group."[96]

Since taking over as associate secretary of the Concilio, Ortíz had witnessed increased Latino membership numbers in the Mennonite Church. By the early 1980s, Latino membership in the church had reached more than 1,500 in close to 50 congregations, with 11 new Latino churches in the process of being organized.[97] Ortíz also highlighted the fact that all of the Latino congregations had either US Latino pastors or pastors from Mexico, Honduras, Bolivia, Dominican Republic, or Puerto Rico. Meanwhile, *Ecos Menonitas*, the magazine for Meno-Latinos, had reached a peak circulation of nearly 1,000 and had become the central news source for Spanish-speaking Mennonites in Latin America and the United States.[98]

The Concilio came full circle in 1982 when it chose a young pastor from Mathis, Texas—Samuel Hernandez—as its new leader for the 1980s. The same boy who in the 1950s accidentally stumbled into a Mennonite Church because he thought they were going to show a film now found himself representing all Latinos and Latinas in the Mennonite Church. The arrival of Hernandez symbolized a new direction for Meno-Latinos in the 1980s. With the number of churches growing, increased numbers of Latinos in theological schools, and a sense that their time had come, Latinos were cautiously optimistic about the 1980s. If the 1960s and 1970s had given rise to politically potent and theologically grounded Latino religious communities, the 1980s would bring significant challenges in the areas of immigration politics and increased needs for church leadership. However, it was clear that Latino Mennonites and their evangelical counterparts, *hermanos* and *hermanas*, had marched in the vanguard of a changing nation where faith had become inextricably tied to the struggles for peace, justice, and dignity.

Conclusion

Latino Mennonites and the Politics of Belonging

Some will say, well, they were instigators but they really didn't accomplish much. That is especially hard to hear when it comes from people who have yet to accept the fact that because of what we did back then, the doors of the church have been opened for minorities.
—Ted Chapa, Cross-Cultural Youth Convention organizer, 2007

The events that led to the involvement of Latino Mennonites in the civil rights movement, the farmworker struggle, and the coalition they built with African American coreligionists in the Mennonite Church are now little more than distant memories. Most of the religious activists of those days no longer belong to the Mennonite Church; some left the church in frustration, and of these many believe they will never be welcomed back. Those who do still attend Mennonite churches are often quiet about their past, perhaps doubting its significance in the annals of Mennonite history. Aside from a small reunion of black and brown Minority Ministries Council (MMC) leaders in Florida in 1997, there are no visible markers of the time when Latinos engraved their stories, ideas, and cultures into Mennonite life.

In fact, most white Mennonites know more about the origins of their religious movement in sixteenth-century Europe than they do about the struggles of Latinos and other people of color in the twentieth century.

And yet it is precisely those struggles that helped usher in a religious transformation in the Mennonite Church. Beginning in the 1940s, concerns over racism in the church produced collaborative movements by Latinos and African Americans that compelled white Mennonites to reconsider their relationship to American society, politics, religious activism, and their own racial identity. Out of this emerged struggles and debates over race, gender, faith, and identity that solidified the place of Latinos in the Mennonite Church.

A New Chicano and Puerto Rican Civil Rights History

At the heart of studies on Latino evangelicals lies the question of belonging. Cultural, political, spiritual, and denominational belonging has prompted historians and religious studies scholars to critically engage the place of Latino evangelicals in American society. In the past 15 years, scholars have produced new histories of Latino evangelicals that have convincingly argued for the ways Latinos have struggled, reshaped, and participated in American evangelicalism while remaining tied to their ethnic communities. According to Luis D. León, Latino evangelicalism has manifested itself as a "borderlands phenomenon, one that combines Mexican, American, and Christian archetypes, mythologies, religious practices, and complex spirituality into a fresh identity, one that can produce and support *evangélico* mariachis."[1] These struggles and new identities have characterized how the politics of belonging have taken shape in the twentieth century and how they continue to play out in churches in the twenty-first century.

Understanding these dynamics is more important than ever, as the once popular truism that to be Latino is to be Catholic is no longer the case. Of the more than 50 million Latinos now in the United States, nearly 30 percent identify as "born again" or are affiliated with some form of Protestantism, often Pentecostalism.[2] This percentage also represents a younger segment of the population, as second- and third-generation Latinos are moving into evangelical churches faster than their elders did. These days Latinos are credited with rescuing denominations whose memberships have decreased as denominational loyalty has waned in the past 30 years.[3] A National Public Radio report went so far as to suggest that "Latinos are saving American Christianity."[4]

The shift to Protestant and Pentecostal Christianity, however, has a longer history of both Anglo-Protestant missions and urban revival, first with the arrival of white missionaries in Mexico, the Southwest, and Puerto Rico in the late nineteenth century and second with the Azusa Street Revival in Los Angeles in 1906.[5] These events initiated a religious conversion that moved Mexican Americans and Puerto Ricans to rethink the boundaries of ethnic and religious identity. The small number of Latinos who joined Protestant and Pentecostal movements during the first half of the twentieth century were busy forging their own churches, making their own music (in the form of *coritos*), and imbuing mainline Protestantism with the indigenous flair of Pentecostalism. For the most part these movements remained tied to their ethnic communities and were marginal to the broader reach of American religion. That began to change somewhat after World War II as white missionaries increased funding for home and foreign missionary programs and Latino Pentecostal churches grew as a result of increased immigration from Mexico and Puerto Rico.[6]

But it was not until the 1960s and 1970s, with the rise of the farmworker and Brown Power movements that Latino evangelicals made their presence felt on a national stage. The politics and rhetoric of the Chicano and Puerto Rican civil rights movements not only compelled Latino evangelicals to reconsider their faith but also redefined the paternalistic relationships they held with their white religious counterparts. These civil rights movements also deeply shaped the political and theological responses of Latino Catholics in the 1960s and 1970s. During this time religious groups such as PADRES, Las Hermanas, and Católicos por la Raza were organized by both religious and student leaders to pressure the Catholic Church to respond to the needs of Spanish-speaking communities.[7]

For this reason, sociologist Antonio M. Stevens Arroyo has called the 1960s and 1970s an era of "resurgence" of Latino religion in the United States. But for Latino evangelicals it was not so much a "resurgence" as a new and defining moment that merged the politics of the civil rights movement with the evangelical impulses of church life. It was a moment when the critique of white missionaries, church structures, and paternalistic relationships finally gained serious traction. That is, it was a time when the politics and language of the black, Chicano, and Puerto Rican freedom movements prompted Latino church leaders to rethink their relationship to white evangelicals and society in general. But unlike African American churches that were at the center of the black freedom struggle, Latino evangelical churches struggled to find a voice in Chicano and Puerto Rican civil rights struggles.

For the most part, Latino evangelical churches were not places to which civil rights leaders looked for moral fortitude, nor were they places to hold voter registration drives or other civil rights activities. In many places, in fact, Latino evangelicals were called out for being "cultural sell-outs" or challenged for not responding to the needs of barrio communities.[8] But that began to change in the late 1960s. When members of the Mexican American Youth Organization (MAYO) in Alice, Texas, needed a place to print their small newspaper, a local Mennonite church provided them with the necessary space and resources. When suspicions were raised about MAYO activities in South Texas, church leaders insisted that Mexican American youth were simply working on their newspaper and nothing more.[9]

While some churches were beginning to open their doors to Chicano activists in South Texas, in East Harlem the Puerto Rican Young Lords literally took over the Spanish Methodist Church in December 1969 and renamed it "The People's Church." The church became a space for breakfast programs, clothing drives, and other political activities. A similar scene played out in 1970 when MAYO activists posted a "Manifesto of the People" on the doors of the Juan Marcos Presbyterian Church in Houston. MAYO activists demanded the church establish a community outreach program that attended to the "secular needs" of the surrounding Mexican American community. The church responded by organizing neighborhood outreach programs.[10] These events in Texas and East Harlem, as Elias Ortega-Aponte reminds us, helped "breath new meaning, in this case militant meaning, into the gospel preached in the church."[11]

As the tense and uneven relationship between churches and their surrounding communities slowly changed by the mid-1970s, it gave rise to a new and progressive Latino evangelical movement that today is at the center of American politics and religion. According to Amy Sherman of the Center for the Study of Religion at Notre Dame, Latino churches are "just as likely to be involved in social services as are black churches who have a long history of community and political involvement."[12] The politics of Latino faith, as Catherine Wilson argues, are informed by a consistent engagement with politics, community involvement, and an evangelical impulse to spread the Gospel.

This has led to new and important studies by Mexican American and Latino religious studies scholars, who have ably documented the importance of both cultural and civic activism in the history of Latino churches.[13] These scholars agree that while public institutions segregated and offered inferior services to Latinos, the church was one of the few spaces that allowed Latinos room for reflection and a space to build community and develop leadership skills. During the civil rights movement, churches—like other community organizations—were often the training grounds where more effective and direct politics emerged.

For Latino Mennonites it was precisely in the church that their understandings of peace and justice developed. Even if their work did not lead to political or social change on a large scale, the case of Latino Mennonites shows that religious identity politics did not vanish with the ubiquitous rise of a white and conservative evangelicalism in the 1970s. These "Christian counterpolitics," to use Peter Goodwin Heltzel's phrase, present a different way to think about Latino religious identity politics in an era of increased conservatism. The 1970s, in other words, were not only about the emergence of American evangelicalism as a conservative force in American politics. The decade also witnessed the rise of Latino evangelicals (specifically Latino Mennonites) who worked to make the church more responsive to the cultural, educational, and political needs of Latino communities. In the 1970s churches became sites of struggle as Latinos clamored for their rightful place within the mostly white, middle-class, and rural Mennonite Church.[14]

Resituating the church as a site of struggle required using what historian David Montejano has called a "ground-level" analysis in order to interrogate how the crossings of civil rights, faith, and evangelical culture led to the movements for belonging in the Mennonite Church.[15] A ground-level assessment of the Mennonite Church helped to explore multiple identities, the variations in church work, and the contradictions and complexities inherent in them. What emerged was an understanding of how everyday people translated the politics and discourses of the Chicano and Puerto Rican movements to transform the social and religious context of the Mennonite Church. Instead of motivating Latinos to leave the Mennonite Church, or religion in general, the energy of the Chicano and

Puerto Rican movements only confirmed the need to work at changing a denomination about which many Latinos cared deeply.

Yet this was also multidimensional story that revealed the tenuous relationship between movement politics and religious faith. Nestled within the spaces between estrangement and belonging, a sampling of the origins of Latino evangelicalism emerged revealing a structure filled with the religious and political strands of racial and ethnic politics, gender identities, theology, and evangelicalism. Unfortunately, there is often no clear order to this structure. This is why political pundits are at a loss when trying to categorize Latino evangelicals, who appear to ally themselves with progressives on issues of civil rights but stand alongside conservative evangelicals on a number of issues related to sexuality and the domestic sphere. Political analyst Steffen Schmidt commented that "Hispanic evangelicals are really a different trend within the evangelical movement" in that they have concerns about faith-based issues like "family values," poverty, immigration, and education.[16]

The complexities of Latino evangelicalism make the connection to the energy and activism of the Chicano and Puerto Rican Movements all the more important. Though these movements challenged Latinos to rethink racial identity and feminism and to work to end segregation, they also gave rise to religious activism that prompted Latinos to rethink their relationship to the church. The religious activism that emerged in the 1960s and 1970s shows that the reach of the Chicano and Puerto Rican movements was far greater, and more religious in nature, than previously thought.

Integration or Autonomy?

From the moment the MMC was organized in 1968, there was a genuine optimism that black and brown leaders could transform Mennonite institutions from protected ethnic enclaves to welcoming spaces. What made the MMC leaders believe they could do this? In part, it was the grassroots nature of the MMC, most of whose members were not familiar with church politics but came from working-class backgrounds with almost no experience in how church politics worked. But an even greater factor was how black and brown leaders understood Mennonite theology. Black and brown leaders understood Mennonite theology to be open, inclusive, and most of all, critical of American aggression and militarization. These were issues that were at the forefront for black and brown Mennonites. Even as they critiqued white Mennonite modes of dress, church structures, and quiet nature, they also gravitated toward Mennonite theological positions on peace, justice, community, and the "priesthood of all believers."[17]

In their struggles, Latinos and African Americans created strong friendships with the farmers, preachers, and progressives they met and worked with in the Mennonite Church. There was also a belief that white Mennonites, who had a keen understanding of their own ethnic history, could also somehow understand the contemporary struggles of black and brown communities. In his book *Black and Mennonite*, MMC leader Hubert Brown insisted that while he could not "identify with their [Mennonite] biological past . . . I must be cognizant of their ethnic experience . . . just as I think it necessary for Mennonites to become aware of a black past."[18] But even as they were cognizant of Mennonite ethnic identity, Latino and African American Mennonites were adamant that they were not "cultural Mennonites."[19] For them, the power of Mennonite religious identity rested solely on the progressive theological positions of peace and nonviolence.

MMC leaders were also confident that a joint movement of black and brown Mennonites would prove too powerful to stop. As an interethnic movement, the MMC proved critical to the formation of the oppositional politics of Latino Mennonites. First and foremost, the MMC was one of the few groups that brought together African Americans, Mexican Americans, and Puerto Ricans. Inspired by Martin Luther King's vision of the Poor People's Campaign, the MMC sought to establish an interethnic movement that moved beyond a black-white framework of race relations. Yet the politics of the MMC were new for many Latinos, who were more comfortable citing Bible verses than talking about the struggles of low-wage workers or racial discrimination. While African Americans had a history of working for racial justice in the Mennonite Church that dated back to the 1950s, Latinos entered the conversations on race and the church only in the late 1960s.

Without question, joining African Americans in forming the MMC radically repositioned Latinos in the Mennonite Church. They moved from being thought of as marginal missionary projects to central political players in the discussions of race in the 1960s and 1970s. Building a movement with African American Mennonites not only shows how Latinos moved beyond their ethnic community but also points to the power of interethnic activism in forging movements for social change. Examining the complex interactions and political outcomes of interethnic activism revealed the importance of a comparative approach in uncovering the motivations behind the rise of Latino evangelicals in the 1970s.

True, Latino evangelicals took many of their activist cues from other Latino activists in the United States and Latin America, but there were also many instances of black-brown cooperation in religious settings and a clear influence by the black civil rights movement that has largely remained outside the purview of religious scholars and historians.[20] In the Mennonite Church, Latinos not only disrupted the black-white binary that had dominated discussions on race since the 1950s; they also helped expand the discussion to include their needs as a Spanish-language minority, their unique cultural differences, and their support for the farmworker movement even as white Mennonite leaders remained neutral. In each case, white Mennonites, and in some cases black Mennonites, struggled with how best to respond.

In 1973, pressured by white Mennonite leaders who promised to integrate African American and Latino Mennonites into every facet of church leadership, the MMC officially agreed to disband. The end of the MMC raised new and important questions about how the politics of belonging would actually play out. The most important question was whether integration or autonomy presented the best option for minorities in the Mennonite Church. Some black and brown leaders believed that white Mennonites were deliberately pushing for integration in order to move toward a position where questions about race and identity took on less importance. Others saw it as an important step toward integrating black and brown Mennonites into every facet of leadership in the Mennonite Church.

Unfortunately, the opportunity to think about how integration might actually work against the development of black and Latino Mennonite churches was missed. Instead of continuing on a track by which minority congregations could develop their own brand and style, integration urged them to assimilate and embrace traditional, and overwhelmingly white, notions of Mennonite theology and culture. In the end, the disagreement over whether to integrate or remain autonomous fractured the black-brown coalition and ended the era of interethnic activism in the Mennonite Church. But even as the MMC coalition floundered, the politics and energy it emanated in the church spurred new movements that highlighted the role of women in church leadership and showed the power religious identity politics played in mobilizing Latino evangelicals in the 1970s.

Mixing Race, Gender, and Faith

While the politics behind the interethnic coalition of black and brown Mennonites stemmed from racial and ethnic pride, how those politics were articulated often reinforced hierarchies of gender as MMC men expressed race in explicitly gendered language. For Latino men, who often talked about their refashioned racial identity, strong masculine rhetoric helped ease the tensions being raised over whether one could be both a "macho" and Christian. In the Mennonite Church, with its tradition of peacemaking, the tension was even more daunting. MMC leaders worried about how to convince black and brown men in the pews that forgoing military service was not cowardly or unpatriotic but in fact that peacemaking required "Machismo integrity."[21] But the strong talk from Latino leaders was often more performance than reality. At the heart of gendered race talk was the need felt by Latino men to "man-up" in their religious beliefs in order to offset assertions by Brown Power activists that to be an evangelical and belong to the peace-loving Mennonite Church disqualified one from serious political activism. In church sermons, public talks, and writings, masculine rhetoric helped carve out both a religious and militant ethos in the MMC that countered the perceived passiveness of the Mennonite Church.[22] It also led to the growing estrangement of women in the MMC.

Frustrated by a lack of opportunities to showcase their leadership abilities, in 1973 Latinas began organizing their own conferences, separate from the men, where they could gather to preach, support one another, and discuss issues that were most relevant to them. By holding separate conferences, Latinas in the Mennonite Church challenged what appeared to be the normal and casual practices of sexism in the church. They did so by creating spaces where they could demonstrate their skills as preachers, Bible interpreters, and of course singers and musicians. Gender norms in an evangelical home, where the man was considered the spiritual leader, were understood as biblical mandates and often dictated familial relations.

Rather than challenging traditional family models, Latinas focused on changing the place of women in the church by highlighting their preaching, spiritual, and leadership abilities. And while they rejected the politics of feminism, they were nonetheless attentive and sympathetic to the calls for change that feminists were making in the 1970s. Women like Iris Navarro, who attended the Latina Mennonite conference in Corpus Christi in 1976, urged church leaders to acknowledge that "the church is truly integrated only when each sister can participate fully and with equal conditions."[23]

Simply to assume that evangélicas, particularly Latina Mennonites, were turned off by the feminist movement or apathetic to its politics ignores many of the real and sustained engagements they had with a movement that was perceived to be fundamentally secular. The borderlands of faith and feminism, in other words, created a space where Latinas blended the biblical mandates they held sacred with the very best of the feminist movement in terms of acknowledging the abilities of women to lead, preach, and participate in religious movements.

The public discourses that emerged around faith, race, and gender also carried implications for how Latino leaders related to grassroots churches and youth. The movement to belong in the Mennonite Church was led mostly by a select few Latino leaders who emerged out of working-class churches but whose politics had often distanced them from many of the people in those churches. The criticisms about the extent of political involvement came from some Mexican American leaders in South Texas who believed that politics had no place in the church. Evangelism and saving souls, not politics and civil rights activities, were central to the mission of the church. Many of these criticisms came from pastors and other church leaders who believed that people like Lupe De León and Ted Chapa had simply taken things too far. And while youth were the engines of activism in the Chicano and Puerto Rican movements, evangelical Latino youth demanded that MMC leaders talk more about "God power" along with Chicano and black power. At the 1972 Cross-Cultural Youth Convention, black, Latino, and Native American youth pushed back the ethnic nationalist rhetoric they heard from the speakers throughout the week. They did so even as they praised convention organizers for creating a space to talk about identity, culture, and religion.

That these struggles even took place at the level they did confirms what

historian Mario T. García has argued about the important but often ignored religious dimensions of the Chicano movement and other Latino
civil rights causes.[24] The tentacles of these movements spread to churches
across the Midwest and affected the activities of civic and religious institutions in regions outside the Southwest and Northeast. But more than
correcting a previously forgotten chapter of history, the struggles of Latinos in the Mennonite Church reveal how questions of gender, race, activism, and faith carried deep and important meanings for those who were
part of the church and the movements for civil rights. They demonstrate
that Latino evangelicals have a history of social engagement that counters
any notion that they were strictly worried about saving souls or getting
into heaven. The church was not immune to the important questions that
many activists were raising about feminism and institutional racism. In
fact, those questions were central to Latino leaders who were challenging
their own denominational bodies.

Moreover, these struggles show how the Chicano and Puerto Rican
movements impressed on Latino evangelicals a way to think about their
own cultural and social standing in relation to their understanding of theology and church doctrine. Historian Paul Barton makes this point clear
when he discusses church organizations like La Raza Churchmen and programs like the Migrant Ministry in Texas, which organized movements to
bridge the chasm between churches and their surrounding communities.[25]
For the first time Mexican Americans and other Latinos were challenging white religious leaders about the needs of Spanish-speaking communities, social injustice, and religious activism. More important, the work
of these and other organizations shows us how the civil rights movement
catapulted Latino religious leaders to the center of national debates about
race and religion. Latino religious communities were marginal no more.

Race and Mennonite Church History

It is no secret that the membership of mainline Protestant denominations
with historic European roots is now declining.[26] The same is true of the
Mennonite Church. A church-wide study found that the church is largely
made up of an aging white Mennonite population, less than 10 percent
of whom attend church more than once a week, and that only about half
of the members believe they will remain with the denomination.[27] The

loyalty that people once felt to their denominations has been on a slow decline for the past 40 years as new religious movements, nondenominational churches, and Pentecostal groups have increased in numbers. Today people are much more fluid in their religious choices and often mix and match religious allegiances depending on circumstances and contexts.

The flipside to the decreasing membership in the Mennonite Church is the increasing number of racial-ethnic congregations that include Latino, African American, Native American, Asian American, and new immigrant members. Of the 169 racial-ethnic Mennonite churches, nearly half are Latino, largely located in urban areas, and most of their members are younger than the aging white Mennonite membership. The new religious body that emerged in 2001 as Mennonite Church USA (a merger between the General Conference and the "Old" Mennonite Church) is today more evangelical, more politically involved, and more urban, and its Latino and African American members are more charismatic in their worship styles. A little over 80 percent of Latinos and African Americans in the Mennonite Church believe in the "charismatic gifts of healing, prophesying and speaking in tongues."[28] It is these evangelical Mennonite churches, as Mennonite scholar J. Nelson Kraybill suggests, "that have been most successful at reaching across ethnic, racial and economic boundaries."[29] Thus the future of the Mennonite Church is likely to be more diverse and evangelical.

The changing demographics of the Mennonite Church are part of a larger set of issues facing white Mennonites. In the past 30 years white Mennonites have struggled to balance their increasingly normative place in American society with their desire to remain an alternative to mainstream evangelicalism. They have addressed this somewhat by maintaining an active presence as a "historic peace church" and an active voice on issues of peace and nonconformity. In the 1970s Mennonite peace theology was lauded as "an Anabaptist vision of communitarianism and peace" by eager members of the evangelical left who were searching for a theology grounded in social justice concerns.[30] But the attention they received from progressive evangelicals was also a sign that white Mennonites were more urban, wealthier, and more evangelical than ever. The "quiet in the land" identity to which they had clung for much of the twentieth century could not resist the forces of radically changing contexts.

The 1970s stood as a critical moment for white Mennonites, who pushed social justice while also feeling the pull of church leaders who wished the church would take a more evangelical stance. Historian Perry Bush methodically demonstrates this point in his work *Two Kingdoms, Two Loyalties* by arguing that in the civil rights era "Mennonites continued to take their political cues from a national society that could no longer be described as 'outside' the boundaries of their world."[31]

Yet it is clear that the social and ethnic transformations that white Mennonites experienced in the years after World War II were not only taking place within the dialectics of Anabaptism and evangelicalism.[32] These transformations were also rooted in the dilemmas of race first raised by African Americans in the 1950s. While questions about peace and Anabaptism have been at the center of Mennonite theology and ethnic kinship, race has served as a means for a greater redefinition of Mennonite identity and community. Between the 1950s and the 1970s conversations on race in the church highlighted the anxiety that Mennonites felt about being a "white" church, while also forcing them to take into account the needs of Latinos and African Americans, to diversify their church structures, and for the first time to consider new definitions of Mennonite identity in the United States.

While theological positions on peace and threats of war in the twentieth century forced white Mennonites to rethink their relationship to the state, the racial crisis in the church opened a flurry of debates over how the peace position privileged the social location of white Mennonites and prevented them from forming authentic solidarity movements with minority groups. For many white Mennonites this was difficult to comprehend. How could theologically progressive positions on peace, articulated best by famed Mennonite theologian John Howard Yoder, be considered a roadblock to authentic solidarity with Latinos and African Americans? In part this stemmed from how white Mennonites disassociated the peace position with holding power and privilege in society.

For Latinos, peacemaking was as much a core religious principle as it was a culturally mediated practice that had little relevance in urban barrios and rural communities. In 1976, Lupe De León wrote about the realities of working-class Mexican Americans with limited opportunities who move "from unorganized street violence to sophisticated U.S. Government financially supported training in violence." If several Latino young men grew up in the Mennonite Church with a tradition of peace, De León asked, "why did they die in the Vietnam conflict?"[33] In part, talking about peace and nonresistance in the Mennonite Church revealed the uneven social locations of white, black, and Latino Mennonites and the centrality of race in the church. If Latinos were to practice Mennonite peacemaking, they believed it was important to find "alternatives that are applicable to our culture and tradition within the philosophy of Jesus as peacemaker."[34] The concerns about peace theology and the race conflicts that captured the attention of the Mennonite Church in the years after World War II were responsible for bringing out an "otherwise quiescent [white] racial identity into common view."[35] In other words, the twentieth-century racial crisis in the Mennonite Church turned ethnic Mennonites into white Mennonites.

Countering this "quiescent racial identity," white Mennonites tried to distance themselves from institutional racism by stressing their own history of religious persecution in sixteenth-century Europe. But with an eye toward their own history, white Mennonites were often blind to the racist undertones of their missiology, the exclusion of people of color in positions of power, and their ethnocentric theology. Racism, for white Mennonites, did not need to be addressed because it resulted from the "common sense" embedded in their missionary identity and in their "quiet in the land" ideology. That racism operated "within this sphere of common sense," Ian F. Haney-López has argued, helps explain why white Mennonites were quick to deflect accusations from Latinos that their actions were sometimes paternalistic or racist.[36] But it also directed and shaped how white Mennonites chose to respond to specific causes during the civil rights movement.[37]

Nowhere was this clearer than in some of the theological and philosophical positions white Mennonites took toward specific civil rights issues. While no one questioned that white Mennonites were committed to working against racism, this did not stop them from being suspicious of the tactics that some black and brown leaders employed to bring about social change. In the black freedom struggle, white Mennonites struggled with the notion of "coercive nonviolence" even as they praised Martin Luther King Jr. for his nonviolent intentions. In the context of the Chicano struggle, it was the concern that the farmworker movement was more about unions than about a struggle for civil rights. Even appeals by black and brown leaders for white Mennonites to connect the persecution of sixteenth-century Anabaptists with the racial strife in the 1960s and 1970s were not enough to shift some of the church's rigid positions against civil rights advocacy.

Moving beyond Church History

Writing the history of Latino evangelicals is a difficult task. First and foremost, historians and other scholars must contend with multiple religious traditions and doctrinal and theological differences. Each of these traditions, from Mennonite to Pentecostal, has its own organizational bodies with distinct missionary histories, operational structures, and of course archives—which explains why religious studies scholars are often the ones who dare to wade into these complex waters. Much of the important work on Latino evangelicals that has emerged in the past 15 years has come from religious studies scholars more than from social historians. As a result these works are often not considered in larger debates on race and ethnicity, gender, sexuality, and immigration currently animating the established fields of Chicano and Latino history.

This is changing slowly as scholars such as Rudy Busto and Gastón Espinosa have called for a closer relationship among ethnic studies, history, and religious studies as a way to reveal the complexities and nuances of Chicano and Latino history.[38] Writing the history of Latino evangelicals need not be an aberration or confined to the rubrics of religious or theological studies. Chicana/o and Latina/o historians, for example, would benefit from the lessons Latino evangelicals in the Southwest and Northeast took from the civil rights movement as they worked to transform their religious institutions.

In conceptualizing the history of Latino evangelicals it is also important to understand that the religious choices people make about where they congregate are often shaped by community and cultural familiarity. This was the case for Latinos whose decision to remain in the Mennonite Church was rooted in the deep memories of the "Kool-Aid and cookies" they enjoyed at vacation Bible schools and the strong relationships they formed with white Mennonites. For Mexican Americans, especially those in South Texas, the memories of basketball games, shared meals, and the service projects of white Mennonites were the main reasons they remained connected to the Mennonite Church, whereas for Puerto Ricans on the island and in New York City, it was the social services ethic of the white Mennonites they met in hospitals and drug rehabilitation centers. Years later, those memories were the basis for challenging the church to live up to its own ideals of peace, justice, and community.

But Latinos who remained tied to the mostly white Mennonite Church also understood that they were part of a larger community of evangélicos who worshiped in Spanish, sang the same Pentecostal-influenced *coritos*, and often referred to each other as *hermano* or *hermana*. These shared experiences make up some of the core components of a *cultura evangélica* and show how religious identities often have more to do with culture and community than with doctrinal or theological commitments. Viewing the history of Latino evangelicals from this perspective provides an avenue to talk about Latinos in specific religious traditions—or as a group of evangelicals—without the restrictions and parochialisms of traditional church history.

Understanding the social and cultural dimensions of "brown evangelicals" has today become more important than ever. From the sanctuary movement of the 1980s to pro-immigrant campaigns in the 2000s, Latino evangelicals have entered the political fray in powerful ways. The shape and scope of their increasing influence over the years requires that scholars give attention to the ways in which culture and politics shape religious thought and vice versa. But more important, examining the social and cultural components of Latino evangelicalism provides an avenue for scholars to bridge the identity politics of the civil rights movement with the immigrant rights movement that emerged in the 1980s. In other words, the study of Latino religious history presents new possibilities for thinking about how the civil rights movement helped build an infrastructure of religious support that since the 1980s has positioned churches as an important voice in the struggle for immigrant rights in the past 30 years.

The New Politics of Belonging

In 2013 Elizabeth Soto-Albrecht, originally from Puerto Rico, became the first Latina to serve as moderator of the Mennonite Church USA. Her selection was a historic move that affirms just how far the Mennonite Church has come in its work to become more inclusive. But her tenure began mired in controversy. Soto-Albrecht's commissioning service took place at the biennial Mennonite Church USA convention that in 2013 was held in Arizona. Against the backdrop of some of the strictest anti-immigrant laws in the nation, and with a majority of Latino Mennonites not in attendance—many boycotted the convention—Soto-Albrecht began her tenure as church moderator. Soto-Albrecht herself boycotted the convention, arriving only on the last day to participate in the commissioning service for her new position. As Soto-Albrecht took her place as the new face of the church, the predicament of Latinos in the Mennonite Church remained as precarious as it was in the 1960s and 1970s. Latino leaders continue to advocate for Spanish-language resources, more Latinos in church leadership, and a religious identity that straddles the borders of Anabaptism and evangelicalism.

As the number of Latino immigrants has increased in Mennonite churches in places like Florida and Iowa, Latino leaders continue to struggle with a Mennonite Church structure that places too much power in the hands of regional conferences and therefore limits the possibilities for a national movement of Latino churches similar to what existed in the 1970s. While the number of Latinos in the Mennonite Church continues to rise, along with the number of other people of color in the church, questions concerning the place of Latinos are as salient as they were in the 1960s and 1970s.

Yet even as Latinos remain on the margins of the Mennonite Church and the church continues to struggle to be a more inclusive place, debates over homosexuality reintroduced the question of belonging in the 1990s. Any reader who has followed the fierce debates over openly homosexual clergy and marriages in evangelical churches will not be surprised that Latino Mennonites in particular and Latino evangelicals in general tend to be in disagreement with both. Even as more than half of Latinos support same-sex marriage, Latino evangelicals continue to oppose same-sex marriage by an almost 2 to 1 margin.[39] When the issue surfaced at a recent Mennonite Church USA executive board meeting, nonwhite church leaders reiterated that the "inclusion of lesbian, gay, bisexual and transgender, or LGBT, people is not a major issue for the underrepresented racial-ethnic groups."[40] Interestingly, white Mennonites have supported this opposition under the guise of remaining committed to their aspirations of being an "anti-racist church."[41]

The recent debates over immigrant rights and the place of LGBT Mennonites have once again raised important questions about the paradoxes of belonging. These struggles, like the ones that raged in the 1960s and 1970s, remind us that even as the politics of belonging have benefited insiders and those in positions of power, there have always been vibrant movements of resistance that have called the church to live up to its own ideals of community and peace. But more important, these struggles show us that it is often in the spaces between belonging and exclusion where the politics of religious life compel us to work for what is possible.

Notes

Introduction

Epigraph. Neufeld, *Eight Years among Latin-Americans*, 70.

1. Samuel Hernandez, interview by author, tape recording, Goshen, IN, March 2007.

2. Perfecta De León, interview by author, tape recording, Mathis, TX, December 28, 2006.

3. Markers of ethnicity, nation, and gender have become increasingly complex in an era of heightened immigration, globalization, and debates over the language of identity politics in academia. But for the sake of clarity, throughout the book I use the terms "Latino" and, to a lesser extent, "brown" to identify Mexican Americans and Puerto Ricans that I discuss in this book. I also understand the pitfalls of sexism and heterosexism, but in the interest of clarity I have chosen to use the masculine form "Latino" throughout most of this book except when I am talking specifically about women of Latin American origin. In those cases I use the term "Latina." When more precise language is necessary and appropriate, I sparingly use "Latino/a" or "Latino and Latina." I also use the term "minority" because it is the one consistent way that black and brown people in this study are identified. I use the term "ethnic Mexican" to describe the Mexican population, regardless of citizenship. The labels "Mexican American" and "Chicana/o" are reserved for the Mexican-origin population either born or raised in the United States and those that self-identify as such. See Itzigsohn, "The Formation of Latino and Latina Panethnic Identities"; Gutiérrez, *Walls and Mirrors*; Arredondo, *Mexican Chicago*; and Oboler, *Ethnic Labels, Latino Lives*.

4. Klaassen, *Anabaptism*, 1. The work of J. Denny Weaver is most helpful in defining Anabaptism. Weaver suggests three "priorities" of Anabaptism: (1) "the nor-

mativeness of Jesus for truth," which emphasizes praxis and discipleship; (2) "community," placing community over individualism and stressing the priesthood of all believers; and (3) "peace," standing against violence in any form and believing that Anabaptists are to work for peace and justice. Weaver, *Becoming Anabaptist*. Most recently the work of Stuart Murray has reignited a debate over the "bare essentials" of Anabaptism. See Murray, *The Naked Anabaptist*.

5. My work builds on the call by Chicana/o studies scholars to expand our understandings, timelines, and geographies of Chicana/o history and social movements. See Davalos et al., "Roundtable," 143.

6. Gastón Espinosa and Rick Hunter, "Latino Religions and Politics Survey Voter Report: Pre-2012 Election Findings," nationally representative bilingual telephone survey of 1,000 Latino Christian likely voters, conducted October 4–10, 2012, Claremont McKenna College, 7.

7. The last 10 years have seen a flurry of books on the Latino religious experience during the civil rights movement. Among the more influential works are Sánchez Walsh, *Latino Pentecostal Identity*; Busto, *King Tiger*; R. Martínez, *PADRES*; Medina, *Las Hermanas*; Barton, "*¡Ya Basta!*"; Espinosa and García, *Mexican American Religions*.

8. Stevens Arroyo, *Prophets Denied Honor*; Espinosa, Elizondo, and Miranda, *Latino Religions and Civic Activism in the United States*; Watt, *Farm Workers and the Churches*.

9. Other interethnic religious movements in the mid-twentieth century include the Catholic Interracial Council, which worked in New York and places across the Midwest, and the Christian Friends for Racial Equality, which worked in Seattle. See Walker, *Religion and the Public Conscience*, and Janet Weaver, "From Barrio to '¡Boicoteo!'"

10. M. García, "Religion and the Chicano Movement," 125; R. Martínez, *PADRES*; Treviño, *The Church in the Barrio*; Medina, *Las Hermanas*.

11. Pinn and Valentin, *The Ties That Bind*.

12. One key example of this is Gordon Mantler's treatment of Chicano involvement, including that of Chicano religious leaders, in the Poor People's Campaign in 1968. Mantler, "Black, Brown and Poor," 158–228. For more on multiracial dynamics see Kurashige, *The Shifting Grounds of Race*. I make this argument knowing that some Latino evangelicals were ambivalent about the politics of the civil rights movement. Historians Edwin Sylvest Jr. ("Hispanic American Protestantism in the United States") and Paul Barton ("*¡Ya Basta!*") make this point clear. In this book I also highlight parts of the Latino church that struggled with how to relate to the movement. But no matter the dissent, it is hard to ignore the very real and practical changes that the civil rights movement had on Latino churches. Throughout this book, I demonstrate exactly what those gains were and how they helped shape the experience of Latino Mennonites in the 1970s.

13. Alvarez, "From Zoot Suits to Hip Hop," 56.

14. Brilliant, *The Color of America Has Changed*, 14. For works that employ a comparative approach, see Bernstein, *Bridges of Reform*; Alvarez, *The Power of the Zoot*; Kurashige, *The Shifting Grounds of Race*; L. Fernandez, *Brown in the Windy City*; Medina, *Las Hermanas*.

15. J. Hall, "The Long Civil Rights Movement and the Political Uses of the Past."

16. See, for example, Dudziak, *Cold War Civil Rights*. Curtis Evans has also argued that the focus on anticommunism that initiated evangelical engagements with race eventually shifted toward developing a conservative political movement in the 1960s and 1970s. Evans, "White Evangelical Protestant Responses to the Civil Rights Movement."

17. L. Nieto, "The Chicano Movement and the Gospel," 157.

18. See Swartz, "Identity Politics and the Fragmenting of the 1970s Evangelical Left." I disagree with Swartz's premise that identity politics were at fault for bringing down the evangelical left. Swartz's argument ignores the interplay of race and gender among the white and mostly male leadership of the evangelical left. Therein lies the problem with critics of identity politics. In their attempts to defend the common good, they disregard the power that some groups have to name what exactly that common good is. Blaming identity politics shifts blame to minority groups who were fighting for a place at the table instead of placing blame on white evangelicals—especially white men—who were not willing to institute a race and gender critique as they organized for social change. What Swartz calls the "profound misfortune" of the "corrosive debates over identity" was actually a necessary step in the making of an evangelical and progressive movement in which multiple perspectives and voices were welcomed. My thoughts on theories of identity politics were greatly influenced by Paula Moya, *Learning from Experience*; Rosaldo, "Identity Politics"; and José David Saldívar, "Border Thinking, Minoritized Studies, and Realist Interpellations."

19. M. García, "Religion and the Chicano Movement," 125. In recent years, García has been the most important Chicano historian to include religion in his treatment of Chicano history. See, for example, his *Católicos: Resistance and Affirmation in Chicano Catholic History* (2010). The reverse is true in Mennonite history, where scholars have largely ignored the important contributions of Latinos. Aside from Rafael Falcón's *Hispanic Mennonite Church in North America* (1986), the Latino experience within the Mennonite Church has largely been overlooked. Works by Mennonite historians such as Paul Toews's *Mennonites in American Society* (1996), Perry Bush's *Two Kingdoms, Two Loyalties* (1998), and Tobin Miller Shearer's *Daily Demonstrators* (2010) say little of the contributions and stories of Latinos and Latinas in the Mennonite Church.

20. Montejano, *Quixote's Soldiers*, 27.

21. In part, this is a response to George Mariscal's important call to integrate Chicano movement history "into scholarship focused on the 1960s." Mariscal, *Brown-Eyed Children of the Sun*, 5.

22. Heltzel, *Jesus and Justice*, 7–11.

23. I am careful not to assume that Latinos, African Americans, Native Americans, and Asian Americans share one particular brand of evangelical politics. But I do subscribe to the notion that, while theological and political orientations among these groups range over a broad spectrum, the politics of minority racial and ethnic groups differ from the politics of white evangelicals. In other words, talking about one "evangelicalism" in the United States is problematic, as it tends to ignore problems around identity politics, race, gender, and social location. Religious communities of color have historically differed from their white evangelical counterparts along lines of race, gender, and poverty. See Heltzel, *Jesus and Justice*; A. Smith, *Native Americans and the Christian Right*; Kim, *A Faith of Our Own*; and Espinosa, Elizondo, and Miranda, *Latino Religions and Civic Activism in the United States*.

24. Sánchez Walsh, *Latino Pentecostal Identity*, 157.

25. Works that consider Latino evangelical identity include Walker, *Protestantism in the Sangre de Cristos*; Banker, *Presbyterian Missions and Cultural Interaction in the Far Southwest*; Yohn, *A Contest of Faiths*; Deutsch, *No Separate Refuge*; Machado, *Of Borders and Margins*; Sánchez Walsh, *Latino Pentecostal Identity*; Barton, *Hispanic Presbyterians, Methodists, and Baptists in Texas*; Martínez and Scott, *Los Evangélicos*.

26. I follow the work of religious historian Gastón Espinosa, who asserts that "most Latino Protestants regardless of family grouping see themselves as *evangélicos* in the Spanish-speaking community." Theologians such as Loida Martell-Otero and David Maldonado have argued that the Spanish term *evangélico* carries different connotations than the popular English term "evangelical." I agree with their assessments. But for the purposes of this study, I have decided to use "evangelical" and *evangélico* interchangeably in order to better identify how Latinos themselves identify in using both English and Spanish forms of the word. Espinosa, "Methodological Reflections," 37. See also Maldonado, *Protestantes/Protestants*, 10–11; Martell-Otero, *Latina Evangélicas*; Martínez and Scott, *Los Evangélicos*, xxi.

27. Here I agree with Espinosa's classification of Latino Mennonites as evangelical not only because their Spanish-language congregations tend to be evangelical in orientation but also because it is the evangelical wings of Mennonites that have historically conducted mission outreach to Latinos. See Espinosa, "Methodological Reflections," 44.

28. With regard to expanding the "boundaries of belief," I find Matthew Pehl's assessment of working-class religion in Detroit helpful. In it Pehl complicates the familiar narrative among some that brands "belief rather than economic structures" as more important among working-class religious communities. Pehl's broader criti-

cism is that scholarship on religious communities often falls along denominational lines (Catholicism or Protestantism) instead of class status, for example. While the present study does focus on one religious group, I am not satisfied with demarcating Latinos solely based on whether they are Pentecostal or mainline Protestant. As important as these identities are, the neat categorizations that scholars ascribe are often muddied in reality, as people's identities remain in flux and religious beliefs and practices are rarely static. Pehl, "Apostles of Fascism," 440–441; Bebbington, *Evangelicalism in Modern Britain*, 12–13. See also Albanese, *America: Religions and Religion*.

29. I take a constructivist approach to the history of Latino evangelicals. A constructivist approach takes a "bottom-up" view of culture as being shaped and reshaped by individual and communal experiences. For more on the constructivist approach to religious identity see Droogers, "Globalisation and Pentecostal Success."

30. Lupe De León, interview by author, tape recording, Mathis, TX, June 2007.

31. L. Nieto, "The Chicano Movement and the Churches in the United States," 37.

32. Maduro, "Notes toward a Sociology of Latina/o Religious Empowerment," 157.

33. "The Venturas," February 3, 1973, Mission History Interview Project, box 1, tape 28, Hist. MS 6-81, MCA.

34. Schlabach, *Gospel versus Gospel*, 37, 226–227.

35. For more discussion on the moniker "the quiet of the land," see Bush, *Two Kingdoms, Two Loyalties*, 18–29.

36. Dyck, *An Introduction to Mennonite History*.

37. The "priesthood of all believers" is a belief held in common by both Protestants and Anabaptists.

38. This book focuses largely on the "Old" Mennonite Church tradition, primarily because it had the largest and most direct mission program in Latino communities.

39. Burkholder and Cramer, *The Activist Impulse*.

40. Bush, *Two Kingdoms, Two Loyalties*; Toews, *Mennonites in American Society*; Stutzman, *From Nonresistance to Justice*. Shearer, *Daily Demonstrators*, takes a different view.

41. Evans, "White Evangelical Protestant Responses to the Civil Rights Movement," 248. Two other important authors who make a strong argument for the social engagement of evangelicalism are T. L. Smith, in *Revivalism and Social Reform in Mid-Nineteenth Century America*, and Donald Dayton, in *Discovering an Evangelical Heritage*.

Chapter 1. Building Up the Temple

Epigraphs. Amsa Kauffman, "Tuleta, Texas," *Gospel Herald*, April 24, 1941; Ofelia Aguilar Garcia, quoted by Seferina Garcia De León, interview by author, tape recording, Goshen, IN, April 17, 2007. According to Seferina, this comment by Ofelia, her mother, referred to the eating habits of Mennonites in Mathis. These quotes highlight the radically different perspectives that these two groups had about each other.

1. Thirtieth Annual Report, MBMC Annual Meeting, Belleville, PA, May 10−12, 1936, box 2, file 1, IV-6-3, MCA. Prior to Hershey and Detweiler's trip, D. H. Bender and S. E. Allgyer conducted their own trip to the borderlands in March 1920. H. F. Reist, "Why and When in Texas," *Blank Notes*, no. 2, Congregation Archives Collections, Calvary Mennonite Church, Mathis, TX, 1948−1955, III-43-7, MCA.

2. For more on the history of Protestants and Pentecostals in the borderlands, see Walker, *Protestantism in the Sangre de Cristos*; Banker, *Presbyterian Missions and Cultural Interaction in the Far Southwest*; J. Martínez, *Sea la Luz*; Ramírez, "Borderlands Praxis."

3. T. K. Hershey Collection, Hist. MS 1-114, box 4, Correspondence 1934−1962, MCA.

4. For excellent coverage of Latino history in Chicago see Arredondo, *Mexican Chicago*; L. Fernandez, *Brown in the Windy City*; M. Innis-Jiménez, *Steel Barrio*.

5. Report by Amsa Kauffman to the Thirty-Third MBMC Annual Meeting, Fairview, MI, June 18−20, 1939, MBMC Annual Meeting, box 4, file 7, IV-6-3, MCA.

6. Arredondo, *Mexican Chicago*, 39−79.

7. Edwin Weaver to S. C. Yoder, July 21, 1934, MBMC Executive Office Correspondence 1908−1945, box 3, Chicago Home Mission 1933−1936, IV-7-1, MCA. In the same archive box, see also Weaver's report on behalf of Illinois Mennonite Conference, August 28, 1934.

8. F. D. King to S. C. Yoder, September 16, 1935, MBMC Executive Office, Correspondence, 1908−1945, box 3, Chicago Home Mission, 1933−1936, IV-7-1, MCA.

9. P. A. Friesen to S. C. Yoder, November 29, 1932, MBMC Executive Office Correspondence 1908−1945, box 3, Chicago Home Mission 1921−1932, IV-7-1, MCA.

10. Letter to MBMC Executive Committee, Executive Office Correspondence, box 3, Chicago Home Mission, 1921−1932, IV-7-1, MCA. Mennonites were not the only religious group providing help to Mexican immigrants. Methodists and Congregationalists were doing more prominent work. Both led settlement houses

in different sections of the city. See Arredondo, *Mexican Chicago*, 21–29, 39; and W. Smith, *Mennonites in Illinois*, 421.

11. Oyer, *What God Hath Wrought in a Half Century at the Mennonite Home Mission*; Kraybill, "The Birth of the Chicago Mexican Mission."

12. Smith, *Mennonites in Illinois*, 421. The Chicago Mexican Mission had several homes throughout its life. The first location was at 1931 Roosevelt Rd. From there it moved to the intersection of Miller and Taylor Streets. Finally, the MBMC purchased a four-story building at 1014 Blue Island Avenue. MBMC Overseas Mission, J. D. Graber Files, 1951–1955, "Mennonite Mexican Mission," boxes 1–3, IV-18-10, MCA.

13. L. Fernandez, *Brown in the Windy City*, 59.

14. Kanter, "Making Mexican Parishes," 41.

15. "The Venturas," February 3, 1973, Mission History Interview Project, Hist. MS 6-81, box 1, tape 28, MCA.

16. Ibid.

17. Barton, *Hispanic Methodists, Presbyterians, and Baptists in Texas*, 44.

18. S. C. Yoder to J. W. Shank, MBMC Executive Committee, Executive Office Correspondence 1908–1945, box 3, Chicago Home Mission 1937–1945, IV-7-1, MCA.

19. Shearer, *Daily Demonstrators*, 137.

20. Raul Tadeo, interview by author, tape recording, July 2010, Dalton, OH.

21. Ruiz, *From Out of the Shadows*, 49.

22. T. K. Hershey, "First Mexican Services," *Gospel Herald*, November 5, 1936; David Alwine, "Two Mexican Services," *Gospel Herald*, March 18, 1937. The only record of Mexican Americans during these early years is a man identified only by his last name, "Del Bosque." In 1909, Del Bosque, whom white Mennonites called by his Christian name, "Simon," became the first Mexican American baptized in the Mennonite Church. Records for the Mennonite families who moved to South Texas during the early part of the twentieth century were found in the Lobrecht Family Oral Histories, container 347, A1991-024, South Texas Archives, Texas A&M University, Kingsville, TX.

23. Alwine, "Two Mexican Services."

24. Harry Neufeld, Report on Mission Work in South Texas, *Zionsbote*, May 25, 1938, translated from German by Tina Hartman, Mennonite Brethren Archives, Tabor College, Hillsboro, KS.

25. T. K. Hershey, "Prospects of Mission Work along the Mexican Border," MBMC Thirty-First Annual Meeting, West Liberty, OH, June 12–15, 1937, and "Mexican Border Work," MBMC Thirty-Second Annual Meeting, Wellman, IA, June 19–21, 1938, box 2, file 1, IV-6-3, MCA.

26. J. Martínez, *Sea la Luz*, 62.

27. Hershey, "First Mexican Services."

28. David Alwine, "Mexican Border Mission," *Gospel Herald*, March 9, 1939.

29. Ibid. Catholicism was viewed by Mennonites as a "false teaching." The feeling was often mutual. Catholic priests warned their parishioners to stay away from the Mennonites and their "false teachings." Neufeld, *Eight Years among Latin-Americans*, 78–79.

30. Neufeld, *Eight Years among Latin-Americans*, 44–45.

31. Ibid., 49.

32. Montejano, *Anglos and Mexicans*, 109, 159.

33. Amsa Kauffman, "Tuleta, Texas," *Gospel Herald*, April 24, 1941.

34. Amsa Kauffman, "Mexican Work in Texas," MBMC Thirty-Sixth Annual Meeting, 1942, box 2, file 2, IV-6-3, MCA. Historian Timothy Matovina argues that religious practices provide "liberating countervisions" that help Latinos deal with the harsh realities of everyday life. Matovina, *Guadalupe and Her Faithful*, 19.

35. Amsa Kauffman and Nona Kauffman, "Premont, TX," *Gospel Herald*, September 16, 1943.

36. Alfredo Tagle, interview by author, tape recording, Mission, TX, September 2003.

37. "Vahlsing's Interests Growth Parallels Mathis' Gain," *Mathis News*, October 17, 1952; Texas Almanac: City Population History, 1850–2000, www.texasalmanac.com/population.

38. Rodriguez, *The Tejano Diaspora*, 4. In this regard, the South Texas farming districts reflected the migratory stream of workers in the San Joaquin and Imperial valleys in California that followed the various harvest cycles across the state. See Weber, *Dark Sweat, White Gold*.

39. "Vahlsing's Interests Growth Parallels Mathis' Gain."

40. MBMC Forty-Fourth Annual Meeting, Goshen, IN, June 10–13, 1950, box 2, file 3, IV-6-3, MCA. The outreach to Mexicans in places like Tuleta and Normanna ceased by 1948.

41. Nelson Kauffman, "Workshop for Workers with Spanish-Speaking People," March 1956, box 1, Latin America Strategy 1956–1965 folder, IV-16-21.1, MCA.

42. Florence B. Lauver, "Sowing the Seed in Texas," *Gospel Herald*, May 6, 1947.

43. Elvin Snyder, "A Brief History of the Mennonite Witness in Mathis, Texas," MBMC Service Ministries Records, 1918–1997, box 16, IV-19-7, MCA.

44. Bush, *Two Kingdoms, Two Loyalties*, 165–166.

45. Toews, *Mennonites in American Society*, 182; Schlabach, *Gospel versus Gospel*, 228; P. Erb, *South Central Frontiers*, 424–428.

46. LULAC Council no. 1, file 21.8, Hector P. García Papers, Jeff Bell Library, Texas A&M University, Corpus Christi (hereafter cited as García Papers).

47. "School Investigation," LULAC Council no. 1, García Papers.

48. Diseases like rheumatic fever, tuberculosis, and diarrhea along with still-births and premature births were a major problem in Texas and occurred disproportionately among Mexicans. Richard M. Morehead, "Child Deaths High in Texas," *Dallas Morning News*, February 23, 1948; "Texas' Infant Death Rate at Lowest Level," *Dallas Morning News*, August 18, 1948; Gladwin Hill, "Peons in the West Lowering Culture," *New York Times*, May 27, 1951.

49. Barbara Miller, "Serving in VS in Mathis," 1962, MBMC Relief and Service VS, IV-19-7, MCA; Gladys Alderfer, RN, "Maternity Home Report," in "Blank Notes," Calvary Mennonite Articles 1948–1955, III-43-7, MCA; Dan Hess "Nursing Service Initiated," 1961, MBMC Relief and Service VS, IV-19-7, MCA. The maternity clinic was licensed by the director of the state Maternal and Child Health Division.

50. J. Weldon and Lorene Martin, "The Expanding Mission-Service Program at Mathis," MBMC Forty-Eighth Annual Meeting, Salem, Oregon, June 17–20, 1954, box 2, file 4, IV-6-3, MCA.

51. Perfecta De León, interview by author, tape recording, Mathis, TX, December 28, 2006.

52. Ibid.

53. "Blank Notes," *La Voz de Mathis* newsletter, Congregation Archives Collections, Calvary Mennonite Church, Mathis, TX, 1948–1955, III-43-7, MCA.

54. Rosario Vallejo, interview by author, tape recording, Mathis, TX, December 28, 2006.

55. Ibid.

56. P. De León, interview. See also Graybill and Arthur, "The Social Control of Women's Bodies in Two Mennonite Communities," 9–10.

57. Vallejo, interview.

58. Ted Chapa, interview by author, tape recording, San Antonio, TX, January 25, 2007.

59. "Group Living Guides for Mathis, Texas," MBMC Service Ministries Records 1918–1997, box 16, IV-19-7, MCA.

60. VS women especially were warned: "For a clear Christian testimony and in view of the differences in Latin and Anglo cultures it is advised that you refrain from activities with the opposite sex." Ibid.

61. *Global Anabaptist Mennonite Encyclopedia Online*, s.v. "Charismatic Movement," by Harold E. Bauman, accessed February 14, 2011, www.gameo.org/encyclopedia/contents/C4602ME.html.

62. Lupe De León, interview by author, tape recording, Mathis, TX, June 2007.

63. When the Vietnam War draft was initiated, Lupe De León, Samuel Hernandez, Ted Chapa, Israel De León, and Raul Hernandez registered as conscientious

objectors and participated in alternatives to military service. Ted served in a boy's home in Denver, Colorado. Israel, Lupe's younger brother, served in a nursing home in Maryland, and Raul worked in a hospital in Indiana. Lupe and Samuel served as church pastors. For an excellent review of Mexican American politics during Vietnam, see Oropeza, ¡Raza Sí! ¡Guerra No!

64. Bush, Two Kingdoms, Two Loyalties, 70−71; William Keeney, "Civilian Public Service and Related World War II Experiences," Henry Fast, CPS Camps, 1941−1944, MS 49, box 32, folder 320, MLA.

65. Holsinger, Serving Rural Puerto Rico, 84.

66. On Puerto Rican history see R. Fernandez, The Disenchanted Island; Briggs, Reproducing Empire; and Ayala and Bernabe, Puerto Rico in the American Century.

67. "Fondos Federales Montantes a la Suma de $119,493,416 Han Venido a Puerto Rico en Calidad de Asignaciones y Prestamos" (Federal Contributions Reaching the Sum of $119,493,416 Have Come to Puerto Rico in Loans and Financial Assignments), El Mundo, November 20, 1938, newspaper microfiche, Universidad de Puerto Rico, Mayagüez.

68. H. Claire Amstutz, "Report of Trip to Puerto Rico," MBMC Service Ministries Records 1918−1997, Puerto Rico Executive Committee Meeting folder, IV-19-7, MCA.

69. This work was carried out by what became the Mennonite Relief and Service Committee administered by the MBMC. Global Anabaptist Mennonite Encyclopedia Online, s.v. "Puerto Rico," by Justus G. Holsinger and David W. Powell, November 2010, accessed October 6, 2012, www.gameo.org/encyclopedia/contents/P853.html.

70. Governor Luis Muñoz Marín to local CPS director John E. Lehman, May 11, 1954, Puerto Rico Mennonite Conference, José Ortíz Collection, box 1, item 92-47, II-20, MCA.

71. José Ortíz, interview by author, tape recording, April 17, 2007, Goshen, IN.

72. Ibid.

73. Ibid.

74. Kathryn S. Troyer, "Women's Work at Pulguillas," MBMC Forty-Fourth Annual Meeting, Goshen, IN, June 10−13, 1950, box 2, file 3, IV-6-3, MCA.

75. Marjorie Shantz, "Work among the Women at La Plata and Rabanal." MBMC Forty-Fourth Annual Meeting, Goshen, IN, June 10−13, 1950, box 2, file 3, IV-6-3, MCA.

76. Ibid.

77. John Driver, "Looking Ahead in Puerto Rico," MBMC Forty-Eighth Annual, Salem, OR, June 17−20, 1954, box 2, file 4, IV-6-3, MCA.

78. Lester T. Hershey, "Puerto Rico," MBMC Fifty-Fifth Annual Meeting, 1961, box 2, file 4, IV-6-3, MCA.

79. "Meet Esteban Rivera," *Rio La Plata* newsletter, June 1955, José Ortíz Collection, Puerto Rican Mennonite Conference, item 92-47, II-20, MCA; Wilbur Nachtigall, "The Church in Palo Hincado and La Cuchilla," Forty-Eighth Annual Meeting of the MBMC, Salem, Oregon, June 17–20, 1954, box 2, file 4, IV-6-3, MCA.

80. Lester T. Hershey, "Puerto Rico," MBMC Fifty-Fifth Annual Meeting, 1961, box 3, file 1, IV-6-3, MCA; *Global Anabaptist Mennonite Encyclopedia Online*, s.v. "Puerto Rico," by Justus G. Holsinger and David W. Powell, accessed October 6, 2012, www.gameo.org/encyclopedia/contents/P853.html.

81. J. Gonzalez, *Harvest of Empire*, 81; Stevens Arroyo and Díaz-Ramírez, "Puerto Ricans in the United States," 200–201. See also L. Fernandez, *Brown in the Windy City*; L. Thomas, *Puerto Rican Citizen*.

82. Lester Hershey, "Into the Future," MBMC Forty-Seventh Annual Meeting, 1953, box 2, file 4, IV-6-3, MCA.

83. Sánchez Korrol, *From Colonia to Community*, 215. But with the monopolization of agriculture on the island, Operation Bootstrap only served to displace many agrarian families, forcing them to make their way north in search of more stable employment opportunities in the 1950s. C. Rodriguez, "Puerto Rican Studies."

84. Rivera, "Las Bases Sociales de la Transformación Ideológica del Partido Popular Democrático en la Década del Cuarenta."

85. Neftali Torres, interview with author, tape recording, Camuy, Puerto Rico, June 18, 2007.

86. L. Thomas, *Puerto Rican Citizen*, 142–144.

87. Sánchez Korrol, *From Colonia to Community*; Dávila, *Barrio Dreams*.

88. Díaz-Stevens, *Oxcart Catholicism on Fifth Avenue*.

89. Levitt, *The Transnational Villagers*, 160.

90. Among the first Puerto Ricans baptized into the Mennonite Church in New York City were Liduvina and Alvado Lopez and their daughter Nelsa, Ada and Angel Rodriguez and their son Edgar, Aida and Jose Luis Fernandez, David Colon, Desiderio and Silita Colon, and Juaquina Lopez. Gladys Widmer, "La Historia de la Primera Iglesia Evangélica Menonita de Brooklyn," Hist. MS, 1-675, Gladys Widmer Collection, Brooklyn, New York, 1957, MCA.

91. Espinosa describes "Nuyorican religion" as "an indigenous expression of Puerto Rican religiosity articulated by and for the population in the New York City *barrio*." See Espinosa, "Borderland Religion," 217.

92. P. Thomas, *Savior, Savior, Hold My Hand*, 325–327.

93. The first Spanish-speaking congregation in Manhattan was established in 1912, but most of the congregations in Manhattan were established between 1941 and 1947. "The Protestant Church and Puerto Ricans in New York City," a report conducted by the Pathfinding Service and the New York City Mission Society

under the auspices of the Protestant Council of the City of New York, New York District 1965–1967 file, Home Missions 1956–1964 drawer, Eastern Mennonite Missions Archives, Salunga, PA.

94. Fitzpatrick, *Puerto Rican Americans*, 87.

95. N. Torres, interview; Stevens Arroyo, "From Barrios to Barricades," 310; León, "Somos un Cuerpo en Cristo."

96. N. Torres, interview.

97. The story of Nicky Cruz looms large in Latino churches. Cruz's story emerged in a Puerto Rican cultural context, and his story of renewal and conversion has attracted Latino evangelicals since the 1970s. *The Cross and the Switchblade* was especially popular among Latino churches when it was released in 1970. See also Cruz, *Run, Baby, Run*.

98. N. Torres, interview.

99. Ibid.

100. Ibid.

Chapter 2. Missionary Motives

Epigraph. Delton Franz, "The Mennonite Church and the Race Revolution," CESR, 1939–1973, box 7, Race Meetings file, I-3-7, MCA.

1. Vincent Harding, "Decade of Crisis: 1954–1964," Conference on Race Relations, Atlanta, February 25–26, 1964, CESR, box 7, Race Conference file, I-3-7, MCA.

2. Ibid.

3. Shearer, *Daily Demonstrators*, 121–126.

4. Toews, *Mennonites in American Society*, 185–197.

5. Shearer, *Daily Demonstrators*, 49–50; Falcón, *The Hispanic Mennonite Church in North America*, 182–186; Lester T. Hershey, "Puerto Rico," Fifty-Fifth MBMC Annual Meeting, 1961, box 5, file 2, IV-6-3, MCA; González-López, *Puerto Rico en Fotos*.

6. Hostetler argued that the 1950s brought on an "awakening" among Mennonites. See Hostetler, *American Mennonites and Protestant Movements*, 273.

7. Toews, *Mennonites in American Society*, 182–183.

8. Ahlstrom, *A Religious History of the American People*, 951; Guy Hersheberger, "The Church Facing the Race Crisis," Board of Christian Service, December 4, 1963, CESR, box 5, Race Relations Meetings file, I-3-7, MCA.

9. Dudziak, *Cold War Civil Rights*; Plummer, *Window on Freedom*; Hulsether, *Religion, Culture, and Politics in the Twentieth-Century United States*, 12–13, 17.

10. Chappell, *A Stone of Hope*, 147.

11. Ibid., 107.

12. *Global Anabaptist Mennonite Encyclopedia Online* s.v. "The Anabaptist Vision," by Harold S. Bender, accessed April 15, 2011, www.gameo.org/encyclopedia/con tents/A534.html.

13. Of the various groups involved, the MCC "operated sixty-five camps and units . . . with a total of 5,830 men." See Goossen, *Women against the Good War*, 26.

14. Since its inception in the 1920s, the MCC has carried this out on a global scale. Its volunteers have provided relief and assistance in countries across the Middle East, Europe, and Asia.

15. Toews, *Mennonites in American Society*, 181−182.

16. James C. Juhnke, "George R. Brunk Tent Revival Sermon," *Mennonite Life*, September 2002; Maurice E. Lehman, "The Lancaster Revival," *Gospel Herald*, September 1951.

17. Paul M. Lederach, "Revival in Franconia," *Gospel Herald*, September 1951.

18. Ibid.

19. Jason Stevens writes, "The New Evangelicals rose to prominence during a decade when liberals felt as if the legacy of the Roosevelt administration was under siege and when Christian anti-communist groups more extreme than the New Evangelicals, such as the John Birch society, were helping mobilize a right wing counter-reaction to the liberalism of the postwar consensus." Stevens, *God-Fearing and Free*, 66.

20. Marsden, *Fundamentalism and American Culture*, 233. Mennonite theologian Wilbert Shenk wrote, "Admittingly, Mennonite missions had followed the typical Protestant interpretation of the gospel in their missionary witness, and heretofore the historical Anabaptist-Mennonite understanding of the gospel of peace had played no significant role in missionary thinking and practice." Shenk, *By Faith They Went Out*, 80.

21. See Hostetler, *American Mennonites and Protestant Movements*.

22. *Global Anabaptist Mennonite Encyclopedia Online*, "Mennonite Board of Missions (Mennonite Church)," by Levi C. Hartzler, accessed March 7, 2011, http://www.gameo.org/encyclopedia/contents/M463734.html.

23. Bush, *Two Kingdoms, Two Loyalties*, 136−137.

24. Graybill, "Finding My Place as a Lady Missionary," 154; Schlabach, *Gospel versus Gospel*, 13.

25. Bush, *Two Kingdoms, Two Loyalties*, 136−146. See also Peachey, *The Church in the City*, 74−75.

26. Lee Lowry, "Symbolic of Brotherhood," *Happenings*, June 1973, MMC Collection 1969−1974, box 2, file 5, IV-21, MCA.

27. Seferina De León, interview by author, tape recording, Goshen, IN, April 17, 2007.

28. Jesus "Chuy" Navarro, interview by author, tape recording, Robstown, TX,

January 21, 2007; Lupe De León, "VS in South Texas," *Gospel Herald*, November 16, 1971.

29. King, "Seeking a Global Vision."

30. Hammond, "In Search of a Protestant Twentieth Century," 281–294; According to Gallup polls, church attendance was especially high in 1955 and 1958. See Ellwood, *The Fifties Spiritual Marketplace*, 1; and Ahlstrom, *A Religious History of the American People*, 953.

31. Kurashige, *The Shifting Grounds of Race*, 5; Gutiérrez, *Walls and Mirrors*, 118–178; Stevens Arroyo and Díaz-Stevens, "Puerto Ricans in the United States"; C. Rodriguez, "Puerto Rican Studies"; Sánchez Korrol, *From Colonia to Community*, 215.

32. T. K. Hershey, "Mexican Border Trip," *Gospel Herald*, April 16, 1936.

33. Loewen and Nolt, *Through Fire and Water*, 294; Shenk, *By Faith They Went Out*, 58, 79.

34. Shearer, *Daily Demonstrators*, 38.

35. Irvin B. Horst, "Mennonites and the Race Question," *Gospel Herald*, July 13, 1945.

36. This important statement was the first made by the Mennonite Church on the issue of race relations. While not without its faults, it nonetheless opened the door to begin talking about racism in society and the church. "The Way of Christian Love in Race Relations," Mennonite General Conference minutes, Reports 1890–1971, box 6, file 6, I-1-1. MCA. This statement was followed by the General Conference Mennonites, who in 1959 drafted their own statement against racism. In 1960, the Lancaster Conference bishops drafted their own statement. See Shearer, *Daily Demonstrators*, 18.

37. Hershberger, "The Way of Christian Love in Race Relations."

38. For a complete listing of Mennonite colleges and conferences that produced statements denouncing segregation and racism, see Shearer, "A Pure Fellowship."

39. Shearer, *Daily Demonstrators*, x–xi; Vincent Harding, "The Task of the Mennonite Church in Establishing Racial Unity," Christ, the Mennonite Churches, and Race Conference, Woodlawn Mennonite Church, Chicago, April 17–19, 1959, CESR 1939–1971, box 5, I-3-7, MCA.

40. "Facts, Considerations, and Membership of Negroes in the Mennonite Church," compiled by Lee Roy Bechler for the Negro Evangelism Committee, 1955, box 5, file 5, I-3-7. MCA.

41. Harding, "The Task of the Mennonite Church in Establishing Racial Unity."

42. Omi and Winant, *Racial Formation in the United States*, 99.

43. Shearer, *Daily Demonstrators*, 101.

44. Shearer's chapter on Vincent Harding in his book *Daily Demonstrators* (98–129) captures white Mennonites' ambivalence about how to engage civil rights.

45. Harding, "The Task of the Mennonite Church in Establishing Racial Unity."

46. Dyck, "Racial Conference," Prairie Street Mennonite Church, Elkhart, IN, September 14, 1963. CESR 1939–1971, box 5, Elkhart Meeting file, 1963, I-3-7, MCA.

47. Here Perry Bush's analysis of the "quiet in the land" is particularly helpful. Bush writes, "This was a self-perception inherited directly from their Anabaptist ancestors, 'the non-complaining people of the land,' summarized one Mennonite writer, 'the people who bore their suffering patiently, faced their persecution without complaint, and went to their death quietly.... It was an ideal that their American descendants took very much to heart.... For centuries, Mennonite two-kingdom theology reinforced their sociocultural isolation by branding cultural incursions and political activism as 'worldly' and sinful. Like good children, they were seen but not heard. This was the primary identity that nonresistance had forged." Bush, *Two Kingdoms, Two Loyalties*, 9, 201.

48. Comment from an unnamed person during Guy Hershberger's trip to Tennessee. Hershberger, "Mennonites and the Current Race Issue," Mennonite Churches, July–August 1963, CESR 1939–1971, box 5, I-3-7, MCA.

49. Shearer, *Daily Demonstrators*, 13.

50. Bush, *Two Kingdoms, Two Loyalties*, 217; Shearer, *Daily Demonstrators*, 22.

51. Melvin Gingerich, "The Color Line," *Gospel Herald*, February 15, 1949.

52. Guy F. Hershberger, "Islands of Sanity," *Gospel Herald*, March 25, 1952.

53. Gingerich, "The Color Line."

54. L. C. Hartzler, "Color-Blind Christians," *Gospel Herald*, January 12, 1954.

55. Chappell, *A Stone of Hope*, 107–108. The southern Presbyterians and the Southern Baptist Convention had passed resolutions against segregation before 1954. See also Ed Cony, "More Southern Pastors Plead for Moderation," *Wall Street Journal*, February 14, 1958; and "Southern Churches Urge Mixing," *Citizens Council*, May 1958.

56. Robert J. McCracken, "Actions Always Speak Louder Than Words," *Gospel Herald*, February 13, 1962.

57. Chappell, *A Stone of Hope*, 107.

58. The main examples include Toews, *Mennonites in American Society*; Bush, *Two Kingdoms, Two Loyalties*; and Hostetler, *American Mennonites and Protestant Movements*.

59. Bush, *Two Kingdoms, Two Loyalties*, 212; Toews, *Mennonites in American Society*, 256–257. Toews cited King's "theology and strategy of nonviolence" that most appealed to Mennonites and prompted them to become more active in the civil rights movement. But even as Mennonite leaders appreciated King's stance on nonviolence, his theological understanding of coercive nonviolence and his associations with liberal theology worried some Mennonites.

60. Bush, *Two Kingdoms, Two Loyalties*, 210.

61. For an excellent analysis of the long relationship between Anabaptism and evangelicalism, see Burkholder and Cramer, *The Activist Impulse*, 2–3.

62. J. D. Graber, "Race Relations in World Evangelism," Christ, the Mennonite Churches, and Race Conference, Woodlawn Mennonite Church, Chicago, April 17–19, 1959, CESR 1939–1971, box 5, I-3-7, MCA.

63. Ibid. Here Graber was citing a story originally shared by J. B. Toews of the Mennonite Brethren mission board.

64. Schultz, "Religion as Identity in Postwar America"; Prothero, *American Jesus*, 117.

65. The General Conference and (Old) Mennonite Church groups also issued statements in 1962 and 1961 that offered a positive view of communism. See Thiessen, "Communism and Labor Unions."

66. Graber, "Race Relations in World Evangelism," 44.

67. Shearer, *Daily Demonstrators*, 13.

68. Guy F. Hershberger served as the secretary of economic and social concerns of the Mennonite Church and was commissioned by the MCC Peace Section.

69. Hershberger, "Mennonites and the Current Race Issue."

70. Norman Kraus, Racial Conference, Prairie Street Mennonite Church, Elkhart, IN, September 14, 1963, box 2, Racial Conference 1963–1969 file, IV-16-21, MCA.

71. Nelson Kauffman to Ernest Bennett, April 14, 1965, box 1, file 3, I-6-5, MCA.

72. Thirty-Seventh MBMC Annual Meeting, Mission Board Report, 1943, box 4, file 7, IV-6-3, MCA.

73. Martin G. Brumbaugh, reconstruction unit newsletter, "What's It Like Down There," Albert M. Gaeddert Collection, MS 50, box 9, MLA.

74. C. Rodriguez, "Puerto Ricans: Between Black and White"; Ginorio, "A Comparison of Puerto Ricans in New York with Native Puerto Ricans and Native Americans on Two Measures of Acculturation"; "Report: NYC Survey Invest.," New York District 1965–1967 file, Home Missions 1956–1964 drawer, Eastern Mennonite Missions Archives, Salunga, PA.

75. Gutiérrez, "Demography and the Shifting Boundaries of 'Community,'" 1.

76. MMC minutes, Executive Committee, December 1970, MMC Minutes 1968–1974, IV-21, MCA. See Powell, "Materials for Home Missions—Minority Ministries Merger Commission," MBM Executive Office, MMC 1970–1973 file, IV-7-6, MCA.

77. Ted Chapa, interview by author, tape recording, San Antonio, TX, January 25, 2007.

78. "Events as Interpreted by John Ventura," John Ventura file, box 2, file 2, IV-16-21, MCA.

79. Ibid.

80. Chapa, interview; John Powell, "Urban Racial Council: Report to Mission Board," MMC Minutes 1968–1974, box 1, file 2, IV-21, MCA.

81. The idea for the URC actually arose at the race conference in Kidron, Ohio (1968). In July 1968, African American leaders gathered in Cleveland to settle final details in preparation for the race conference in Chicago. See John H. Mosemann, "Why an Urban-Racial Council," MBM MMC, URC Materials 1969, IV-21-1, MCA.

82. URC minutes, Chicago, October 4–5, 1968, Race Meetings file, I-3-7, MCA.

83. Urban Racial Council minutes, Chicago, October 4–5, 1968, box 1, file 3, I-6-5, MCA.

84. Ibid.

85. Ogbar, *Black Power*, 192–193; See also "Working in the Inner City 1968," Cleveland, OH, MMC Minutes 1968–1974, box 1, file 3, I-6-5, MCA.

86. Curtis Burrell, "The Church and Black Militancy," URC meeting, Chicago, October 4–5, 1968, Race Meetings file, I-3-7, MCA.

87. Spanish-Speaking Churches Caucus, Chicago, December 5–6, 1969, box 1, Mennonite Church file, Office of Latin Concerns 1969–1972, I-6-6, MCA.

88. Hubert Brown, interview by author, tape recording, Newton, KS, June 2007.

89. Curtis Burrell, "The Church and Black Militancy," URC meeting, Chicago, October 4–5, 1968, Race Meetings file, I-3-7, MCA.

90. Harding, "The Task of the Mennonite Church in Establishing Racial Unity." See also Shearer, "Moving beyond Charisma in Civil Rights Scholarship."

91. Hoffnung-Garskof, *A Tale of Two Cities*, 69, 90.

92. Gutiérrez, "Demography and the Shifting Boundaries of 'Community,'" 1–2.

93. Newspaper headline, *Happenings*, June 1973, MMC Collection 1969–1974, box 2, file 5, IV-21, MCA.

Chapter 3. The Fight over Money

Epigraph. "Recommended Reorganization of the Urban Racial Council," letter to Executive Committee of the URC, January 9, 1970, MMC, Home Missions Task Force, General Board, box 1, file 1, I-6-5, MCA.

1. Known as the "largest street gang in the United States," the Black P. Stone Nation, originally known as the Blackstone Rangers, had a complicated history in

Chicago. See Jeffrey Ogbar, *Black Power*, 121–122. Organized as a street gang some-time around 1962, the Blackstone Rangers gained credibility when, in collabora-tion with the Woodlawn Organization, they received funding from the Office of Economic Opportunity under President Lyndon Johnson's Great Society plan to al-leviate poverty. The grant provided funds for the Woodlawn Organization to work with street gangs to establish employment training programs. James Alan McPher-son, "Chicago's Blackstone Rangers," *Atlantic*, May 1969, accessed July 28, 2008, http://www.theatlantic.com/doc/196905/blackstone-rangers/2.

2. The MMC later provided funding to reopen the day care center at Bethel Mennonite. John Powell, Compassion Fund Report, July 1969–July 1971, Gen-eral Board Files, box 1, file 3, MMC, 1971–1973, I-6-5, MCA.

3. *Global Anabaptist Mennonite Encyclopedia Online*, s.v. "Yoder (Ioder, Joder, Jod-ter, Jotter, Yoeder, Yother, Yothers, Yotter)," by Melvin Gingerich, Melvin, accessed May 26, 2011, www.gameo.org/encyclopedia/contents/Y644ME.html.

4. Lupe De León, "VS in South Texas," *Gospel Herald*, November 16, 1971.

5. Powell, "Recommended Reorganization of the Urban Racial Council," box 1, file 1, Mennonite Church General Board, 1971–1995, I-6-5, MCA.

6. According to historian Gastón Espinosa, the frustration with organized reli-gion in the 1960s and 1970s coupled with a growing interest in humanistic and sec-ular thought, such as Marxism, kept scholars focused on political areas of research that rarely acknowledged the role of the church. See Espinosa, *Latino Religions and Civic Activism in the United States*, 3.

7. Lara-Braud, "The Status of Religion among Mexican Americans," 91. Recent work by Latina and Latino scholars on religion during the civil rights movement includes Medina, *Las Hermanas*; Barton, "¡Ya Basta!"; M. García, *Católicos*; R. Mar-tínez, *PADRES*; Watt, *Farm Workers and the Churches*; Espinosa, Elizondo, and Mi-randa, *Latino Civic Activism and Religion in the United States*.

8. See note 7. In general, such studies have focused on the influence of libera-tion theology in Latin America. Latin American religion played a significant role in shaping Latino religious involvement in the civil rights movement. While theolo-gians have produced important works on the intersections of black and brown the-ology, historians for the most part have ignored the everyday engagement of Latinos with black religion in the United States.

9. A few examples include Toews, *Mennonites in American Society*; Bush, *Two Kingdoms, Two Loyalties*; Shearer, *Daily Demonstrators*.

10. "Working in the Inner-City, 1968," Cleveland, MMC minutes 1968–1974, box 1, file 2, IV-21, MCA.

11. URC meeting minutes, October 4, 1968, MMC Minutes 1968–1974, box 1, file 2, IV-21. MCA; MMC Executive Committee minutes, Elkhart, IN, Decem-ber 17–18, 1970, MMC Minutes 1968–1974, box 1, file 2, IV-21, MCA.

12. Clayson, *Freedom Is Not Enough*, 30–32.

13. Hall, "The Long Civil Rights Movement and the Political Uses of the Past"; Clayson, *Freedom Is Not Enough*, 157; Ashmore, *Carry It On*; Orleck and Hazirjian, *The War on Poverty*.

14. Mantler, "Black, Brown, and Poor," 88.

15. Ibid., 68.

16. James Forman, "Black Manifesto," presentation to National Black Economic Development Conference, Detroit, April 26, 1969, box 3, file 71, GC Voluntary Service, series 11, Gulfport VS Unit, VII.R, MLA.

17. Ibid.

18. Soja, *Thirdspace*. See also L. Pulido, *Black, Brown, Yellow, and Left*, 95.

19. Frye, "The Black Manifesto and the Tactic of Objectification"; Dye, "The Black Manifesto for Reparations in Detroit."

20. Dye, "The Black Manifesto for Reparations in Detroit," 58.

21. John Powell, interview by author, tape recording, Ypsilanti, MI, April 26, 2007.

22. Eleanor High to Beulah Kauffman, September 8, 1969, Beulah Kauffman Collection, Women's Concerns 1969–1971, box 1, file 58, Voluntary Service Requests, IV-20-23.1, MCA.

23. Jacob E. Geyer, "Renewing a Tradition of Radicalism," unpublished paper, Goshen College, 1978, 1, Mennonite Historical Library, Goshen College, Goshen, IN.

24. John Powell, talk presented at Mennonite Church biennial assembly in Turner, OR, 1969, Minority Ministries Home Missions Task Force, General Board Files, box 3, file 40, I-6-5, MCA.

25. Powell, interview.

26. Ibid.

27. John Powell, "Report on Compassion Fund, 1969–70," box 3, II-14-18, MCA.

28. MMC Executive Committee minutes, Chicago, March 8, 1971, MMC Minutes 1968–1974, box 1, file 2, IV-21, MCA. According to the minutes, "The one question which emerged was 'should the Latin Council elect its members to the Executive Committee of MMC rather than the total membership?'"

29. Dan Miller to John Powell, July 14, 1969, Spanish Concilio 1969–1975 file, IV-16-21, MCA.

30. I use the Spanish word *Concilio* instead of the English "Council" at the request of Latino leaders themselves who wanted it to remain *Concilio* to acknowledge the Spanish-language roots of the group.

31. MMC Executive Committee minutes, Elkhart, IN, January 9–10, 1970, General Board, box 1, MMC Minutes file, I-6-5, MCA.

32. Spanish-Speaking Churches Caucus minutes, Chicago, December 1969, Mennonite Church Office of Latin Concerns Minutes 1969–1972, I-6-6, MCA; John Powell, Executive Committee Urban Racial Council, January 2, 1970, General Board Files, Minority Ministries / Home Missions file, I-6-5, MCA.

33. Joel Kauffman, "Lupe De León: From Kool-Aid to the Big House," *Sent: A Magazine about People in Mission*, Fall 1978, 2–4.

34. For the emerging politics of Mexican American youth in the 1960s, see Muñoz, *Youth, Identity, Power*.

35. Lupe De León, interview by author, tape recording, Mathis, TX, 27 June 2007.

36. Ibid.

37. Oropeza, *¡Raza Sí! ¡Guerra No!*, 49.

38. Ibid., 79.

39. The term "Chicano" was used by young Mexican Americans in the 1960s as a way to identify with their Mexican and indigenous heritage, as a form of self-assertion, and as a symbolic act to show the development of a raised political consciousness. See Gutiérrez, *Walls and Mirrors*, 184.

40. John Lehman, "Administrative Visit to South Texas," October 31, 1966, MBMC Service Ministries Records, 1918–1997, Relief and Service, IV-19-7, MCA.

41. Howard Zehr to John Lehman, April 27, 1966, MBMC Service Ministries Records, 1918–1997, Relief and Service, IV-19-7, MCA.

42. MMC Executive Committee minutes, Chicago, March 8, 1971, MMC Minutes 1968–1974, box 1, IV-21, MCA.

43. Oropeza, *¡Raza Sí! ¡Guerra No!*, 95.

44. There was also some hope that the Concilio would better relate to other Latino groups that did not participate with the MMC, especially groups in Pennsylvania and New York. MMC Executive Committee minutes, Eureka, IL, July 3, 1971, General Board Files, MMC Minutes file, I-6-5, MCA.

45. Lupe De León, "VS in South Texas."

46. John Powell, Compassion Fund Report, July 1969–July 1971, General Board Files, MMC 1971–1973, box 3, file 38, I-6-5, MCA. For a complete record of Compassion Fund disbursements, see appendix 2 of Hinojosa, "Making Noise among the 'Quiet in the Land.'"

47. Clayson, *Freedom Is Not Enough*, 139.

48. Ibid., 137.

49. John Powell, "The Compassion Fund Is . . ." *Gospel Herald*, March 24, 1970.

50. "Minority Ministries Fund Disbursement, 1973." General Board Files, Minority Ministries Home Missions Task Force, box 3, file 40, I-6-5, MCA.

51. Carson, *In Struggle*, 295.

52. Shearer, *Daily Demonstrators*, 190–220.

53. Ruperto Gudea Jr., "MMC's Pluses Outweigh Minuses," *Happenings*, November 19, 1971.

54. Warner Jackson, "Multiplied Disciples in the Mennonite Church," *Gospel Herald*, March 14, 1972.

55. With this in mind, MMC leaders sought to become a broader organization that not only addressed black and brown concerns but was inclusive of Native Americans and other minority groups, as well as poor whites. The idea never materialized, but it did open the door to forging a closer funding relationship with the church without being perceived as narrow-minded cultural nationalists. Tony Brown, "Unity Essential For Liberation," *Happenings*, November 19, 1971.

56. Tomás Chávez, "La Nueva Raza," *Happenings*, November 19, 1971, MMC Collection, 1969–1974, box 2, file 5, IV-21, MCA.

57. Also important to note here is that a member of the Brown Berets of Detroit, Rolando Garcia, attended the conference in Detroit. "The conference welcomed his presence and raised an offering in support of the Chicano cause." *Happenings*, November 19, 1971.

58. Espinosa, "History and Theory in the Study of Mexican American Religions," 76–77.

59. Barton, "¡Ya Basta!," 127.

60. "Excerpts from the Speech," *Happenings*, November 19, 1971.

61. L. De León, interview.

62. John Powell to Chuy Navarro, March 12, 1973, box 2, MMC file, II-14-18, MCA. By this time the MBMC had changed its name to Mennonite Board of Missions.

63. Boyd Nelson, "Minority Ministries on the Move," February 15, 1972, box 5, file 142, MMC 1972, MLA.VII.C, MLA.

64. "Random Responses Regarding Detroit Meeting," *Happenings*, November 19, 1971.

65. MMC Report of Annual Meeting in Detroit, 1971, John Powell Collection, box 2, file 1, IV-21-4, MCA.

66. "A Preface to the Compassion Fund Report," in MMC Compassion Fund 1969–1973, IV-21-4, MCA.

67. L. De León, interview.

68. Powell, interview.

69. Dan Shenk, "Report on MMC Gathering in Detroit," *Happenings*, November 19, 1971.

Chapter 4. "Jesus Christ Made a Macho Outta Me!"

Epigraph. Lupe De León to his close friend Neftali Torres. Lupe De León, interview by author, tape recording, Mathis, TX, June 27, 2007.

1. "The Minority What?," MMC brochure, MMC Minutes 1968−1974, IV-21, MCA.

2. Specific numbers are hard to determine because the Mennonite Church did not officially count churches as Latino or African American until the 1983 Yearbook. In a June 28, 1972, *Happenings* article Art Smoker claimed that minority congregations made up about 6 percent of the membership of the Mennonite Church. José Ortiz provided some leads when he indicated that Latinos made up 184 members in 1955, 498 in 1970, and 1,583 in 1981. Ortiz, "The Spirit of Ebenezer," Mennonite Yearbook, 1982, 10; John Powell, "Minority Ministries Council Program Projections, January 1974−1976," letter to Board of Directors of MBM, January 9, 1973, MMC file, IV-7-6, MCA; Dan Shenk, "Minorities Seek Closer Ties with Total Mennonite Church," *Happenings*, December 5, 1972.

3. The plan was first introduced as a "Soul and Spirit" Convention for Minority Youth in the Mennonite Church by John Powell in September 1970. "Projections for 'Soul and Spirit' Convention for Minority Youth in the Mennonite Church," September 24, 1970, Cross-Cultural Convention '72 Planning Meeting minutes, July 12−13, 1971, Cross-Cultural Convention '72 file, IV-21-4, MCA.

4. The official count at the CCYC was 246 youth and 79 counselors and staff. "Cross Cultural Youth Convention 1972," *Gospel Herald*, September 12, 1972; Hubert Brown, "Let's Get behind the Cross-Cultural Youth Convention," *Happenings*, June 28, 1972, MCA.

5. Lipsitz, "The Struggle for Hegemony," 148.

6. Omi and Winant, *Racial Formation in the United States*, 99.

7. Ted Chapa, interview by author, tape recording, San Antonio, TX, January 25, 2007.

8. Ibid.

9. Cross-Cultural Convention '72 Planning Meeting minutes, Bethesda Mennonite Church, St. Louis, MO, July 12−13, 1971, John Powell Collection, Cross-Cultural Convention '72 file, IV-21−4, MCA. Convention planners included Verbena Brown, Ted Chapa, Larry Cruz, Gene Norris, Helen Robinson, Sis-Obed Torres, Al Williams, John Powell, Lupe De León, and Art Smoker.

10. Powell, "Projections for 'Soul and Spirit' Convention for Minority Youth in the Mennonite Church."

11. Warner Jackson first reported the threat to the youth on the first day of the convention. After that, however, it does not seem to have surfaced again. MMC, Warner Jackson, box 2, Information Services Audiovisuals, IV-5-5, MCA.

12. Cross-Cultural '72 Planning Meeting minutes, November 19−20, 1971, John Powell Collection, Cross-Cultural Convention '72 file, IV-21-4, MCA.

13. Ibid.

14. "Cross-Cultural Youth Convention 1972," *Gospel Herald*, September 12, 1972. The choirs were Burnside Community Mennonite Church Choir, Columbus, OH; Canaan Baptist Church Choir, Elkhart, IN; Lawndale Mennonite Church Choir, Chicago; and Rehoboth Mennonite Fellowship Choir, Saint Anne, IL.

15. John Powell, sermon at CCYC, 1972, Information Services Audiovisuals, box 13, Friday morning, part 2, IV-10-5, MCA.

16. Michael T. Kaufman, "Puerto Rican Group Seizes Church in East Harlem in Demand for Space," *New York Times*, December 29, 1969.

17. Enck-Wanzer, "Decolonizing Imaginaries," 2. For many young Puerto Ricans, the Young Lords Party was one of the most visible examples of the rising ethnic nationalism of the late 1960s.

18. "Interview with Yoruba, Minister of Information, Young Lords Organization," in Enck-Wanzer, *The Young Lords*, 203.

19. Abramson, "The People's Church Offensive," in *Palante*, 1971; Enck-Wanzer, *The Young Lords*, 32, 206.

20. Enck-Wanzer, "Decolonizing Imaginaries," 7.

21. Michael T. Kauffman, "8 Hurt, 14 Seized in a Church Clash," *New York Times*, December 8, 1969. Accessed October 2009 in ProQuest Historical Newspapers, *New York Times* (1851−2007), 53.

22. Kauffman, "Puerto Rican Group Seizes Church in East Harlem in Demand for Space." Church members asked that the police not intercede on their behalf; instead, the church filed an injunction to bar the group from further disruptions of its services.

23. Neftali Torres, interview by author, tape recording, Camuy, Puerto Rico, June 18, 2007.

24. "Young Lords Mar Services, Including East Harlem's," *New York Times*, January 12, 1970.

25. N. Torres, interview.

26. Ideological tensions between the church and the Young Lords made any sense of compromise difficult. In addition, pastor Humberto Carranza "was an anti-Castro Cuban exile[,] whereas the Young Lords were pro-Castro." Enck-Wanzer, "Decolonizing Imaginaries," 8.

27. Neftali Torres, talk at Cross-Cultural Theological Consultation, transcribed from tape recording, 1973, MBM Home Missions, box 1, file 8, IV-16-21, MCA.

28. Neftali Torres, sermon at CCYC, 1972, tape recording, Information Services Audiovisuals, box 13, Monday evening—Torres and Music, IV-10-5, MCA.

29. Ibid.

30. Ibid.

31. Flores, "The Diaspora Strikes Back," 213.

32. The scholarship on race and Puerto Rican identity argues that historically Puerto Rican migrants have emphasized their nationality as their race and therefore they consider their race Puerto Rican. See Landale and Oropesa, "White, Black, or Puerto Rican?," 234.

33. C. Rodriguez, "Puerto Rican Studies," 446.

34. Duany, "Nation and Migration," 58.

35. Torres, "Political Radicalism in the Diaspora," 3.

36. For an excellent treatment of this dilemma see L. Thomas, *Puerto Rican Citizen*, 221–244.

37. A. Torres, "Political Radicalism in the Diaspora," 13.

38. See Lorrin Thomas's discussion of the "divided nation" theory in *Puerto Rican Citizen*, 235.

39. Neftali Torres, talk at Cross-Cultural Theological Consultation, transcribed from tape recording, 1973, MBM Home Missions, box 1, file 8, IV-16-21, MCA.

40. Neftali Torres, sermon at CCYC, 1972.

41. Neftali Torres, talk at Cross-Cultural Theological Consultation, 1973, MCA.

42. Cultural critic Paul Gilroy asserts that "gender is the modality in which race is lived." Gilroy, *The Black Atlantic*, 85.

43. Lupe De León, speech at CCYC, 1972, tape recording, Information Services Audiovisuals, box 13, Tuesday and Wednesday evening—music and De León, IV-10-5, MCA.

44. L. De León, interview.

45. Brusco, *The Reformation of Machismo.*

46. Bebout, *Mythohistorical Interventions*, 18, 31. Cultural critic José Limón makes a similar argument when he asserts that Americo Paredes's book *With His Pistol in His Hand* became "like a *corrido* (ballad) and its [the book's] hero for a new generation of Chicano social activists of the sixties." Limón, *Dancing with the Devil*, 82.

47. Blackwell, *¡Chicana Power!*, 66. See also her discussion of "retrofitted memory," 2.

48. "Chicanismo," according to García, represented a political and cultural ideology that served to define Chicanos' sense of community, brotherhood, and activism during the 1960s and 1970s. García, *Chicanismo.*

49. Nieto, "The Chicano Movement and the Churches in the United States," 40.

50. De León, talk at CCYC.

51. Sumner, "Mexican American Minority Churches, USA," 228.

52. Grebler, Moore, and Guzman, "The Urban Mexican-American Parish," 253.

53. L. De León, interview. For an excellent discussion of how Chicano movement leaders criticized the church as an "oppressive institution," see Treviño, *The Church in the Barrio*, 176–205.

54. De León, speech to CCYC.

55. Religious leaders have often sought to protect Christianity from overt feminization. From the early twentieth century evangelist, Billy Sunday, who often prayed, "Lord save us . . . from effeminate, sissified, three-caret Christianity," to the Promise Keepers movement at the end of the twentieth century, gender and religion have always been linked. See Prothero, *American Jesus*, 94; Brusco, *The Reformation of Machismo*.

56. Manuela García, speech to CCYC, 1972, MMC Spanish American Ethnic Meeting, Information Services Audiovisuals, box 1, IV-10-5, MCA.

57. Roth, *Separate Roads to Feminism*, 132.

58. Ibid., 154.

59. Ibid., 3.

60. Chavez responded with a thank you letter addressed to Lupe De León in which he stated: "The churches have been instrumental, as you probably know, in keeping up the courage and morale of the strikers in their struggles these past ten years." Cesar Chavez to Lupe De León, December 18, 1972, MBM Home Missions 1970–1989, box 2, IV-16-21.5, MCA.

61. Open-mike session, CCYC, Information Services Audiovisuals, Wednesday evening, box 13, IV-10-5, MCA.

62. Ibid.

63. Open-mike session, CCYC, 1972, Information Services Audiovisuals, box 13, IV-10-5, MCA.

64. Open-mike session, CCYC, 1972, MCA.

65. Nancy De León, CCYC, 1972, Information Services Audiovisuals, Friday morning part 1, box 13, IV-10-5. MCA.

66. Comment by unidentified "white girl," CCYC, 1972, Cross-Cultural Convention '72 file, IV-21-4, MCA.

67. Sis-Obed Torres, CCYC, 1972, Information Services Audiovisuals, IV-10-5, box 13, MCA.

68. Open-mike session, CCYC, 1972, MCA.

69. Paul Nolt, to organizers of the CCYC, MBM Home Missions 1970–1989, MMC 1970–1973 file, IV-16-21.5, MCA.

70. Sowell's letter was not found, but there is a reference to it in the MMC Executive Committee minutes, September 28, 1971, in General Board Files, Bronx, NY, I-6-5, MCA.

71. Ibid.

72. José A. Santiago, Artemio De Jesus, and Jorge Miller, "The New Structure

for the Council of Spanish Mennonite Churches in Relation to Other Mennonite Organizations in Region V," box 2, I-6-6.1, MCA.

73. Ibid.

74. MMC Executive Committee minutes, October 15, 1971, Detroit, General Board Files, MMC Minutes file, I-6-5, MCA.

75. Chuy Navarro to MMC leadership and MBM Home Missions leadership, South Texas Mennonite Church Council Records, box 2, Chuy Navarro file, II-14-18. MCA.

76. Ibid.

77. Ibid.

78. Concilio Latino, El Acta 3–5, January 1975, Hispanic Mennonite Convention, Minutes and Reports, box 1, I-6-6.1, MCA.

79. John Powell, "Recommended Reorganization of the Urban Racial Council," letter to Executive Committee of the URC, January 9, 1970, Minority Ministries Council, Home Missions Task Force, General Board, box 1, file 1, I-6-5, MCA.

Chapter 5. Social Movement or Labor Union?

Epigraph. "Supplement to the Ted Koontz Report to the MCC Peace Section (Personal views of Guy F. Hershberger)," April 18, 1974, MCC Peace Section, Farm Workers 1973–1976, no. 3, box 7, file 2, IX-7-12, MCA.

1. Paul Conrad, "Experiences in Nurturing a Young Church," *Gospel Herald*, November 20, 1962.

2. Paul and Ann Conrad, interview by author, tape recording, New Carlisle, OH, April 2007. See also Marjorie Vandervelde, "Friends in Southern Texas: The Church Life and Workaday Devotion of Mennonite Families in Mathis," *Christian Living*, December 1962.

3. Barton, "¡Ya Basta!," 138.

4. For more on Mennonite struggles with how nonviolence was used and talked about in the black freedom struggle, see the chapter "Race and Another Look at Nonviolent Resistance" in Schlabach, *War, Peace, and Social Conscience*. Of course, there were varieties of Mennonite activism. For example, Prairie Street Mennonite Church in Elkhart, IN; Community Mennonite Church in Markham, IL; and Woodlawn Mennonite Church in Chicago did engage in direct activism. Leaders of the Lancaster Mennonite Conference, however, voiced concerns about becoming involved in civil rights marches because of the principle of "coercive nonviolence." See Shearer, *Daily Demonstrators*.

5. Quoted in Schlabach, *War, Peace, and Social Conscience*, 225.

6. The first at Bethel College in Kansas in January and the second at Goshen College in Indiana in March.

7. Scholars have begun to reassess the legacy of Cesar Chavez as more than simply a labor leader or civil rights activist. New scholarship emphasizes that religious symbolism and influences that shaped the politics of Chavez and the farmworkers. Luís D. León, "César Chávez and Mexican American Civil Religion," 53–63; Mario T. García, *The Gospel of César Chávez.*

8. Valdés, *Al Norte,* 156.

9. Watt, *Farm Workers and the Churches,* 39–44. Harold Quinley showed that Protestant churches remained conflicted about how to respond adequately to the social issues burning in the late 1960s. Quinley, "The Dilemma of an Activist Church," 14.

10. Miller, "History of the Mennonite Conciliation Service," 9. In his chapter on the history of Mennonite Conciliation Service, Joseph Miller argues that "Mennonites were on both sides of the picket line." Ibid. He cites Hispanic Mennonite farmworkers who he claims were anti-Chavez. But he does so without providing any evidence of exactly who these Hispanic Mennonites were or how many were farmworkers. Hispanic Mennonites did work on some of the larger Mennonite farms, but they were subject to the segregationist patterns common in central California, where there were "grower towns and churches" and "worker towns and churches"—towns such as Reedley (grower) and Orange Cove (worker), for example. In other words, many of the Hispanic Mennonites that Miller contends supported the growers would not have attended church, or other social activities for that matter, with their grower bosses. If indeed Hispanic Mennonite farmworkers did side with the growers, Miller fails to provide any evidence to support his claim and fails to acknowledge the power dynamics at play between growers and farmworkers. See ibid., 9. General Conference leader Harold Regier, confirmed the segregation of workers and growers: "Thus, the Mennonite Brethren church has congregations of growers and congregations of farm workers." Regier, "Report on California Farm/Worker Issue," March 1974, MCC Peace Section, Farm Workers 1973–1976, no. 3, box 7, IX-7-12, MCA.

11. Miller, "History of the Mennonite Conciliation Service," 10.

12. "Farm Workers in Indiana," in 1970 Annual Report on Farm Labor of the State Employment Securities Division, box 3, II-14-18, MCA. Through the advocacy work of the League of United Latin American Citizens, Midwest Council of La Raza, and church-related organizations, farmworkers found some welcome support far from home. See Theron Schlabach, "A Congregation (Prudently) Concerned with Peace and Justice," CMC Centennial History Chapter, part 5, Theron F. Schlabach Papers, Hist. MS 1-544, box 44, file 3, MCA.

13. Associated Press, "Indiana Community Upset by Migrant Labor Project," *Dallas Morning News,* April 17, 1968.

14. Quoted in Ben Noll, "A Community of Brotherhood," unpublished paper, Goshen College, 2009, 4–5, Goshen College, Goshen, IN.

15. Ibid., 1; "Laborer Dies of Gunshot Wound," *Goshen News*, November 5, 1969.

16. Klaassen, "Plea for Migrants," *Goshen News*, November 14, 1969.

17. Noll, "A Community of Brotherhood," 10.

18. Paul Hershberger, "Miller May Close Housing," *Goshen News*, December 1971; Ken Washington, "Protesters to Boycott Pine Manor Products," *Goshen News*, November 19, 1971.

19. Associated Press, "Migrant Worker Tells of Threats, Beatings," *Dallas Morning News*, December 18, 1968.

20. Valdés, *Al Norte*, 185.

21. Associated Press, "Migrants' Housing Criticized: Filthy Conditions of Michigan Camp Result in Arrest," *Corpus Christi Caller-Times*, August 2, 1970.

22. Ibid.

23. Saralee Tiede, "Migrant Stories Biased, Florida Farmer Declares," *Dallas Morning News*, July 25, 1970; Associate Press, "Texas Official Denies Migrants Exploited," *Dallas Morning News*, July 18, 1970.

24. Nancy Hulvershorn, "Pine Manor Boycott to Be Continued," *Elkhart Truth*, November 30, 1971, Sandy and Carolyn Schwartzentruber Collection, MSC Minutes, Hist. MS 1–802, MCA; Paul Hershberger, Mexican Americans, part 1, "Why the Boycott at Pine Manor," *Goshen News*, December 14, 1971. Hershberger cites three central organizations that helped organize the boycott from South Bend: the "Social action committee from First Unitarian Church," "Ladies of Notre Dame," and "El Centro," a Mexican American arm of the Office of Economic Opportunity. See also Sandy and Carolyn Schwartzentruber Collection, MSC Minutes, Hist. MS 1-802, MCA; Washington, "Protestors to Boycott Pine Manor Products."

25. Paul Hershberger, Mexican Americans, part 2, "Community Groups Provide a Helping Hand," *Goshen News*, December 15, 1971.

26. John Powell, Compassion Fund Report, July 1969–July 1971, General Board Files, MMC 1971–1973, box 3, file 38, I-6-5, MCA.

27. "Community Talks Turkey," *Gospel Herald*, January 18, 1972.

28. Paul Hershberger, "Housing Project Proposed," *Goshen News*, December 17, 1971.

29. La Causa (The Cause) came to be how people referred to the farmworker movement. A listing of financial contributions from religious groups in January 1974 showed that a total of 27 (out of 32) granting groups had their base on the East Coast or in the Midwest. NFWM, "Member Organizations and Designated Representatives," January 1974, MCC Peace Section, Farm Workers 1973–1976, no. 3, box 7, IX-7-12, MCA.

30. Over 48 percent of the migrants came from the Midwest, especially Oklahoma and Kansas, but there was also a high percentage of in-state migration. See Enns-Rempel, "They Came from Many Places."

31. Enns-Rempel, "Many Roads to the San Joaquin Valley"; Janzen, "Back to the City"; Enns-Rempel, "Churches That Died on the Vine."

32. Toews, "150 Years Later." See also Barrett, *The Vision and the Reality.*

33. The uneven support for King had to do with Guy Hershberger's beliefs about "coercive non-violence." See Schlabach, *War, Peace, and Social Conscience.*

34. See Hartmann, "Expanding Feminism's Field and Focus."

35. Jocele Meyer to Churchwide WMSC Committee, January 18, 1974, MCC Peace Section, Farm Workers 1973–1976, no. 3, box 7, IX-7-12, MCA.

36. Ibid.

37. Thiessen, "Communism and Labor Unions."

38. Ibid., 23.

39. By 1954 the Mennonite Church changed its position when the committee on economic and social relations acknowledged that unions "serve a useful purpose for the maintenance of justice and a balance of power in a sib-Christian society." Mennonites were free to cooperate with unions "in so far as doing so does not conflict with . . . Christian testimony." *Global Anabaptist Mennonite Encyclopedia Online,* s.v. "Labor Unions," by Guy F. Hershberger and John H. Redekop, accessed July 12, 2011, www.gameo.org/encyclopedia/contents/L205ME.html.

40. Del Castillo and Garcia, *César Chávez,* 33.

41. Vargas, *Labor Rights Are Civil Rights,* 8. Vargas notes there was optimism that farmworkers would be guaranteed organizing and collective bargaining rights. But as Vargas shows, "Southern Dixiecrats weakened key New Deal reforms by exempting agriculture and domestic work from the National Labor Relations Act and the Social Security Act." Ibid.

42. Ferris and Sandoval, *The Fight in the Fields,* 4.

43. Felipe Hinojosa, "From the Voice of the Farm Worker to the Cry of Internal Dissent: The Short but troubled History of the UFW newspaper *El Malcriado,*" unpublished paper presented at the Southwestern Social Science Association Conference, San Antonio, March 2003.

44. Elaine Graves, "*El Malcriado* Anthology, 1965–1972," 16; Doug Adair, interview by author, e-mail, November 18, 2002.

45. Ganz, *Why David Sometimes Wins,* 7.

46. Daniel, "Cesar Chavez and the Unionization of California Farm Workers," 351. Ferris and Sandoval also note that "Chávez made a calculated decision to avoid calling their association a union." Ferris and Sandoval, *The Fight in the Fields,* 65.

47. Jenkins, *The Politics of Insurgency,* x–xi.

48. Vargas, *Labor Rights Are Civil Rights,* 5.

49. Agricultural Workers Organizing Committee leader Al Green, quoted in Jenkins, *The Politics of Insurgency*, 155.

50. Daniel, "Cesar Chavez and the Unionization of California Farm Workers," 351.

51. Ganz, *Why David Sometimes Wins*, 6.

52. See Cesar Chavez, "The Mexican-American and the Church"; Watt, *Farm Workers and the Churches*, 69–77.

53. Barton, ¡*Ya Basta!*, 127.

54. McNamara, "Social Action Priests," 182.

55. Jonathan Nathan, "Buena Gente, Jefes Duros: The Relationship of Mennonite Farmers and the United Farm Workers Union in California," unpublished paper, Bethel College, North Newton, KS, 2008, 23.

56. Ted Koontz, "Peace Section Involvement in the Farm Labor Situation," March 26, 1974, series 4, box 9, file 28, IX-7-12, MCA.

57. Harold R. Regier, "Report on California Farm/Worker Issue," March 1974, MCC Peace Section, Farm Workers 1973–1976, no. 3, box 7, IX-7-12, MCA.

58. This suspicion first came after a phone call MCC Peace Section leader Ted Koontz received from California grower William Snyder alerting the MCC that Mennonites were "carrying guns in the fields." Ted Koontz, "Peace Section Involvement in the Farm Labor Situation," March 26, 1974, Farm Workers 1973–1976, box 7, IX-7-12, MCA. The point was later challenged by General Conference leader Harold Regier, who reported that "Mennonites did not carry guns." See his "Report on California Farmer/Worker Issues," March 12–16, 1974, Farm Workers 1973–1976, box 7, IX-7-12, MCA.

59. Koontz, "Peace Section Involvement in the Farm Labor Situation."

60. The first meeting took place in Washington, DC, in January 1974 at the offices of the MCC. Mennonite growers and others concerned traveled from California to meet with Ted Koontz and Luann Habegger of the MCC Peace Section and share the "grower perspective" with their fellow Mennonites on the East Coast. Ted Koontz, "Conversation with California Mennonites Regarding Farm Workers," January 17, 1974, March 12–16, 1974, MCC Peace Section, Farm Workers 1973–1976, box 7, IX-7-12, MCA.

61. MCC Executive Committee Meeting, March 11, 1974, MCC Peace Section files, as reported by Regier in "Report on California Farmer/Worker Issues."

62. Nathan, "Buena Gente, Jefes Duros," 10.

63. "Study of the Farm Labor Situation by Arizona Ecumenical Council," 1972, MCC Peace Section, Farm Workers 1973–1976, box 7, IX-7-12, MCA; Guy F. Hershberger, "Meeting with Arizona UFW," Supplement to Hershberger Supplementary Report of April 18, 1974, MCC Peace Section, Farm Workers 1973–1976, box 7, IX-7-12, MCA.

64. Quinley, "The Dilemma of an Activist Church," 4.

65. Regier wrote that "farmers in California feel that easterners have been misinformed about the facts." See his "Report on California Farmer/Worker Issue."

66. Ibid.

67. Ruth Sutter, Dan Hertzler, and Beth Sutter, "Labor Study Diary," May 1974, Guy F. Hershberger Collection, Hist. MS 1-171, CA/UFW, box 28, file 2, MCA.

68. Ibid.

69. Ted Koontz, "Report to the MCC Peace Section on Conversations in California Regarding the Farm Labor Situation," March 12—16, 1974, MCC Peace Section, Farm Workers (1973—1976), box 7, IX-7-12, MCA.

70. Ibid.

71. Regier, "Report on California Farmer/Worker Issues."

72. Koontz, "Report to the MCC Peace Section on Conversations in California Regarding the Farm Labor Situation."

73. Ibid.

74. Dating back to the 1940s, Mennonite growers had forged a consistent pattern financial giving to MCC relief programs, as they strongly believed that "the hungry people of Europe must be fed!" As early as 1935 at the First Mennonite Church in Upland, California, a number of Mennonite citrus growers at the "Jubilee Session" of the General Conference denomination, brought oranges from nearby groves, and all participants were provided with "an unlimited quantity" of freshly squeezed orange juice. Lester Hostetler, "Mennonite Citrus Fruit Growers," *Mennonite Life*, October 1947. Some from Southern California contributed nearly $90,000 worth of raisins to the relief center in Reedley. See Arnold C. Ewy, "The Grape and Raisin Industry," *Mennonite Life*, 1950, 9.

75. Ted Koontz, telephone conversation with author, August 2011.

76. Regier, "Report on California Farmer/Worker Issues."

77. "Supplement to the Ted Koontz Report to the MCC Peace Section (Personal Views of Guy F. Hershberger)."

78. Regier, "Report on California Farmer/Worker Issues."

79. Chris Hartmire, "The Farm Bureau & The Farm Worker," May 1972, accessed June 2010, www.farmworkermovement.org.

80. Ted Koontz to Walt Hackman and William Snyder, "Call from Jack Angell of the American Farm Bureau," April 8, 1974, MCC Peace Section, series 4, Farm Workers, box 9, file 28, IX-7-12.8, MCA.

81. Lupe De León, to Dan Clark, May 4, 1973, De León file, IV-16-21, MCA.

82. "Task Force Report to the Spanish Concilio of the Mennonite Church on the Farm Worker Issue in California," May 6—8, 1974, MCC Peace Section, Farm Workers 1973—1976, no. 3, box 7, IX-7-12, MCA.

83. "Supplement to the Ted Koontz Report to the MCC Peace Section (Personal

Views of Guy F. Hershberger)"; Schlabach, *War, Peace, and Social Conscience,* 224, 476.

84. Schlabach, *War, Peace, and Social Conscience,* 449.

85. MCC News Service, "Mennonites Explore Farm Labor Conflict in California," April 12, 1974, 2, MCC Peace Section, Farm Workers 1973–1976, no. 3, box 7, file 2, IX-7-12, MCA.

86. "Task Force Report to the Spanish Concilio of the Mennonite Church on the Farm Worker Issue in California."

87. This is also a point that historian Theron Schlabach makes regarding Hershberger's "message about racial acceptance and justice." Schlabach, *War, Peace, and Social Conscience,* 437. It made Hershberger, as Schlabach describes him, "part of the old guard" and not necessarily reflective of a younger generation of Mennonites—white, black, and Latino—who were taking different approaches to social activism. Ibid., 462.

88. Neftali Torres, Cross-Cultural Student Seminar, Chicago, 1976, MBM Home Missions, box 1, file 8, Seminar Booklet, IV-16-21, MCA.

89. Historian Lois Barrett Janzen added that MCC members "instructed its staff to undertake any other efforts only in consultation with West Coast Mennonites." Janzen, "The Dialog That Hasn't Begun," *The Mennonite,* May 14, 1976, 316–317.

90. Hubert Schwartzentruber, United Farm Worker–Grower Issues minutes, Goshen College, July 30, 1974, MCC Peace Section, Farm Workers 1973–1976, no. 3, box 7, IX-7-12, MCA.

91. Watt, *Farm Workers and the Churches,* 106.

92. This point was clearly communicated to Ted Koontz by two growers, Richard Hofer and Stanley Warkentin. Ted Koontz, "Conversation with California Mennonites Regarding Farm Workers."

93. Regier, "Report on California Farmer/Worker Issues," 23.

94. For an excellent discussion of Chicano nationalism see E. Chávez, *¡Mi Raza Primero!,* 5–7.

95. De Genova and Ramos-Zayas, *Latino Crossings,* 21.

96. Torres, Cross-Cultural Student Seminar, Chicago, 1976.

Chapter 6. Mujeres Evangélicas

Epigraph. María Tijerina, "Funciones del Hombre y la Mujer a Prueba, según la Biblia," *Ecos Menonitas* 3, no. 3 (July 1981). Translation by author.

1. Dan Shenk, "Spanish-Speaking Women Meet in Moline," *Happenings,* June 1, 1973.

2. Maria Bustos, "Entrevista con Mary Bustos" [Interview with Mary Bustos], by Lupe De León, *Ecos Menonitas,* March 1974.

3. Seferina De León, interview by author, tape recording, Goshen, IN, April 17, 2007.

4. Religious historian Ann Braude has argued that scholars should "take as their point of departure the fact that women constitute the majority of participants in all sizable religious groups throughout American history." Braude, "Women's History Is American Religious History," 233.

5. Martell-Otero, "Women Doing Theology." See also Martell-Otero , Pérez, and Conde-Frazier, Latina Evangélicas.

6. S. De León, interview.

7. Brusco, Reforming Machismo, 2–3. This chapter also follows Sharon Sievers call "to expand our sense of what feminism is, and has been, in order to effectively write its history" Sievers, "Six (or More) Feminists in Search of a Historian," 325.

8. Denise Segura and Patricia Zavella outline four key dimensions of borderlands: "structural, discursive, interactional, and agentic." This chapter takes an agentic perspective that recognizes the agency of Latinas in the Mennonite Church and takes seriously their perceptions of the possibilities for gender equity in the church. Segura and Zavella define these expressions of agency as the ways in which "borderland subjects often take extraordinary creative measures and assert their own sense of selves." Segura and Zavella, "Gendered Borderlands," 539.

9. Blackwell, ¡Chicana Power!, 21.

10. Sánchez Korrol, "In Search of Unconventional Women," 141–150.

11. Garza, "The Influence of Methodism on Hispanic Women through Women's Societies," 80. For more on the lack of literature on "mujeres evangélicas," see Espinosa, "Your Daughters Shall Prophesy," 25–48.

12. Brusco, Reforming Machismo; Adams, "Perception Matters"; Medina, Las Hermanas.

13. Brusco, Reforming Machismo, 3.

14. Berkowitz, Something Happened, 5, 6.

15. Bustos, "Entrevista con Mary Bustos."

16. S. De León, interview.

17. Ibid.

18. "Spanish-Speaking Churches Caucus," Chicago, December 1969, Mennonite Church Office of Latin Concerns 1969–1972, I-6-6, MCA.

19. Falcón, The Hispanic Mennonite Church in North America, 111–122.

20. Shenk, "Spanish-Speaking Women Meet in Moline."

21. Mary Bustos, "Asi Fue el Principio: Conferencia Femenil Hispana Menonita, 1973–1982," Hispanic Mennonite Church, I-6-6.2, MCA; Lupe De León to Beulah Kauffman, January 22, 1974, Hispanic Mennonite Women's Conference 1974–1980, MBM Home Missions, box 2, Lupe De León file, IV-16-21, MCA.

22. Mary Bustos, "Corta Historia de la Conferencia Hispana Femenil," *Ecos Menonita*, April 1978.

23. Mary Bustos, "Los Donativos de la Última Conferencia," *Ecos Menonitas*, October 1977.

24. Shirley Powell, "Making Our Theology Practical," *Happenings*, June 1, 1973.

25. Dan Shenk, "Church Becoming Multiethnic Brotherhood," *Happenings*, June 1, 1973.

26. Ibid.

27. S. De León, interview.

28. Gracie Torres, interview by author, tape recording, Utuado, Puerto Rico, June 20, 2007.

29. Minutes of the Spanish-speaking churches caucus, Chicago, December 1969, Mennonite Church Office of Latin Concerns 1969–1972, box 1, file 1, I-6-6, MCA; Criselda's time was brief, but in searching for a representative, the council hoped to "choose someone from the Midwest, preferably a woman." MMC, Latin Concilio minutes, October 15, 1971, Office of Latin Concerns, box 1, file 1, I-6-6, MCA.

30. In his work on Latino masculinity, Alfredo Mirandé argues that there are distinct ways to categorize what it means to be "macho." Negative conceptions of machismo, for example, highlight its "exaggerated masculinity, male dominance, aggressiveness, and self-centeredness" (*Hombres y Machos*, 70–71). Positive attributes include "responsibility, general code of ethics, standing up for rights, and respect" (ibid., 74). Mirandé suggests that these polarities tend to blur the continuum on which Latino men operate. Latinos within the MMC often crossed between negative and positive associations. But what is clear is that being "machista" did not connote abuse or disregard of women. It did mean, however, responsibility in the private and public sphere.

31. Manuela García, "Small Group," Cross-Cultural Youth Convention, 1972, Information Services Audiovisuals, box 1, file 15, IV-10-5, MCA.

32. Ibid.

33. Roth, *Separate Roads to Feminism*, 163.

34. Baca Zinn, "Political Familialism."

35. Lozano, "Faithful in the Struggle," 127.

36. Ibid., 128.

37. A. Nieto, "From 'Black-Eyed Girls' to the MMU (*Mujeres Metodistas Unidas*)," 96.

38. Rios, "The Ladies Are Warriors," 205.

39. In our interview I found it quite interesting that even as Yolanda began doing Protestant missionary work, her commitment to la Virgen de Guadalupe did

not waver. Yolanda Villareal, interview by author, tape recording, Mission, TX, January 8, 2004.

40. Braude, "Faith, Feminism, and History," 239.

41. Ibid., 237.

42. Offen, "Rethinking Feminist Action in Religious and Denominational Contexts," 63; Brusco, *The Reformation of Machismo.*

43. "Women in the Church: A Study Document," prepared by the MBCM in cooperation with the WMSC, General Board, data set 1, box 4, Women in the Church file, I-6-5, MCA.

44. Ibid.

45. Graybill, "Finding My Place as a Lady Missionary," 155. See also "Women in the Church: A Study Document."

46. *Global Anabaptist Mennonite Encyclopedia Online,* s.v. "Biblical Understandings Concerning Women and Men (Mennonite Church, 1975)," accessed October 27, 2011, www.gameo.org/encyclopedia/contents/B539.html.

47. Ibid.

48. Lupe De León to Ross T. Bender (executive secretary of the MBCM), June 12, 1973, Lupe De León file, IV-16-21, MCA.

49. Bustos, "Entrevista con Mary Bustos."

50. Ibid.

51. G. Torres, interview.

52. S. De León, interview.

53. Espinosa, "Your Daughters Shall Prophesy," 26.

54. Manuelita "Nellie" Treviño Bazán was one of the first Mexican American Pentecostal women ordained in 1920. Ibid., 35.

55. Bustos, "Entrevista con Mary Bustos."

56. Maria Rivera Snyder, "Educación para el Parto sin Temor," *Ecos Menonitas,* November 1976; Seferina De León, "El Que Huye: ¿Es Posible que nos pase a nosotros?," *Ecos Menonitas,* April 1977; Esperanza Gutierrez, "Fe, Determinación y Esfuerzo," *Ecos Menonitas,* July 1979; Iris Navarro, "Ayuda Para Amas de Casa," *Ecos Menonitas,* July 1979.

57. Maria L. Rivera Snyder, "Educación para el Parto sin Temor," *Ecos Menonitas,* November 1976. Translation by author.

58. Ibid., translation by author.

59. Martell-Otero, "Women Doing Theology."

60. Espinosa, "Your Daughters Shall Prophesy," 42.

61. See Medina, *Las Hermanas*; Hartmann, "Expanding Feminism's Field and Focus"; Nabhan-Warren, "Little Slices of Heaven and Mary's Candy Kisses"; and Braude, "Faith, Feminism, and History."

62. Hartmann, "Expanding Feminism's Field and Focus," 50.

63. Medina, *Las Hermanas*, 1–4.

64. Blackwell, *¡Chicana Power!*, 174.

65. Adams, "Perception Matters," 113.

66. G. Torres, interview.

67. Martell-Otero, "Women Doing Theology," 76.

68. *Coritos*, literally "little songs," are sung in Latino evangelical churches. They usually have an upbeat rhythm and repetitive lyrics. They have come to shape and define Latino evangelical worship services. Historian Edwin Aponte defines *coritos* as "religious symbols in Hispanic Protestant popular religion," and historian Daniel Ramírez contends that they have also influenced Latino Catholic religiosity. See Aponte, "Coritos as Active Symbol" and Ramírez, "Alabaré a mi Señor," 149–170.

69. Navarro, "Conferencia Femenil Hispana Menonita," *Ecos Menonitas*, 1976.

70. G. Torres, interview.

71. Ibid.

72. Espinosa, "Your Daughters Shall Prophesy," 37–38.

73. Sánchez Korrol, "In Search of Unconventional Women," 148–149.

74. Ibid., 149.

75. G. Torres, interview.

76. S. De León, interview.

77. Marjorie Vandervelde, "Friends in Southern Texas: The Church Life and Workaday Devotion of Mennonite Families in Mathis," *Christian Living*, December 1962.

78. According to Guadalupe San Miguel Jr., "traditional conjunto," of which I speak of here, "was based primarily on the one-row or two-row button accordion; it also typically used two guitars, one of which was a bajo sexto, and a drum." Conjunto music forms part of the diverse and complex heritage of "border music" that came of age in the twentieth century in South Texas. See San Miguel, *Tejano Proud*, 5–17.

79. Little has been written about Bernal's influence on Pentecostal music in the late 1960s. However, scholars have begun to pay closer attention to this phenomenon. See Sharp, "Conjunto Conversions." For more on Paulino Bernal's influence on South Texas conjunto music beginning in the 1950s, see Manuel Peña, *The Texas-Mexican Conjunto*.

80. S. De León, interview.

81. Lupe De León, interview by author, tape recording, Mathis, TX, June 2007.

82. Iris Navarro, "Conferencia Femenil Hispana: Spiritual Fiesta," *Ecos Menonitas*, 1976.

83. In an oral history interview, Esther Ventura talks about how Mennonite missionary Lester Hershey often demonized Mexican cultural music. See "The

Venturas," February 3, 1973, Mission History Interview Project, box 1, tape 28, Hist. MS 6-81, MCA.

84. Advertisement in *Happenings*, June 28, 1972.

85. Back cover of *Everything Is Beautiful*, Mennonite Board of Missions Minority Ministries Council, 1969—1974, 1997—1999, box 5, Phonograph Record Albums, 1970—1972, IV-21, MCA.

86. In her work on Pentecostal Latinas in Pennsylvania, Anna Adams has argued that "the process of individuation, coupled with the assertion of a primary responsibility to God, rather than to spouse or family, . . . transforms women into active, responsible agents." Adams, "Perception Matters," 110.

87. Enriqueta Dias, "Recordando la Segunda Conferencia Femenil Hispana," *Happenings*, July 1974.

88. Arnoldo J. Casas, "Un paso adelante para los Menolatinos," *Ecos Menonitas*, October 1977.

Chapter 7. "Remember Sandia!"

"Christian Faith and Ethnic Awareness," Cross-Cultural Student Seminar, Chicago, 1976, MBM Home Missions, box 1, file 8, IV-16-21, MCA. Native Americans involved in the work of the Minority Ministries Council such as Lawrence Hart and Emma LaRocque were allies in the struggle but were not as comfortable with the level of institutional involvement of the mostly Latino and African American leadership. Shortly before making this comment, Emma LaRocque informed the group that this was her "farewell speech to the cross-cultural scene. I'm going back to where I come from, which is Canada, where I want to expend my energies for Indian people."

1. Office of Latin Concerns, minutes, Hispanic Mennonite Convention, box 1, Minutes 1973—1976 file, I-6-6.1, MCA.

2. José Ortíz, "The Spirit of Ebenezer," Mennonite Yearbook, 1982, 10. A survey conducted that year by José Ortíz counted 34 Latino Mennonite congregations across the United States with a total membership of 1,061. This was up from less than 200 members in 1955 and 500 members in 1970. Personal collection of the author.

3. Lupe De León, "Leadership for the Latino Mennonite Churches," *Gospel Herald*, August 5, 1975.

4. José Ortíz, "Hispanic Programming Observations and Projections," December 23, 1980, Hispanic Mennonite Convention, box 2, I-6-6.1, MCA.

5. Harvey and Goff, *The Columbia Documentary History of Religion in America since 1945*, 365.

6. Berger, introduction to *The Hidden 1970s*, 3.

7. Oboler, *Ethnic Labels, Latino Lives*; Gutiérrez, "Demography and the Shifting Boundaries of 'Community,'" 1.

8. Lara-Braud, "The Status of Religion among Mexican Americans," 91.

9. Catherine Wilson defines religious identity politics as the "content and context of religious values, beliefs, and culture that drive social and political action in community life." Wilson, *The Politics of Latino Faith*, 14.

10. "The Merger Then and Now," Minority Staff Report, May 1976, Afro-American Mennonite Association, box 5, Minority Affairs Committee file, I-6-7, MCA.

11. "Staff Report on the Merger," May 5, 1976, MBM Home Missions, series 5, box 2, Minority Ministries and Home Missions Merger folder, 1976, IV-16-21, MCA.

12. Office of Latin Concerns, minutes, 1981–1988, Hispanic Mennonite Convention, box 1, I-6-6, MCA.

13. Part of those funds were funneled to the General Board to help pay the salary of the appointed minority associate secretaries. The rest of the funds were simply absorbed into the Home Missions budget to help pay for the travel expenses of the newly formed Minority Affairs Committee. But as that committee quickly disintegrated a year later and only one minority secretary (José Ortíz) was appointed in 1974, much of those funds were lost and simply blended into the Home Missions general budget. "Minority Involvement Expands in New Plan," *Happenings* February 1974. See also Paul N. Kraybill, "Minority Progress Report," memo to General Board, February 11, 1974, General Board Files, box 3, I-6-5, MCA.

14. MMC Executive Committee minutes, Bronx, NY, September 28, 1970, MMC Minutes, box 1, file 2, IV-21, MCA.

15. Ernest Bennett, "Letter to Tito Guedea, Lupe De León, John Powell," February 7, 1973, General Board, MMC file, I-6-5, MCA.

16. Dorsa J. Mishler, "Memo to Ernest Bennett," September 11, 1972, MBM Executive Office, Minority Ministries file, IV-7-6, MCA.

17. Dorsa J. Mishler, "Memo to Ernest Bennett," September 28, 1972. MBM Executive Office, Minority Ministries file, IV-7-6, MCA.

18. Ibid.

19. Mishler, "Memo to Ernest Bennett," September 11, 1972. MCA; John Powell, interview by author, tape recording, Ypsilanti, Michigan, April 26, 2007.

20. John Powell, interview.

21. Mishler, "Memo to Ernest Bennett," September 11, 1972.

22. John Powell, "Minority Ministries Council De-centralization," April 10, 1973, Home Missions Task Force, General Board Files, box 3, file 40, I-6-5, MCA.

23. MMC Executive Committee, "Reflections and Visions of the Minority

Ministries Council," 1973, General Board Files, Minority Ministries / Home Missions Task Force 1973 file, I-6-5, MCA.

24. Tito Guedea, telephone call to Paul Kraybill, May 14, 1973, Minority Ministries Home Ministries Merger file, General Board, MMC file, I-6-5, MCA.

25. John Powell, interview; MMC Mass Assembly minutes, October 19, 1973, Sandia, TX, MMC Minutes 1968–1974, box 1, file 2, IV-21, MCA.

26. Minutes of Executive Committee Meeting of MMC, Sandia, TX, October 19–21, 1973, General Board Files, box 3, Minorities–Sandia Model file, I-6-5, MCA.

27. Ibid.

28. MMC Executive Committee minutes, February 1974, box 2, Minority Ministries file, II-14-18, MCA.

29. Ivan Kaufman, "The Future for General Board Black and Latin Staff," box 2, 3/5/80 file, I-6-6.1, MCA.

30. Mennonite Church, Office of Latin Concerns minutes, 1973–1976, Spanish Concilio minutes file, Corpus Christi Mennonite Church, February 22–23, 1974, I-6-6, MCA.

31. "José Ortiz to General Board," *Happenings,* July 1974.

32. "¿Hacia Donde Vamos?," *Ecos Menonitas,* June 1975.

33. Tom Navarro, "Una Perspectiva de un Servicio de Instalación," *Ecos Menonitas,* January 1975.

34. José Ortíz, "El Verano del '75," *Ecos Menonitas,* November 1975, translated by author. See also Falcón, *The Hispanic Mennonite Church in North America,* 51.

35. José Ortíz, "Reporte, Secretario General Asociado," November 1974, translation by author, Hispanic Mennonite Convention, box 1, Minutes 1973–1976 file, I-6-6.1, MCA.

36. Paul Kraybill, General Secretary's Report, August 22, 1974, Hispanic Mennonite Convention, box 1, Minutes 1973–1976 file, I-6-6.1, MCA.

37. This was the second letter that Jackson had written. In January 1974 he wrote a letter in which he criticized the lack of clarity over the roles of the Latin and black caucuses. Jackson wrote: "It appears that this system we have created, when I see how it is turning out is turning EVERY OUNCE of Black control to one man, and this we do not want, nor will we tolerate!" Warner Jackson, "Material Defects in the Merger Plan Which Must Be Corrected before Implementation," January 6, 1974,. General Board Files, box 3, file 45, I-6-5, MCA.

38. Warner Jackson, "The Black Church and the Home Ministries: Minority Ministries Council Merger," June 3, 1974, MBM Executive Office 1967–1987, General Board Files, box 3, file 43, IV-7-6, MCA.

39. Ibid.

40. Paul N. Kraybill, "Minority Progress Report," memo to General Board, February 11, 1974, General Board, box 3, I-6-5, MCA.

41. Black Council, Latin Concilio, and Home Missions Conjoint Meeting, Rosemont, IL, May 28, 1976, MBM Home Missions, Lupe De León file, 1971–1982, IV-16-21, MCA.

42. José Ortíz, "Report of Latin Associate Secretary," September 9, 1976, Hispanic Mennonite Convention, box 1, I-6-6.1, MCA.

43. José M. Ortíz, "Hispanics and Free Church Tradition," *Mennonite Weekly Review*, January 24, 1980.

44. Ivan Kaufman, "The Future for General Board Black and Latin Staff," box 2, 3/5/80 file, I-6-6.1, MCA.

45. Ortíz, "Hispanics and the Free Church Tradition."

46. Ibid.

47. Lupe De León to José Ortíz, September 10, 1976, MBM Home Missions, Lupe De León file, 1971–1982, IV-16-21, MCA.

48. Ibid.

49. Office of Latin Concerns, Administrative Committee of Concilio, 1975, Hispanic Mennonite Convention, box 1, Minutes 1973–1976 file, I-6-6, MCA.

50. Office of Latin Concerns, Hispanic Mennonite Convention minutes, box 1, Minutes 1979–1980 file, I-6-6, MCA.

51. Reunion Comité Administrativo Concilio Nacional de Iglesias Menonitas Hispanas, Davenport, IA, September 11–12, 1976, Hispanic Mennonite Convention, box 2, Appendix A file, I-6-6.1, MCA.

52. Ibid.

53. "It was moved, seconded and carried that having heard the concern of the Spanish Concilio through Lupe De León, we realize that information on the problem needs to go to our churches, that our Washington office should give attention to the matter." MCC Peace Section, November 18, 1976. Lupe De León, "Informe al Comité Administrativo del Concilio Nacional de Iglesias Menonitas Hispanas," February 15–16, 1980, Hispanic Mennonite Convention, box 1, Latin Concerns Minutes 1979–1980 file, I-6-6, MCA.

54. J. Martínez, "Latin American Anabaptist-Mennonites," 464.

55. Jaime Prieto Valladares, *Mission and Migration*, 354.

56. Reunion Comité Administrativo Concilio Nacional de Iglesias Menonitas Hispanas, Davenport, IA, September 11–12, 1976, Hispanic Mennonite Convention, box 2, Appendix A file, I-6-6.1, MCA.

57. H. Brent Weaver, "Hispanic Ministries News Release," [ca. 1980], Hispanic Ministries, box 2, file 6, V-4-40, MCA.

58. Falcón, *The Hispanic Mennonite Church in North America*, 55–56.

59. Mejido, "U.S. Hispanics/Latinos and the Field of Graduate Theological Education."

60. Hernández et al., "A Demographic Profile of Latino/a Seminarians," 2.

61. Falcón, *The Hispanic Mennonite Church in North America*, 151.

62. John Lederach, Report of the Meeting with the Concilio Nacional, January 31, 1978, Hispanic Mennonite Convention, box 2, I-6-6.1, MCA.

63. Comité Administrativo, "Mennonite Theological Training for Spanish Leadership," Rosemont, IL, February 25–26, 1977, General Board, Office of Latin Concerns, Minutes 1977–1978 file, I-6-6, MCA.

64. Rafael Falcón, "Goshen College: ¿Integración o Separación?," *Ecos Menonitas*, October 1979.

65. Ibid.

66. Quoted in Arnoldo Casas, "Menoticias: Hesston College / Seminario Nazareno," *Ecos Menonitas*, July 1978.

67. Saulo Padilla, "Attempts and Challenges to the Development of a Hispanic Mennonite Identity," unpublished paper, Goshen College, Goshen, IN, April 2005, personal collection of author.

68. Hispanic Leadership Training Program, August 17, 1978, box 1, file 27, V-4-40, MCA.

69. Hispanic Ministries, box 1, file 1, V-4-40, MCA.

70. The roll of first-year students in 1979 included, among others, Héctor Vázquez, Eva Vázquez, Samuel López, Ramiro Hernández, Marta Hernández, Leonicio Gutiérrez, David Acosta, Miguel Cruz, Fidencia Flores, Eliel Núñez, Margarita Pequeño, Daniel Pérez, Orlando Rivera, Elizabeth Santiago, and Alfa Tijerina. Ibid.

71. Falcón, *The Hispanic Mennonite Church in North America*, 151.

72. Ibid., 57.

73. Miguel Angel Cruz, "El Primer Graduado de Ministerios Hispanos," *Ecos Menonitas*, April 1981.

74. Quoted in Wayne North, "Future Latin Leaders Find Dreams Come True," *Gospel Herald*, February 22, 1980.

75. Quoted in H. Brent Weaver, "Hispanic Ministries News Release."

76. Hispanic Ministries, box 1, file 39, V-4-40, MCA.

77. "A List of Priorities as Stated by the Latin Representation in Sandia, TX, Conference," General Board Files, Minorities–Sandia Model file, October 1973, I-6-5, MCA.

78. "Reporte Concilio Nacional de Iglesias Menonitas Hispanas," Cachipay, Colombia, December 3–6, 1980, MBM Home Missions Records 1970–1980, series 4, Anabaptist Curriculum file, 1981, IV-16-21, MCA.

79. Ibid.

80. Rafael Falcón, "La Iglesia Meno-Latina en Norte América: Una Interpretación," *Ecos Menonitas*, July 1983.

81. Gilberto Flores, interview with author, e-mail, May 17, 2012.

82. Lupe De León, "Are We Ready for Church Growth?," *Gospel Herald*, 1976.

83. José Ortíz, "The Melting Pot Is Not Melting," *Gospel Herald*, December 27, 1977.

84. Sánchez Walsh, *Latino Pentecostal Identity*, 1.

85. Wilson, *The Politics of Latino Faith*, 216.

86. Stevens-Arroyo, *Prophets Denied Honor*, 182.

87. Sánchez Walsh, *Latino Pentecostal Identity*, 66.

88. E. Fernández, *La Cosecha*, 36.

89. Ibid., 37.

90. Barton, "¡Ya Basta!," 139.

91. Treviño, "Race and Ethnicity," 276–290.

92. Montejano, *Quixote's Soldiers*, 266.

93. Berkowitz, *Something Happened*, 161–162.

94. Treviño, *The Church in the Barrio*, 203.

95. Lupe De León, "Informe al Comité Administrativo del Concilio Nacional de Iglesias Menonitas Hispanas," Goshen College Hispanic Ministries, box 2, V-4-40, MCA.

96. José Ortíz, associate general secretary, "Report to the General Board," Office of Latin Concerns, July 5, 1979, General Board—Office of Latin Concerns, Minutes 1979–1980 file, I-6-6, MCA.

97. Saulo Padilla, "Attempts and Challenges to the Development of a Hispanic Mennonite Identity."

98. José Ortíz, associate general secretary, "Report to the General Board," Office of Latin Concerns, October 22, 1979, General Board—Office of Latin Concerns, Minutes 1979–1980 file, I-6-6, MCA.

Conclusion

Epigraph. Ted Chapa, interview by author, tape recording, San Antonio, TX, January 25, 2007.

1. León, *La Llorona's Children*, 240.

2. Two important studies have helped develop a better understanding of the religious shifts in the Latino community: Espinosa, Elizondo, and Miranda, *Hispanic Churches in American Public Life*; and Pew Forum on Religion and Public Life and Pew Hispanic Project, *Changing Faiths: Latinos and the Transformation of American Religion*, 2007, www.pewforum.org/uploadedfiles/Topics/Demographics/hispanics-religion-07-final-mar08.pdf.

3. Barbara Bradley Hagerty, "US Hispanics Choose Churches outside Catholicism," accessed March 29, 2012, www.npr.org/2011/10/19/141275979/u-s-his panics-choose-churches-outside-catholicism.

4. Ibid.

5. Some of the important studies of twentieth-century Latino Protestantism and Pentecostalism that suggest a broader engagement include Espinosa, "El Azteca"; Ramírez, "Borderlands Praxis"; J. Martínez, *Sea la Luz*; and Banker, *Presbyterian Missions and Cultural Interaction in the Far Southwest*.

6. Ramírez, "Borderlands Praxis."

7. Much has been written about Latino Catholic involvement in the civil rights movement and the influences of liberation theology in Latin America. See Elizondo, *Galilean Journey*; Medina, *Las Hermanas*; R. Martínez, *PADRES*.

8. Treviño, *The Church in the Barrio*, 176–205.

9. Felipe Hinojosa, "Mennonites in the Barrio: The Rancho Alegre Youth Center in Mathis, Texas," *Mennonite Life*, Summer 2011; Dan and Mary Miller, interview by author, digital recording, Boerne, TX, August 30, 2010.

10. Behnken, *Fighting Their Own Battles*, 178–179.

11. Ortega-Aponte, "Raised Fist in the Church!," 150.

12. Amy L. Sherman, "The Community Serving Activities of Hispanic Protestant Congregations," copublished by Hudson Institute's Faith in Communities Initiative and the Center for the Study of Latino Religion, Notre Dame University, December 2003; Barton, "¡Ya Basta!"

13. Many of these works have been cited throughout this book. They include Espinosa, Elizondo, and Miranda, *Latino Religions and Civic Activism in the United States*; Sánchez Walsh, *Latino Pentecostal Identity*; and Barton, *Hispanic Methodists, Presbyterians, and Baptists in Texas*.

14. Heltzel, *Jesus and Justice*, 205.

15. Montejano, *Quixote's Soldiers*, 263.

16. Schmidt quoted in Carlos Harrison, "Hispanic Evangelicals, Longtime Republican Stronghold, at Odds with GOP on Key Issues," *Huffington Post*, January 18, 2012, accessed April 28, 2012, www.huffingtonpost.com/2012/01/17/latino -vote-hispanic-evangelicals-florida_n_1210909.html.

17. The notion of a "priesthood of all believers" is central to Anabaptist/Mennonite theology. In its basic form, it asserts that everyone has been gifted with the ability to share the Gospel, interpret scripture, and lead religious services. It challenges the hierarchies of the church by allowing everyone to partake in leadership and community development.

18. Brown, *Black and Mennonite*, 25.

19. "I Am Not a Cultural Mennonite," *Festival Quarterly*, 1976, cited in Emma LaRocque, "Christian Faith and Ethnic Awareness," Cross-Cultural Student Semi-

nar, Chicago, 1976, MBM Home Missions, box 1, file 8, IV-16-21, MCA. In the article African American, Latino, and Native American Mennonites were asked about their positions on ethnic and religious identity.

20. While there have been theological treatments of the shared struggles of Latinos and African Americans, historical accounts for the most part point to the influence of the farmworker movement, Latin American liberation theology, and the Chicano movement. On theology, See Pinn and Valentin, *The Ties That Bind*.

21. Lupe De León, "Peacemaking from My Perspective," unpublished paper, April 1976, MBM Home Missions, box 2, Articles folder, 1971, MCA.

22. From the early twentieth-century evangelist Billy Sunday, who often prayed, "Lord save us . . . from effeminate, sissified, three-caret Christianity," to the Promise Keepers movement at the end of the twentieth century, gender and religion have had a close and sometimes tense relationship. See Prothero, *American Jesus*, 94; and Brusco, *The Reformation of Machismo*.

23. Iris Navarro, "Conferencia Femenil Hispana: Spiritual Fiesta," *Ecos Menonitas*, 1976. Navarro was reporting on the third conference organized by Latina Mennonites, which took place on April 9–11, 1976, in Corpus Christi, TX.

24. M. García, "Religion and the Chicano Movement."

25. Barton, "¡Ya Basta!"

26. Richard Yeakley, "Growth Stalls, Falls for Largest US Churches," *USA Today*, February 15, 2011. This reports cites declining membership dating back to the 1970s. But while mainline Protestantism loses members, numbers for evangelical churches continue to rise.

27. However, denominational loyalty among Mennonites is higher than it was in 1972 (when only 25 percent believed they would remain with the denomination) and higher than mainline or conservative Protestant groups. Conrad L. Kanagy, "A Landscape of Change," *The Mennonite*, February 6, 2007, accessed March 30, 2012, www.themennonite.org/issues/10–3/articles/A_landscape_of_change.

28. Conrad L. Kanagy, "Key Growth among Racial/Ethnic Members," *Mennonite Weekly Review*, February 12, 2007.

29. J. Nelson Kraybill, "Is Our Future Evangelical?" *The Mennonite*, March 5, 2002.

30. Swartz, "Re-Baptizing Evangelicalism," 271.

31. Bush, *Two Kingdoms, Two Loyalties*, 259–260.

32. See, for example, the essays in Burkholder and Cramer, *The Activist Impulse*.

33. Lupe De León, "Peacemaking from My Perspective."

34. Ibid.

35. Shearer, "Conflicting Identities," 22.

36. Haney-López, *Racism on Trial*, 6.

37. In the same way, Montejano notes that how "individuals and organizations

might be mobilized depended on how an issue, action, or cause was framed or identified." Montejano, *Quixote's Soldiers*, 266.

38. Both scholars have bridged ethnic and religious studies, and their works serve as models for pushing church history beyond its own parochialisms. See Busto, *King Tiger*; and Espinosa, "History and Theory in the Study of Mexican American Religions."

39. Fernanda Santos, "Same-Sex Marriage Support Has Grown among Latinos, Survey Finds," *New York Times*, October 18, 2012; Gastón Espinosa and Rick Hunter, "Latino Religions and Politics Survey Voter Report: Pre-2012 Election Findings," nationally representative bilingual telephone survey of 1,000 Latino Christian likely voters, fielded October 4–10, 2012, Claremont McKenna College, 14.

40. Anna Groff, "Board Seeks Ways to Deal with Conflict," *The Mennonite*, March 1, 2010.

41. One of the core principles of Mennonite Church USA, the denomination that emerged as a result of the General Conference and (Old) Mennonite Church merger, is to be an antiracist church. What that means and how it actually plays out in the church remains to be seen.

Bibliography

Abramson, Michael. *Palante: Young Lords Party.* 1971. Reprint, Chicago: Haymarket Books, 2011.

Adams, Anna. "Perception Matters: Pentecostal Latinas in Allentown, Pennsylvania." In *A Reader in Latina Feminist Theology: Religion and Justice,* edited by María Pilar Aquino, Daisy L. Machado, and Jeannette Rodríguez, 98–113. Austin: University of Texas Press, 2002.

Ahlstrom, Sydney E. *A Religious History of the American People.* 2nd ed. New Haven, CT: Yale University Press, 2004.

Albanese, Catherine. *America: Religion and Religions.* 4th ed. Belmont, CA: Wadsworth, 2006.

Alcoff, Linda Martín, Michael Hames-García, Satya P. Mohanty, and Paula M. L. Moya, eds. *Identity Politics Reconsidered.* New York: Palgrave Macmillan, 2006.

Alvarez, Luis. "From Zoot Suits to Hip Hop: Towards a Relational Chicana/o Studies," *Latino Studies* 5 (2007): 53–75.

———. *The Power of the Zoot: Youth Culture and Resistance during World War II.* Berkeley: University of California Press, 2009.

Anzaldúa, Gloria. *Borderlands / La Frontera: The New Mestiza.* 3rd ed. San Francisco: Aunt Lute Books, 2007.

Aponte, Edwin. "Coritos as Active Symbol in Latino Protestant Popular Religion." *Journal of Hispanic/Latino Theology* 2 (1995): 57–66.

———. "Views from the Margins: Constructing a History of Latina/o Protestantism." In *Hispanic Christian Thought at the Dawn of the 21st Century,* edited by Alvin Padilla et al., 85–97. Nashville, TN: Abingdon, 2005.

Arredondo, Gabriela F., *Mexican Chicago: Race, Identity, and Nation, 1916–39.* Urbana: University of Illinois Press, 2008.

Arredondo, Gabriela F., Aida Hurtado, Norma Klahn, Olga Najera-Ramirez, and Patricia Zavella, eds. *Chicana Feminisms: A Critical Reader*. Durham, NC: Duke University Press, 2003.

Ashmore, Susan Youngblood. *Carry It On: The War on Poverty and the Civil Rights Movement in Alabama, 1964–1972*. Athens: University of Georgia Press, 2008.

Ayala, Cesar J., and Rafael Bernabe. *Puerto Rico in the American Century: A History since 1898*. Chapel Hill: University of North Carolina Press, 2009.

Baca Zinn, Maxine. "Political Familialism: Toward Sex Role Equality in Chicano Families." *Aztlán* 6 (1975): 13–26.

Badillo, David A. *Latinos and the New Immigrant Church*. Baltimore: Johns Hopkins University Press, 2006.

Banker, Mark T. *Presbyterian Missions and Cultural Interaction in the Far Southwest, 1850–1950*. Urbana: University of Illinois Press, 1992.

Barrett, Lois. *The Vision and the Reality: The Story of Home Missions in the General Conference Mennonite Church*. Newton, KS: Faith and Life, 1983.

Barton, Paul. *Hispanic Methodists, Presbyterians, and Baptists in Texas*. Austin: University of Texas Press, 2006.

———. "¡Ya Basta! Latino/a Protestant Activism in the Chicano/a and Farm Worker Movements." In *Latino Religions and Civic Activism in the United States*, edited by Gastón Espinosa, Virgilio Elizondo, and Jesse Miranda, 127–144. New York: Oxford University Press, 2005.

Beaver, Pierce, ed. *American Missions in Bicentennial Perspective: Papers Presented at the Fourth Annual Meeting of the American Society of Missiology at Trinity Evangelical Divinity School, Deerfield, Illinois, June 18–20, 1976*. South Pasadena, CA: William Carey Library, 1977.

Bebbington, David. *Evangelicalism in Modern Britain: A History from the 1730s to the 1980s*. 1989. Reprint, New York: Routledge, 1993.

Bebout, Lee. *Mythohistorical Interventions: The Chicano Movement and Its Legacies*. Minneapolis: University of Minnesota Press, 2011.

Behnken, Brian D. *Fighting Their Own Battles: Mexican Americans, African Americans, and the Struggle for Civil Rights in Texas*. Chapel Hill: University of North Carolina Press, 2011.

———. "'We Want Justice!': Police Murder, Mexican American Community Response, and the Chicano Movement." In *The Hidden 1970s: Histories of Radicalism*, edited by Dan Berger, 195–213. New Brunswick, NJ: Rutgers University Press, 2010.

Bendroth, Margaret, and Virginia Brereton, eds. *Women and Twentieth-Century Protestantism*. Urbana: University of Illinois Press, 2001.

Bennett, Scott H. *Radical Pacifism: The War Resisters League and Gandhian Nonviolence in America, 1915–1963*. Syracuse, NY: Syracuse University Press, 2004.

Berger, Dan. Introduction to *The Hidden 1970s: Histories of Radicalism*, edited by Dan Berger, 1–17. New Brunswick, NJ: Rutgers University Press, 2010.

Berkowitz, Edward, ed. *Something Happened: A Political and Cultural Overview of the Seventies*. New York: Columbia University Press, 2007.

Bernstein, Shana. *Bridges of Reform: Interracial Civil Rights Activism in Twentieth-Century Los Angeles*. New York: Oxford University Press, 2011.

Blackwell, Maylei. *¡Chicana Power! Contested Histories of Feminism in the Chicano Movement*. Austin: University of Texas Press, 2011.

Brackenridge, R. Douglas, and Francisco O. Garcia-Treto. *Iglesia Presbiteriana: A History of Presbyterians and Mexican Americans in the Southwest*. 2nd ed. San Antonio, TX: Trinity University Press, 1987.

Braude, Ann. "Faith, Feminism, and History." In *The Religious History of American Women: Reimagining the Past*, edited by Catherine A. Brekus, 232–252. Chapel Hill: University of North Carolina Press, 2007.

———. "Women's History Is American Religious History." In *Retelling US Religious History*, edited by Thomas Tweed, 87–107. Berkeley: University of California Press, 1997.

Briggs, Laura. *Reproducing Empire: Race, Sex, Science, and US Imperialism in Puerto Rico*. Berkeley: University of California Press, 2002.

Brilliant, Mark. *The Color of America Has Changed: How Racial Diversity Shaped Civil Rights Reform in California, 1941–1978*. New York: Oxford University Press, 2010.

Brown, Hubert L. *Black and Mennonite: A Search for Identity*. Scottdale, PA: Herald, 1976.

Brusco, Elizabeth E. *The Reformation of Machismo: Evangelical Conversion and Gender in Columbia*. Austin: University of Texas Press, 2010.

Burkholder, Jared, and David Cramer, eds. *The Activist Impulse: Essays on the Intersection of Evangelicalism and Anabaptism*. Eugene, OR: Pickwick, 2012.

Bush, Perry. *Two Kingdoms, Two Loyalties: Mennonite Pacifism in Modern America*. Baltimore: Johns Hopkins University Press, 1998.

Busto, Rudy V. *King Tiger: The Religious Vision of Reies López Tijerina*. Albuquerque: University of New Mexico Press, 2006.

Carson, Clayborne. *In Struggle: SNCC and the Black Awakening of the 1960s*. Cambridge, MA: Harvard University Press, 1981.

Chappell, David L. *A Stone of Hope: Prophetic Religion and the Death of Jim Crow*. Chapel Hill: University of North Carolina Press, 2005.

Chavez, Cesar E. "The Mexican-American and the Church." *El Grito* (Summer 1968): 215–218.

Chávez, Ernesto. *¡Mi Raza Primero! Nationalism, Identity, and Insurgency in the Chicano Movement in Los Angeles, 1966-1978*. Berkeley: University of California Press, 2002.

Clayson, William. *Freedom Is Not Enough: The War on Poverty and the Civil Rights Movement in Texas*. Austin: University of Texas Press, 2010.

Cornell, Stephen, and Douglas Hartmann. "Conceptual Confusions and Divides: Race, Ethnicity, and the Study of Immigration." In *Not Just Black and White: Historical and Contemporary Perspectives on Immigration, Race, and Ethnicity in the United States*, edited by Nancy Foner and George M. Fredrickson, 23–41. New York: Russell Sage Foundation, 2004.

Corten, André, and Ruth R. Marshall-Fratani, eds. *Between Babel and Pentecost: Transnational Pentecostalism in Africa and Latin America*. Bloomington: Indiana University Press, 2001.

Cruz, Nicky, with Jamie Buckingham. *Run, Baby, Run*. Plainfield, NJ: Logos International, 1968.

Daniel, Cletus E. "Cesar Chavez and the Unionization of California Farm Workers." In *Labor Leaders in America*, edited by Melvyn Dubofsky and Warren Van Tine, 350–382. Urbana: University of Illinois Press, 1987.

Davalos, Karen, Eric R. Avila, Rafael Pérez-Torres, and Chela Sandoval. "Roundtable on the State of Chicana/o Studies." *Aztlán* 27 (Fall 2002): 139–152.

Dávila, Arlene. *Barrio Dreams: Puerto Ricans, Latinos, and the Neoliberal City*. Berkeley: University of California Press, 2004.

Dayton, Donald. *Discovering an Evangelical Heritage*. New York: Harper and Row, 1976.

De Genova, Nicholas, and Ana Y. Ramos-Zayas. *Latino Crossings: Mexicans, Puerto Ricans, and the Politics of Race and Citizenship*. New York: Routledge, 2003.

De La Torre, Miguel A., and Edwin David Aponte. *Introducing Latino/a Theologies*. Maryknoll, NY: Orbis Books, 2001.

De La Torre, Miguel A., and Gastón Espinosa, eds. *Rethinking Latino(a) Religion and Identity*. Cleveland, OH: Pilgrim, 2006.

Del Castillo, Richard Griswold, and Richard A. Garcia. *César Chávez: A Triumph of Spirit*. Norman: University of Oklahoma Press, 1997.

De León, Arnoldo. *They Called Them Greasers: Anglo Attitudes toward Mexicans in Texas, 1821–1900*. Austin: University of Texas Press, 1983.

Deutsch, Sarah. *No Separate Refuge: Culture, Class, and Gender on an Anglo-Hispanic Frontier in the American Southwest, 1880–1940*. Oxford: Oxford University Press, 1987.

Díaz-Stevens, Ana María. *Oxcart Catholicism on Fifth Avenue: The Impact of the Puerto Rican Migration upon the Archdiocese of New York*. South Bend, IN: University of Notre Dame Press, 1993.

Droogers, André. "Globalisation and Pentecostal Success." In *Between Babel and Pentecost: Transnational Pentecostalism in Africa and Latin America*, edited by André Corten and Ruth R. Marshall-Fratani, 41–61. Bloomington: Indiana University Press, 2001.

Duany, Jorge. "Nation and Migration: Rethinking Puerto Rican Identity in a Trans-national Context." In *None of the Above: Puerto Ricans in the Global Era*, edited by Frances Negrón-Muntaner, 51–64. New York: Palgrave Macmillan, 2007.

———. *The Puerto Rican Nation on the Move: Identities on the Island and in the United States*. Chapel Hill: University of North Carolina Press, 2002.

Dubofsky, Melvyn, and Warren Van Tine, eds. *Labor Leaders in America*. Urbana: University of Illinois Press, 1987.

Dudziak, Mary. *Cold War Civil Rights: Race and the Image of American Democracy*. Princeton, NJ: Princeton University Press, 2000.

Dyck, Cornelius. *An Introduction to Mennonite History*. 3rd ed. Scottdale, PA: Herald, 1993.

———, ed. *Jesus Christ Reconciles: Proceedings of the Ninth Mennonite World Conference*. Elkhart, IN: Mennonite World Conference, 1972.

Dye, Keith. "The Black Manifesto for Reparations in Detroit." *Michigan Historical Review* 35 (Fall 2009): 53–83.

Ellwood, Robert S. *The Fifties Spiritual Marketplace: American Religion in a Decade of Conflict*. New Brunswick, NJ: Rutgers University Press, 1997.

Elizondo, Virgilio P. *Galilean Journey: The Mexican-American Promise*. Maryknoll, NY: Orbis Books, 1983.

Enck-Wanzer, Darrel. "Decolonizing Imaginaries: Rethinking 'the People' in the Young Lords' Church Offensive." *Quarterly Journal of Speech* 98 (2012): 1–23.

———, ed. *The Young Lords: A Reader*. New York: New York University Press, 2010.

Enns-Rempel, Kevin. "Churches That Died on the Vine: Short-Lived California Mennonite Congregations." *California Mennonite Historical Society Bulletin* 49 (Summer 2008): 1–5.

———. "Many Roads to the San Joaquin Valley: Sources of Mennonite Settlement in the Reedley/Dinuba Area." *California Mennonite Historical Society Bulletin* 24 (April 1991): 1–4.

———. "They Came from Many Places: Sources of Mennonite Migration to California, 1887–1939." *California Mennonite Historical Society Bulletin* 28 (May 1993): 1–8.

Erb, Paul. *South Central Frontiers: A History of South Central Mennonite Conference*. Scottdale, PA: Herald, 1974.

Espinosa, Gastón. "Borderland Religion: Los Angeles and the Origins of the Latino Pentecostal Movement in the US, Mexico, and Puerto Rico, 1900–1945." PhD diss., University of California, Santa Barbara, 1999.

———. "El Azteca: Francisco Olazábal and Latino Pentecostal Charisma, Power, and Faith Healing in the Borderlands." *Journal of the American Academy of Religion* 63 (September 1999): 597–616.

———. "History and Theory in the Study of Mexican American Religions." In *Rethinking Latino(a) Religion & Identity*, edited by Miguel A. De La Torre and Gastón Espinosa, 69–100. Cleveland, OH: Pilgrim, 2006.

———. "Methodological Reflections on Social Science Research on Latino Religions." In *Rethinking Latino(a) Religion & Identity*, edited by Miguel A. De La Torre and Gastón Espinosa, 13–45. Cleveland, OH: Pilgrim, 2006.

———. "Your Daughters Shall Prophesy: A History of Women in Ministry in the Latino Pentecostal Movement in the United States." In *Women and Twentieth-Century Protestantism*, edited by Margaret Lamberts Bendroth and Virginia Lieson Brereton, 25–48. Urbana: University of Illinois Press, 2002.

Espinosa, Gastón, Virgilio Elizondo, and Jesse Miranda. *Hispanic Churches in American Public Life: Summary of Findings.* Institute for Latino Studies, Notre Dame University, Interim Reports 2003.2 (March 2003).

———, eds. *Latino Religions and Civic Activism in the United States.* New York: Oxford University Press, 2005.

Espinosa, Gastón, and Mario T. García, eds. *Mexican American Religions: Spirituality, Activism, and Culture.* Durham, NC: Duke University Press, 2008.

Evans, Curtis. "White Evangelical Protestant Responses to the Civil Rights Movement." *Harvard Theological Review* 102 (2009): 245–273.

Falcón, Rafael. *The Hispanic Mennonite Church in North America, 1932–1982.* Scottdale, PA: Herald, 1986.

Fernández, Eduardo C. *La Cosecha: Harvesting Contemporary United States Hispanic Theology (1972–1998).* Collegeville, MN: Liturgical, 2000.

Fernandez, Lilia. *Brown in the Windy City: Mexicans and Puerto Ricans in Postwar Chicago.* Chicago: University of Chicago Press, 2012.

Fernandez, Ronald. *The Disenchanted Island: Puerto Rico and the United States in the Twentieth Century.* 2nd ed. Westport, CT: Praeger, 1996.

Ferriss, Susan, and Ricardo Sandoval. *The Fight in the Fields: Cesar Chavez and the Farmworkers Movement.* New York: Harcourt Brace, 1997.

Fitzpatrick, Joseph. *Puerto Rican Americans: The Meaning of Migration to the Mainland.* New York: Prentice Hall, 1971.

Flores, Juan. "The Diaspora Strikes Back: Nation and Location." In *None of the Above: Puerto Ricans in the Global Era*, edited by Frances Negrón-Muntaner, 211–216. New York: Palgrave Macmillan, 2007.

Foley, Neil. *The White Scourge: Mexicans, Blacks, and Poor Whites in Texas Cotton Culture.* Berkeley: University of California Press, 1999.

Foner, Nancy, and George M. Fredrickson, eds. *Not Just Black and White: Historical and Contemporary Perspectives on Immigration, Race, and Ethnicity in the United States.* New York: Russell Sage Foundation, 2005.

Frye, Jerry K. "The Black Manifesto and the Tactic of Objectification." *Journal of Black Studies* 5 (September 1974): 65–76.

Ganz, Marshall. *Why David Sometimes Wins: Leadership, Organization, and Strategy in the California Farm Worker Movement.* New York: Oxford University Press, 2010.

García, Alma. "The Development of Chicana Feminist Discourse, 1970–1980." In *Unequal Sisters: A Multicultural Reader in US Women's History*, edited by Ellen DuBois and Vicki Ruiz, 418–431. New York: Routledge, 1990.

García, Ignacio M. *Chicanismo: The Forging of a Militant Ethos among Mexican Americans.* Tucson: University of Arizona Press, 1997.

García, Mario T. *Católicos: Resistance and Affirmation in Chicano Catholic History.* Austin: University of Texas Press, 2010.

———. *The Gospel of César Chávez: My Faith in Action.* Lanham, MD: Sheed and Ward, 2007.

———. "Religion and the Chicano Movement: Católicos por la Raza." In *Mexican American Religions: Spirituality, Activism, and Culture*, edited by Gastón Espinosa and Mario T. García, 125–152. Durham, NC: Duke University Press, 2008.

Garza, Minerva. "The Influence of Methodism on Hispanic Women through Women's Societies." *Methodist History* (January 1996): 78–89.

Gilroy, Paul. *The Black Atlantic: Modernity and Double Consciousness.* Cambridge, MA: Harvard University Press, 1993.

Ginorio, Angela. "A Comparison of Puerto Ricans in New York with Native Puerto Ricans and Native Americans on Two Measures of Acculturation: Gender Role and Racial Identification." PhD diss., Fordham University, 1979.

Goldschmidt, Henry, and Elizabeth McAlister, eds. *Race, Nation, and Religion in the Americas.* New York: Oxford University Press, 2004.

Gonzalez, Juan. *Harvest of Empire: A History of Latinos in America.* New York: Penguin Books, 2000.

González, Ray, ed. *Muy Macho: Latino Men Confront Their Manhood.* New York: Anchor Books, 1996.

González-López, Lyvia M., ed. *Puerto Rico en Fotos: La Colección Menonita, 1940–1950.* San Juan, PR: Fundación Luis Muñoz Marín, 2009.

Goossen, Rachel Waltner. *Women against the Good War: Conscientious Objection and Gender on the American Home Front.* Chapel Hill: University of North Carolina Press, 1997.

Graves, Elaine F. "El Malcriado Anthology, 1965–1972." MA thesis, Fairfield University, 1973.

Graybill, Beth E. "Finding My Place as a Lady Missionary: Mennonite Women Missionaries to Puerto Rico, 1945–1960." *Journal of Mennonite Studies* 17

(1999): 152–173.

Graybill, Beth E., and Linda B. Arthur. "The Social Control of Women's Bodies in Two Mennonite Communities." In *Religion, Dress and the Body*, edited by Linda B. Arthur, 9–30. Oxford: Berg, 1999.

Grebler, Leo, Joan W. Moore, and Ralph C. Guzmán. "The Urban Mexican-American Parish." In *Introduction to Chicano Studies: A Reader*, edited by Livie Isauro Duran and H. Russell Bernard, 252–261. New York: Macmillan, 1973.

Grijalva, Joshua. *A History of Mexican Baptists in Texas, 1881–1981: Comprising an Account of the Genesis, the Progress, and the Accomplishments of the People called "Los Bautistas de Texas."* Dallas: Office of Language Missions, Baptist General Convention of Texas, in cooperation with the Mexican Baptist Convention of Texas, 1982.

Guthrie, Keith. *The History of San Patricio County.* N.p.: San Patricio County Commission, 1986.

Gutiérrez, David G. "Demography and the Shifting Boundaries of 'Community': Reflections on 'US Latinos' and the Evolution on Latino Studies." In *The Columbia History of Latinos in the United States since 1960*, edited by David G. Gutiérrez, 1–42. New York: Columbia University Press, 2006.

———. *Walls and Mirrors: Mexican Americans, Mexican Immigrants, and the Politics of Ethnicity.* Berkeley: University of California Press, 1995.

Hall, Jacquelyn Dowd. "The Long Civil Rights Movement and the Political Uses of the Past." *Journal of American History* 91 (2005): 1233–1263.

Hall, Stuart. "New Ethnicities." In *Stuart Hall: Critical Dialogues in Cultural Studies*, edited by David Morley and Kuan-Hsing Chen, 441–450. New York: Routledge, 1996.

Hammond, Phillip E. "In Search of a Protestant Twentieth Century: American Religion and Power since 1900." *Review of Religious Research* 24 (June 1983): 281–294.

Hammond, Phillip E., and Kee Warner. "Religion and Ethnicity in Late-Twentieth-Century America." *Annals of the American Academy of Political and Social Science* 527 (May 1993): 55–66.

Haney-López, Ian F. *Racism on Trial: The Chicano Fight for Justice.* Cambridge, MA: Harvard University Press, 2003.

Hartmann, Susan M. "Expanding Feminism's Field and Focus: Activism in the National Council of Churches in the 1960s and 1970s." In *Women and Twentieth-Century Protestantism*, edited by Margaret Lamberts Bendroth and Virginia Lieson Brereton, 49–69. Urbana: University of Illinois Press, 2002.

Harvey, Paul, and Philip Goff, eds. *The Columbia Documentary History of Religion in America since 1945.* New York: Columbia University Press, 2007.

Heltzel, Peter Goodwin. *Jesus and Justice: Evangelicals, Race, and American Politics.* New Haven, CT: Yale University Press, 2009.

Hernández, Edwin, Milagros Peña, Caroline Sotello Viernes Turner, Jeffrey Smith, and Kari Jo Verhulst. "A Demographic Profile of Latino/a Seminarians." *Latino Research @ND* 4 (March 2007): 2.

Hernández Hiraldo, Samiri. *Black Puerto Rican Identity and Religious Experience.* Gainesville: University Press of Florida, 2006.

Hinojosa, Felipe. "From the Voice of the Farm Worker to the Cry of Internal Dissent: The Short but Troubled History of the UFW Newspaper *El Malcriado.*" Paper presented at the Southwestern Social Science Association Conference, San Antonio, TX, March 2003.

———. "Making Noise among the 'Quiet in the Land': Mexican American and Puerto Rican Ethno-Religious Identity in the Mennonite Church, 1932–1982." PhD diss., University of Houston, 2009.

Hoffnung-Garskof, Jesse. *A Tale of Two Cities: Santo Domingo and New York after 1950.* Princeton, NJ: Princeton University Press, 2008.

Holsinger, Justus G. *Serving Rural Puerto Rico: A History of Eight Years of Service by the Mennonite Church.* Scottdale, PA: Mennonite Publishing, 1952.

Hostetler, Beulah Stauffer. *American Mennonites and Protestant Movements.* Scottdale, PA: Herald, 1987.

Hulsether, Mark. *Religion, Culture, and Politics in the Twentieth-Century United States.* New York: Columbia University Press, 2007.

Innis-Jiménez, Michael. *Steel Barrio: The Great Mexican Migration to South Chicago, 1915–1940.* New York: New York University Press, 2013.

Itzigsohn, José. "The Formation of Latino and Latina Panethnic Identities." In *Not Just Black and White: Historical and Contemporary Perspectives on Immigration, Race, and Ethnicity in the United States,* edited by Nancy Foner and George M. Fredrickson, 197–216. New York: Russell Sage Foundation, 2005.

Janzen, Rod. "Back to the City: Mennonite Community Church, Fresno, California, 1954–2004." *California Mennonite Historical Society* 43 (Winter 2006): 1–15.

Jenkins, J. Craig. *The Politics of Insurgency: The Farm Worker Movement in the 1960s.* New York: Columbia University Press, 1985.

Juhnke, James C. "George R. Brunk Tent Revival Sermon." *Mennonite Life* 57 (September 2002). http://tools.bethelks.edu/mennonitelife/2002sept/brunk.php.

———. "Shaping Religious Community through Martyr Memories." *Mennonite Quarterly Review* 73, no. 3 (July 1999): 546–557.

———. *Vision, Doctrine, War: Mennonite Identity and Organization in America, 1890–1930.* Scottdale, PA: Herald, 1989.

Kanter, Deborah. "Making Mexican Parishes: Ethnic Succession in Chicago Churches, 1947–1977." *US Catholic Historian* (Winter 2012): 35–58.

Kessler-Harris, Alice. *In Pursuit of Equity: Women, Men, and the Quest for Economic Citizenship in 20th Century America*. Oxford: Oxford University Press, 2001.

Kim, Sharon. *A Faith of Our Own: Second-Generation Spirituality in Korean American Churches*. New Brunswick, NJ: Rutgers University Press, 2010.

King, David P. "Seeking a Global Vision: The Evolution of World Vision, Evangelical Missions and American Evangelicalism." PhD diss., Emory University, 2011.

Klaassen, Walter. *Anabaptism: Neither Catholic nor Protestant*. Waterloo, ON: Conrad, 1973.

Kraybill, Nelson. "The Birth of the Chicago Mexican Mission." Unpublished paper, Goshen College, 1978. Mennonite Historical Library, Goshen, IN.

Kurashige, Scott. *The Shifting Grounds of Race: Black and Japanese Americans in the Making of Multiethnic Los Angeles*. Princeton, NJ: Princeton University Press, 2010.

Kyle, Richard. *From Sect to Denomination: Church and Their Implications for Mennonite Brethren History*. Hillsboro, KS: Center for Mennonite Brethren Studies, 1985.

Lampe, Philip E. "Religion and the Assimilation of Mexican Americans." *Review of Religious Research* 18 (1977): 243–253.

Landale, Nancy S., and R. S. Oropesa. "White, Black, or Puerto Rican? Racial Self-Identification among Mainland and Island Puerto Ricans." *Social Forces* 81 (2002): 231–254.

Lara-Braud, Jorge. "The Status of Religion among Mexican Americans." In *La Causa Chicana: The Movement for Justice*, edited by Margaret M. Mangold, 87–94. New York: Family Service Association of America, 1972.

León, Luis D. "César Chávez and Mexican American Civil Religion." In *Latino Religions and Civic Activism in the United States*, edited by Gastón Espinosa, Virgilio Elizondo, and Jesse Miranda, 53–64. New York: Oxford University Press, 2005.

———. *La Llorona's Children: Religion, Life, and Death in the US-Mexican Borderlands*. Berkeley: University of California Press, 2004.

———. "Somos un Cuerpo en Cristo: Notes on Power and the Body in an East Los Angeles Chicano/Mexicano Pentecostal Community." *Latino Studies Journal* 5 (September 1994): 60–86.

Levitt, Peggy. *The Transnational Villagers*. Berkeley: University of California Press, 2001.

Limón, José. *Dancing with the Devil: Society and Cultural Poetics in Mexican-American South Texas*. Madison: University of Wisconsin Press, 1994.

Lipsitz, George. *American Studies in a Moment of Danger*. Minneapolis: University of Minnesota Press, 2001.

———. "The Struggle for Hegemony." *Journal of American History* 75 (June 1988): 146–150.

Loewen, Harry, and Steven Nolt. *Through Fire and Water: An Overview of Mennonite History*. Rev. 2nd ed. Scottdale, PA: Herald, 2010.

Lozano, Nora O. "Faithful in the Struggle: A Historical Perspective on Hispanic Protestant Women in the United States." In *Los Evangélicos: Portraits of Latino Protestantism in the United States*, edited by Juan F. Martínez and Lindy Scott, 151–173. Eugene, OR: Wipf and Stock, 2009.

Machado, Daisy L. *Of Borders and Margins: Hispanic Disciples in Texas, 1888–1945*. New York: Oxford University Press, 2003.

Maduro, Otto. "Notes toward a Sociology of Latina/o Religious Empowerment." In *Hispanic/Latino Theology: Challenge and Promise*, edited by Ada María Isasi-Díaz and Fernando F. Segovia, 151–166. Minneapolis, MN: Fortress, 1996.

Maldonado, David, Jr. *Crossing Guadalupe Street: Growing Up Hispanic and Protestant*. Albuquerque: University of New Mexico Press, 2001.

———. *Protestantes/Protestants: Hispanic Christianity within Mainline Traditions*. Nashville, TN: Abingdon, 1999.

Mantler, Gordon. "Black, Brown and Poor: Martin Luther King Jr., the Poor People's Campaign, and Its Legacies." Ph.D. diss., Duke University, 2008.

Mariscal, George. *Brown-Eyed Children of the Sun: Lessons from the Chicano Movement, 1965–1975*. Albuquerque: University of New Mexico Press, 2005.

Mariz, Cecilia Loreto, and Maria Campos Machado. "Pentecostalism and Women in Brazil." In *Power, Politics, and Pentecostals*, edited by Edward L. Cleary and Hannah W. Stewart-Gambino, 41–54. Boulder, CO: Westview, 1997.

Marsden, George M. *Fundamentalism and American Culture*. 2nd ed. New York: Oxford University Press, 2006.

Martell-Otero, Loida I. "Women Doing Theology: Una Perspectiva Evangélica." *Apuntes* 14 (1994): 67–85.

Martell-Otero, Loida I., Zaida Maldonado Pérez, and Elizabeth Conde-Frazier. *Latina Evangélicas: A Theological Survey from the Margins*. Eugene, OR: Cascade Books, 2013.

Martínez, Juan F. "Latin American Anabaptist-Mennonites: A Profile." *Mennonite Quarterly Review* 74 (2000): 463–478.

———. "Mennonite Brethren, Latinos and Mission." *Direction Journal* 23 (1994): 43–49.

———. *Sea la Luz: The Making of Mexican Protestantism in the American Southwest, 1829–1900*. Denton: University of North Texas Press, 2006.

Martínez, Juan F., and Lindy Scott, eds. *Los Evangélicos: Portraits of Latino Protestantism in the United States.* Eugene, OR: Wipf and Stock, 2009.

Martínez, Richard Edward. *PADRES: The National Chicano Priest Movement.* Austin: University of Texas Press, 2005.

Matovina, Timothy M. *Guadalupe and Her Faithful: Latino Catholics in San Antonio, from Colonial Origins to the Present.* Baltimore: Johns Hopkins University Press, 2005.

———. *Tejano Religion and Ethnicity: San Antonio, 1821–1860.* Austin: University of Texas Press, 1995.

McNamara, P. H. "Social Action Priests in the Mexican American Community." *Sociological Analysis* 29 (1968): 177–185.

Medina, Lara. *Las Hermanas: Chicana/Latina Religious-Political Activism in the US Catholic Church.* Philadelphia: Temple University Press, 2005.

Mejido, Manuel Jesús. "U.S. Hispanics/Latinos and the Field of Graduate Theological Education." *Theological Education* 34 (1998): 51–72.

Miller, Donald E., and Tetsunao Yamamori. *Global Pentecostalism: The New Face of Christian Social Engagement.* Berkeley: University of California Press, 2007.

Miller, Joseph S. "A History of the Mennonite Conciliation Service, International Conciliation Service, and Christian Peacemaker Teams." In *From the Ground Up: Mennonite Contributions to International Peacebuilding,* edited by Cynthia Sampson and John Paul Lederach, 3–29. New York: Oxford University Press, 2000.

Mirandé, Alfredo. *Hombres y Machos: Masculinity and Latino Culture.* Boulder, CO: Westview, 1997.

Moffett, Stephen Lloyd. "The Mysticism and Social Action of César Chávez." In *Latino Religions and Civic Activism,* edited by Gastón Espinosa, Virgilio Elizondo, and Jesse Miranda, 35–51. New York: Oxford University Press, 2005.

Montejano, David. *Anglos and Mexicans in the Making of Texas, 1836–1986.* Austin: University of Texas Press, 1987.

———. *Quixote's Soldiers: A Local History of the Chicano Movement, 1966–1981.* Austin: University of Texas Press, 2010.

Moore, Joan W., and Ralph C. Guzmán. "New Wind from the Southwest." *Nation,* May 30, 1966, 645–648.

Moya, Paula. *Learning from Experience: Minority Identities, Multicultural Struggles.* Berkeley: University of California Press, 2002.

Muñoz, Carlos. *Youth, Identity, Power: The Chicano Movement.* Rev. and exp. ed. New York: Verso, 2007.

Murray, Stuart. *The Naked Anabaptist: The Bare Essentials of a Radical Faith.* Scottdale, PA: Herald, 2010.

Nabhan-Warren, Kristy. "Little Slices of Heaven and Mary's Candy Kisses: Mexican American Women Redefining Feminism and Catholicism." In *The Religious History of Women: Reimagining the Past*, edited by Catherine A. Brekus, 294–318. Chapel Hill: University of North Carolina Press, 2007.

Nañez, Alfredo. *History of the Rio Grande Conference of the United Methodist Church.* Dallas, TX: Bridwell Library, Southern Methodist University, 1980.

Negrón-Muntaner, Frances, ed. *None of the Above: Puerto Ricans in the Global Era.* New York: Palgrave Macmillan, 2007.

Neufeld, Harry M. *Eight Years among Latin-Americans.* Hillsboro, KS: Mennonite Brethren, 1947.

Nieto, Adriana Pilar. "From 'Black-Eyed Girls' to the MMU (*Mujeres Metodistas Unidas*): Race, Religion and Gender in the US-Mexico Borderlands." PhD diss., University of Denver, 2010.

Nieto, Leo D. "The Chicano Movement and the Churches in the United States / El Movimiento Chicano y las Iglesias en Los Estados Unidos." *Perkins Journal* 29 (Fall 1975): 32–41.

———. "The Chicano Movement and the Gospel: Historical Accounts of a Protestant Pastor." In *Hidden Stories: Unveiling the History of the Latino Church*, edited by David Cortés-Fuentes and Daniel R. Rodríguez-Díaz, 143–157. Decatur, GA: Asociación para la Educación Teológica Hispana, 1994.

Nolt, Steve. "A Two-Kingdom People in a World of Multiple Identities: Religion, Ethnicity, and American Mennonites." *Mennonite Quarterly Review* 73 (July 1999): 485–502.

Oboler, Suzanne. *Ethnic Labels, Latino Lives: Identity and the Politics of (Re)Presentation in the United States.* Minneapolis: University of Minnesota Press, 1995.

Offen, Karen. "Rethinking Feminist Action in Religious and Denominational Contexts." In *Globalizing Feminisms, 1789–1945*, edited by Karen Offen, 63–66. New York: Routledge, 2010.

Ogbar, Jeffrey O. G. *Black Power: Radical Politics and African American Identity.* Baltimore: Johns Hopkins University Press, 2005.

Omi, Michael, and Howard Winant. *Racial Formation in the United States: From the 1960s to the 1990s.* 2nd ed. New York: Routledge, 1994.

Oppenheimer, Mark. *Knocking on Heaven's Door: American Religion in the Age of Counterculture.* New Haven, CT: Yale University Press, 2003.

Orleck, Annelise, and Lisa Gayle Hazirjian, eds. *The War on Poverty: A New Grassroots History, 1964–1980.* Athens: University of Georgia Press, 2011.

Oropeza, Lorena. *¡Raza Sí! ¡Guerra No! Chicano Protest and Patriotism during the Viet Nam War Era.* Berkeley: University of California Press, 2005.

Ortega-Aponte, Elias. "Raised Fist in the Church! Afro-Latino/a Practice among the Young Lords Party: A Humanistic Spirituality Model for Radical

Latino/a Religious Ethics." PhD diss., Princeton Theological Seminary, 2011.

Ortíz, José, and David Graybill. *Reflections of an Hispanic Mennonite*. Intercourse, PA: Good Books, 1989.

Oyer, Emma. *What God Hath Wrought in a Half Century at the Mennonite Home Mission*. Elkhart, IN: Mennonite Board of Missions and Charities, 1949.

Peachey, Paul. *The Church in the City*. Newton, KS: Faith and Life, 1963.

Pehl, Matthew. "'Apostles of Fascism,' 'Communist Clergy,' and the UAW: Political Ideology and Working-Class Religion in Detroit, 1919–1945." *Journal of American History* 99 (September 2012): 440–465.

Peña, Manuel. *Música Tejana: The Cultural Economy of Artistic Transformation*. College Station: Texas A&M University Press, 1999.

———. *The Texas-Mexican Conjunto: History of a Working-Class Music*. Austin: University of Texas Press, 1985.

Pinn, Anthony B., and Benjamin Valentin, eds. *The Ties That Bind: African American and Hispanic American / Latino/a Theologies in Dialogue*. New York: Continuum, 2001.

Plummer, Brenda Gayle, ed. *Window on Freedom: Race, Civil Rights, and Foreign Affairs, 1945–1988*. Chapel Hill: University of North Carolina Press, 2007.

Portes, Alejandro, and Min Zhou. "The Second Generation: Segmented Assimilation and Its Variants." *Annals of the American Academy of Political and Social Science* 530 (November 1993): 74–96.

Prentiss, Craig, ed. *Religion and the Creation of Race and Ethnicity: An Introduction*. New York: New York University Press, 2003.

Prothero, Stephen. *American Jesus: How the Son of God Became a National Icon*. New York: Farrar, Straus and Giroux, 2004.

Pulido, Albert. "Are You an Emissary of Jesus Christ? Justice, the Catholic Church, and the Chicano Movement." In *American Mosaic: Selected Readings on America's Multicultural Heritage*, edited by Young I. Song and Eugene C. Kim. Englewood Cliffs, NJ: Prentice Hall, 1993.

Pulido, Laura. *Black, Brown, Yellow, and Left: Radical Activism in Los Angeles*. Berkeley: University of California Press, 2006.

Quinley, Harold E. "The Dilemma of an Activist Church." *Journal for the Scientific Study of Religion* 13 (March 1974): 1–21.

Ramírez, Daniel. "Alabaré a mi Señor: Culture and Ideology in Latino Protestant Hymnody." In *Los Evangélicos: Portraits of Latino Protestantism in the United States*, edited by Juan F. Martínez and Lindy Scott, 151–173. Eugene, OR: Wipf and Stock, 2009.

———. "Borderlands Praxis: The Immigrant Experience in Latino Pentecostal

Churches." *Journal of the American Academy of Religion* 67 (September 1999): 573–596.

Remy, Martha. "Protestant Churches and Mexican Americans in South Texas." PhD diss., University of Texas, Austin, 1971.

Rios, Elizabeth. "The Ladies Are Warriors: Latina Pentecostalism and Faith-Based Activism in New York City." In *Latino Religions and Civic Activism in the United States*, edited by Gastón Espinosa, Virgilio Elizondo, and Jesse Miranda, 197–218. New York: Oxford University Press, 2005.

Rivera, A. G. Quintero. "Las Bases Sociales de la Transformación Ideológica del Partido Popular Democrático en la Década del Cuarenta." In *Cambio y Desarrollo en Puerto Rico: La Transformación Ideológica del Partido Popular Democrático*, edited by G. Navas Dávila, 36–119. Río Piedras, PR: Editorial Universitaria, Universidad de Puerto Rico, 1980.

Robert, Dana L., ed. *Converting Colonialism: Vision and Realities in Mission History, 1706–1914*. Grand Rapids, MI: William B. Eerdmans, 2008.

Rodriguez, Clara E. "Puerto Ricans: Between Black and White." *New York Affairs* 1 (1974): 92–101.

———. "Puerto Rican Studies." *American Quarterly* 42 (September 1990): 437–455.

Rodriguez, Marc Simon. *The Tejano Diaspora: Mexican Americanism and Ethnic Politics in Texas and Wisconsin*. Chapel Hill: University of North Carolina Press, 2011.

Rodriguez, José David, and Loida I. Martell-Otero, eds. *Teología en Conjunto: A Collaborative Hispanic Protestant Theology*. Louisville, KY: Westminster John Knox, 1997.

Rosaldo, Renato. "Identity Politics: An Ethnography by a Participant." In *Identity Politics Reconsidered*, edited by Linda Martín Alcoff et al., 118–125. New York: Palgrave Macmillan, 2006.

Roth, Benita. *Separate Roads to Feminism: Black, Chicana, and White Feminist Movements in America's Second Wave*. New York: Cambridge University Press, 2003.

Ruiz, Vicki L. *From Out of the Shadows: Mexican Women in Twentieth-Century America*. New York: Oxford University Press, 1998.

———, ed. *Unequal Sisters: An Inclusive Reader in US Women's History*. 3rd ed. New York: Routledge, 2000.

Saldivar, José David. "Border Thinking, Minoritized Studies, and Realist Interpellations: The Coloniality of Power from Gloria Anzaldúa to Arundhati Roy." In *Identity Politics Reconsidered*, edited by Linda Martín Alcoff et al., 152–170. New York: Palgrave Macmillan, 2006.

Sampson, Cynthia, and John Paul Lederach, eds. *From the Ground Up: Mennonite Contributions to International Peacebuilding*. New York: Oxford University Press, 2000.

Sánchez, George J. *Becoming Mexican American: Ethnicity, Culture, and Identity in Chicano Los Angeles, 1900–1945.* New York: Oxford University Press, 1995.

Sánchez Korrol, Virginia. *From Colonia to Community: The History of Puerto Ricans in New York City.* Berkeley: University of California Press, 1983.

———. "In Search of Unconventional Women: Histories of Puerto Rican Women in Religious Vocations before Midcentury." In *Unequal Sisters: An Inclusive Reader in US Women's History*, 4th ed., edited by Vicki Ruiz with Ellen Carol Dubois, 141–150. New York, Routledge, 2008.

Sánchez Walsh, Arlene M. *Latino Pentecostal Identity: Evangelical Faith, Self, and Society.* New York: Columbia University Press, 2003.

Sandoval, Moises, ed. *Fronteras: A History of the Latin American Church in the USA since 1513.* Vol. 10. San Antonio, TX: Mexican American Cultural Center, 1983.

San Miguel, Guadalupe, Jr. *Let All of Them Take Heed: Mexican Americans and the Campaign for Educational Equality in Texas, 1910–1981.* College Station: Texas A&M University Press, 2000.

———. *Tejano Proud: Tex-Mex Music in the Twentieth Century.* College Station: Texas A&M University Press, 2002.

Schlabach, Theron F. *War, Peace, and Social Conscience.* Scottdale, PA: Herald, 2009.

———. *Gospel versus Gospel: Mission and the Mennonite Church, 1863–1944.* Scottdale, PA: Herald, 1980.

Schultz, Kevin M. "Religion as Identity in Postwar America: The Last Serious Attempt to Put a Question on Religion in the United States Census." *Journal of American History* 93 (September 2006): 359–384.

Segura, Denise A., and Patricia Zavella. "Gendered Borderlands." *Gender and Society* 22 (October 2008): 537–544.

Sharp, Ethan. "Conjunto Conversions: Musical Adaptations in Mexicano Pentecostal Communities." Paper presented at the American Academy of Religion Conference, San Diego, CA, November 2007.

Shearer, Tobin Miller. "Conflicting Identities: White Racial Formation among Mennonites, 1960–1985." *Identities: Global Studies in Culture and Power* 19 (June 2012): 268–284.

———. *Daily Demonstrators: The Civil Rights Movement in Mennonite Homes and Sanctuaries.* Baltimore: Johns Hopkins University Press, 2010.

———. "Moving beyond Charisma in Civil Rights Scholarship." *Mennonite Quarterly Review* 82 (April 2008): 213–248.

———. "'A Pure Fellowship': The Danger and Necessity of Purity in White and African-American Mennonite Racial Exchange, 1935–1971." PhD diss., Northwestern University, 2008.

Shenk, Wilbert R. *By Faith They Went Out: Mennonite Missions, 1850–1999.* Elkhart, IN: Institute of Mennonite Studies, 2000.

Sievers, Sharon. "Six (or More) Feminists in Search of a Historian." In *Expanding the Boundaries of Women's History: Essays on Women in the Third World*, edited by Cheryl Johnson-Odim and Margaret Strobel, 319–330. Bloomington: Indiana University Press, 1992.

Smith, Andrea. *Native Americans and the Christian Right: The Gendered Politics of Unlikely Alliances*. Durham, NC: Duke University Press, 2008.

Smith, T. L. *Revivalism and Social Reform in Mid-Nineteenth-Century America*. Baltimore: Johns Hopkins University Press, 1980.

Smith, Willard H. *Mennonites in Illinois*. Scottdale, PA: Herald, 1983.

Soja, Edward W. *Thirdspace: Journeys to Los Angeles and Other Real-and-Imagined Places*. Cambridge: Wiley-Blackwell, 1996.

Song, Young I., and Eugene C. Kim, eds. *American Mosaic: Selected Readings on America's Multicultural Heritage*. Englewood Cliffs, NJ: Prentice Hall, 1993.

Stevens, Jason W. *God-Fearing and Free: A Spiritual History of America's Cold War*. Cambridge, MA: Harvard University Press, 2010.

Stevens Arroyo, Anthony M. "From Barrios to Barricades: Religion and Religiosity in Latino Life." In *The Columbia History of Latinos in the United States since 1960*, edited by David Gutiérrez, 303–354. New York: Columbia University Press, 2004.

———. *Prophets Denied Honor: An Anthology on the Hispanic Church in the United States*. Maryknoll, NY: Orbis Books, 1980.

Stevens-Arroyo, Anthony M., and Ana María Díaz-Ramírez. "Puerto Ricans in the United States: A Struggle for Identity." In *The Minority Report: An Introduction to Racial, Ethnic, and Gender Relations*, 2nd ed., edited by Anthony Gary Dworkin and Rosalind J. Dworkin, 196–232. New York: Holt, Rinehart and Winston, 1982.

Stutzman, Ervin. *From Nonresistance to Justice: The Transformation of Mennonite Church Peace Rhetoric, 1908–2008*. Scottdale, PA.: Herald, 2011.

Sumner, Margaret. "Mexican American Minority Churches, USA." In *Mexican Americans in the United States: A Reader*, edited by John Burma, 225–233. New York: HarperCollins, 1970.

Swartz, David R. "Identity Politics and the Fragmenting of the 1970s Evangelical Left." *Religion and American Culture: A Journal of Interpretation* 21 (Winter 2011): 81–120.

———. "Re-baptizing Evangelicalism: American Anabaptists and the 1970s Evangelical Left." In *The Activist Impulse: Essays on the Intersection of Evangelicalism and Anabaptism*, edited by Jared Burkholder and David Cramer, 262–291. Eugene, OR: Pickwick, 2012.

Sylvest, Edwin, Jr. "Hispanic American Protestantism in the United States." In *Fronteras: A History of the Latin American Church in the US since 1513*, edited by Moises Sandoval, 279–338. San Antonio, TX: Mexican American Cultural Center, 1983.

Taylor, Paul S. *An American-Mexican Frontier.* Chapel Hill: University of North Carolina Press, 1934.

Thiessen, Janis. "Communism and Labor Unions: The Changing Perspectives of Mennonites in Canada and the United States." *Direction Journal* 38 (Spring 2009): 17–28.

Thomas, Lorrin. *Puerto Rican Citizen: History and Political Identity in Twentieth-Century New York City.* Chicago: University of Chicago Press, 2010.

Thomas, Piri. *Savior, Savior, Hold My Hand.* New York: Doubleday, 1972.

Toews, Paul. *Mennonites in American Society, 1930–1970: Modernity and the Persistence of Religious Community.* 4th ed. Scottdale, PA: Herald, 1996.

———. "150 Years Later: Revisiting the Beginnings of the General Conference Mennonites and Mennonite Brethren." *California Mennonite Historical Society Bulletin* 53 (Fall 2010): 1–6.

Torres, Andrés. "Political Radicalism in the Diaspora: The Puerto Rican Experience." In *The Puerto Rican Movement: Voices from the Diaspora,* edited by Andrés Torres and José E. Velázquez, 1–24. Philadelphia: Temple University Press, 1998.

Torres, Andrés, and José E. Velázquez, eds. *The Puerto Rican Movement: Voices from the Diaspora.* Philadelphia: Temple University Press, 1998.

Treviño, Roberto. *The Church in the Barrio: Mexican American Ethno-Catholicism in Houston.* Chapel Hill: University of North Carolina Press, 2006.

———. "Facing Jim Crow: Catholic Sisters and the 'Mexican Problem' in Texas." *Western Historical Quarterly* 34 (Summer 2003): 139–164.

———. "Race and Ethnicity." In *The Blackwell Companion to Religion in America,* edited by Philip Goff, 276–290. Malden, MA: Wiley-Blackwell, 2010.

Valdés, Dennis. *Al Norte: Agricultural Workers in the Great Lakes Region.* Austin: University of Texas Press, 1991.

Valladares, Jaime Prieto. *Mission and Migration: A Global Mennonite History.* Intercourse, PA: Good Books, 2010.

Vargas, Zaragosa. *Labor Rights Are Civil Rights: Mexican American Workers in Twentieth-Century America.* Princeton, NJ: Princeton University Press, 2007.

Vásquez, Manuel A., and Marie Friedmann Marquardt. *Globalizing the Sacred: Religion across the Americas.* New Brunswick, NJ: Rutgers University Press, 2003.

Walker, Randi Jones. *Protestantism in the Sangre de Cristos, 1850–1920.* Albuquerque: University of New Mexico Press, 1991.

————. *Religion and the Public Conscience: Ecumenical Civil Rights Work in Seattle, 1940–1960*. Washington, DC: Circle Books, 2012.

Waters, Mary C. *Black Identities: West Indian Immigrant Dreams and American Realities*. Cambridge, MA: Harvard University Press, 2001.

Watt, Alan J. *Farm Workers and the Churches: The Movement in California and Texas*. College Station: Texas A&M University Press, 2010.

Weaver, J. Denny. *Becoming Anabaptist: The Origin and Significance of Sixteenth-Century Anabaptism*. Scottdale, PA: Herald, 1987.

Weaver, Janet. "From Barrio to '¡Boicoteo!': The Emergence of Mexican American Activism in Davenport, 1917–1970." *University Libraries Staff Publications* (2009): 215–254.

Weber, Devra. *Dark Sweat, White Gold: California Farm Workers, Cotton, and the New Deal*. Berkeley: University of California Press, 1996.

Wilson, Catherine. *The Politics of Latino Faith: Religion, Identity, and Urban Community*. New York: New York University Press, 2008.

Yohn, Susan M. *A Contest of Faiths: Missionary Women and Pluralism in the American Southwest*. Ithaca, NY: Cornell University Press, 1995.

Zamora, Emilio. *Claiming Rights and Righting Wrongs in Texas: Mexican Workers and Job Politics during World War II*. College Station: Texas A&M University Press, 2008.

Index

Page numbers in *italics* indicate photographs.

Concilio Nacional de Iglesias Menonitas
Hispanas: agenda of, 189–90; concerns of, 186–89; Hispanic Ministries
Program, 192–94; MMC and, 174, 177;
Office of Spanish Literature, 194, 195;
progress of, 200–201; Rivera Snyder
and, 173
Congress of Racial Equality, 80
conjunto music, 256n78
Conrad, Paul and Ann, 122–23, 123
conscientious objectors: De León as, 87;
programs for, 35–36, 51; in Puerto Rico,
38–39; registration as, 35
constructivist approach, 225n29
coritos, 256n68
Council of Spanish Mennonite Churches,
119
CPS (Civilian Public Service) program,
35–36, 51
The Cross and the Switchblade (film), 43
Cross-Cultural Theological Consultation,
155–56
Cross-Cultural Youth Convention (CCYC),
103, 104, 117, 118; concerns about,
101–2; demographics of, 102; de-
scription of, 99–100, 101, 120–21;
farmworker movement and, 114–15,
135–36; feedback about, 116–17,
212; M. García at, 157; hunger strike
at, 115–16; music at, 171; reaction to,
117–18, 119–20; speakers at, 102–4,
107–14
Cruz, Nicky, 43
curanderos (folk healers), 26

Daniel, Cletus, 134
Declaration of Cachipay, 195–96
De León, Lupe: on becoming Protestant,
9; on Bernal, 169; at CCYC, 103, 104;
Chicano movement and, 123; civil rights
movement and, 96–97; on Compassion
Fund, 95; Concilio and, 200; Ewy and,
139; gender debate and, 162; on gender

identity, 110–13; at Hesston College,
54, 55; immigration conference and,
190; influence of, 44; on Mennonite
surnames, 76; Meyer and, 131; migrant
farmworkers and, 129, 141–43; MMC
and, 86–89, 94, 96; peacemaking and,
34–35; Powell and, 180–81, 182, 186;
on regionalization, 187–88; at Sandia
conference, 179; on violence and war,
215–16
De León, Perfecta, 32
De León, Seferina: conferences and,
149–50, 152, 179; dress of, 165; gender
debate and, 162–63; at Hesston College,
54–55; influence of, 44; music and,
168–73, 171
Derstine, Gerald, 34–35
Detweiler, William G., 17, 18
Díaz-Stevens, Ana María, 41
Dowd Hall, Jacquelyn, 79
dress codes, 54–55, 165
Driver, John, 38, 41
drug rehabilitation programs, 167
Duany, Jorge, 108
Dyck, Cornelius, 59

East Harlem, New York, 40–41, 42,
105–7, 108–9, 206
Eatmon, K. D., 127
Ecos Menonitas (magazine), 189, 201
Elizondo, Virgilio, x, 197
El Malcriado (newspaper), 133
Elwood, Indiana, 126
Enck-Wanzer, Darrel, 106
Epworth Forest Park, Indiana, 101, 103
Espinosa, Gastón, 41, 163, 164, 217
ethnic identity: CCYC and, 104; of Chicanos, 240n39; of Latinos, 64–67, 145;
of Mennonites, 21–22, 76; MMC and,
91; of Puerto Ricans, 107–10; religious
faith and, 2, 46–47, 95; terminology,
221n3; of youth, 99. See also interethnic
alliances; race and racism

165, 166, 170; fundraising by, 155;
MMC and, 153, 156–57; music and,
165–73; Role of Women Task Force,
160, 161–62; as street preachers, 167.
See also Latinas
Women's Missionary and Service Auxiliary, 82
Women's Missionary and Service Commission (WMSC), 130–31, 154
women's movement, 114. *See also* feminism

World Vision, 55–56
World War II, 27, 35–36, 49
worship services, 34. *See also* music in
churches

Yoder, John Howard, 215
Yoder, S. C., 22
Young Lords, 105–7, 206

Zehr, Howard J., 88

About the Author

Felipe Hinojosa is an assistant professor of history at Texas A&M University. He received his PhD in history from the University of Houston and has published articles on race, the Chicano movement in Texas, Latino/a religion, and the relationship between ethnic studies and religious studies. His teaching and research interests include Latina/o-Chicana/o studies, American religion, social movements, gender, and comparative race and ethnicity. Hinojosa is the recipient of numerous awards and fellowships such as the Hispanic Theological Initiative Dissertation Fellowship and a First Book Grant for Minority Scholars from the Louisville Institute.

Donald B. Kraybill and Carl Desportes Bowman, *On the Backroad to Heaven: Old Order Hutterites, Mennonites, Amish, and Brethren*

Donald B. Kraybill and Steven M. Nolt, *Amish Enterprise: From Plows to Profits*, 2nd edition

Werner O. Packull, *Hutterites Beginnings: Communitarian Experiments during the Reformation*

Benjamin W. Redekop and Calvin W. Redekop, eds., *Power, Authority, and the Anabaptist Tradition*

Calvin Redekop, ed., *Creation and the Environment: An Anabaptist Perspective on a Sustainable World*

Calvin Redekop, Stephen C. Ainlay, and Robert Siemens, *Mennonite Entrepreneurs*

Steven D. Reschly, *The Amish on the Iowa Prairie, 1840 to 1910*

Kimberly D. Schmidt, Diane Zimmerman Umble, and Steven D. Reschly, *Strangers at Home: Amish and Mennonite Women in History*

Diane Zimmerman Umble, *Holding the Line: The Telephone in Old Order Mennonite and Amish Life*

David Weaver-Zercher, *The Amish in the American Imagination*